GULLIVERIANA
III

TRAVELS INTO SEVERAL REMOTE NATIONS OF THE WORLD VOL. III (1727) AND MEMOIRS OF THE COURT OF LILLIPUT (1727)

FACSIMILE REPRODUCTIONS
WITH AN INTRODUCTION
BY JEANNE K. WELCHER
AND GEORGE E. BUSH, JR.

SCHOLARS' FACSIMILES & REPRINTS
DELMAR, NEW YORK
1972

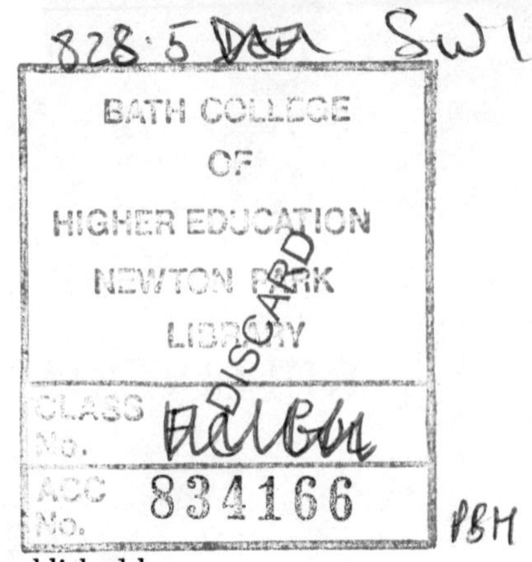

Gulliveriana III

Facsimile re-editions published by
Scholars' Facsimiles & Reprints, Inc.,
P.O. Box 344, Delmar, New York 12054

Reproduced from copies in
and with permission of
The Yale University Library

Printed in the United States of America

Library of Congress Cataloging in Publication Data

Main entry under title:
Travels into several remote nations of the world.
(Gulliveriana, 3)
"Facsimile reproductions."
1. Voyages, Imaginary. I. Memoirs of the court of Lilliput. 1972.
PZ1.G974 vol. 3 [PR3291.G8] 823′.5′08s [823′.5′08]
ISBN 0-8201-1101-5 72-4431

INTRODUCTION

As ONE might readily suppose, the name of Gulliver and of the lands he visited, Lilliput in particular, had such currency in the eighteenth century as to be part of the everday vocabulary. What is surprising, then, is the limited use writers made of Swift's hero. Neither as an author of their works nor as a character does he loom large in the Gulliveriana.

Only a dozen works besides Swift's are actually signed Lemuel Gulliver or Capt. Gulliver. Even including other forms of the pseudonym—Martin Gulliver, Gulliver Lilliputus—the total is not two dozen. Most of the works ascribed to Gulliver are extraordinarily unlike the original. Few of the authors borrowing his name mention his nautical and medical interests or respect his avowed tastes. There are such anomalies as poems and collections of drawings by Gulliver. He turns his hand to political speeches and letters, advice on matrimony, and satiric footnotes to a scientific work in Italian. Those works which use Gulliver's established genius—his style, subjects, or genres—are rare.

As a character Lemuel Gulliver plays an even smaller part in the Gulliveriana. In half a dozen items, he is mentioned prominently but briefly. For example, Diderot in *Les Bijoux Indiscrets or The Indiscreet Toys*, 1749, has Gulliver make a quick appearance to serve as an interpreter (I, 251-53). Murtagh McDermot, the fictional author and hero of *A Trip to the Moon*, 1728, writes a "Dedication in the Rear" to the "Thrice-renown'd, and Victorious Captain Lemuel Gulliver" (*Gulliveriana* I, 1970, pp. [91-92]), but Gulliver does not enter the tale itself. In fact, it is in only four works that Swift's hero is again central: *Memoirs of the Court of Lilliput* and *Travels into Several Remote Nations of the World*, Vol. III, both 1727; a pamphlet, *An Account of the State of Learning*, 1728; and Garrick's play *Lilliput*, 1756.

Of these four, only the *Memoirs* and *Travels* III are full-length narratives giving Gulliver a role, scope, and prominence similar to the original. These are the two works reprinted here (H. Teerink, *Bibliography of Jonathan Swift*, rev. Arthur Scouten, 1963. *Memoirs* is no. 1221; *Travels* III is nos. 1219, 292, 373, etc.) In their manner of imitating Swift's work they are, therefore, unique among eighteenth-century Gulliveriana.

A further feature associating them closely with the Swift is that both mention the name of "Sympson" (*Memoirs*, vi & 44; *Travels* III, Part I, 6). Richard Sympson became familiar to readers of Swift after "A Letter from Capt. Gulliver to His Cousin Sympson" appeared as a preface to *Gulliver's Travels* in 1735 (Faulkner's edition of the *Works*, Vol. III; see Teerink, p. 192). Before that, the name did not appear in the *Gulliver*. However, it had been in use from the start, Sympson having been the pseudonym of the epistolary negotiator who arranged with Benjamin Motte for the publication of Gulliver. In August 1726 several letters passed between Sympson and Motte (*Correspondence of Jonathan Swift*, ed. Harold Williams, 1963, III, 152-55) but none of these letters was published until years later (Harold Williams, *Text of Gulliver's Travels*, 1952, pp. 46 ff.) The authors of both *Memoirs* and of *Travels* III obviously had some private access to Gulliver's publishing history.

Other likenesses between the *Memoirs* and *Travels* III are readily evident. Both works are far more concerned with matters amatory than was the *Gulliver*. Both are extremely episodic, freely introducing separable tales and anecdotes common to travel romances and loosely tying these to the main story line. Both existed for the same reason, to exploit the Gulliverian market. They appeared, anonymously of course, within months after the original.

The *Memoirs* was advertised early in January (*Mist's Weekly Journal*, 14 January 1727); *Travels* III, the following month (*The Craftsman*, by Caleb D'Anvers, No. XXV, 27 February-3 March 1727). Since such notices were not necessarily very precise in their dating, we may view the works as having appeared practically simultaneously.

Memoirs of the Court of Lilliput
Written by Captain Gulliver
1727

Memoirs of the Court of Lilliput opens with an introduction, signed by its alleged publisher Lucas Bennet, which gives its pretended source. These memoirs, a part of Gulliver's original travel journal which he kept from Sympson and instead gave personally to his old friend Bennet, tell of the "Amours" of the "several People he has been among" (p. vi). Thus the formula for this sequel was set.

The advantages of the scheme are manifest. It allowed for wholly new material, of a very remarkable sort. It prepared the reader for a side of Gulliver hitherto unknown. It automatically provided a structure for the work, as a series of separate love tales with a framework of Gulliver's hearing them or observing the events. The sequel could profit by references to the *Gulliver*. Yet it did not have to strain for likenesses, as the keynote is contrast. It did not even have to presume that its readers knew the *Gulliver*.

The pseudonymous Bennet is unlike most Gulliverian imposters in frankly admitting the anomalous features of his work. Apparently he anticipated that his readers would be aware, perhaps even critical, of the incongruities. His comments may indicate a somewhat exceptional respect for Swift's principles and tone, or perhaps only an overestimate of public discrimination. Later imitators saw that such concern was unnecessary.

Although the introduction suggests that the work will encompass all the Gulliverian lands, in fact it deals with Lilliput only, as the title proposes. Even Blefescu is summarily written off (p. 153). Within this scope the author introduces many of Swift's characters, events, and their setting, with varying degrees of detail and of faithfulness to the original.

Most out of character is Gulliver himself because of his delight in idle gossip. He mentions that *Gulliver's Travels* (Part I, Chap. VI) referred to court scandals. But where Swift's Gulliver turned rapidly away from the subject, the new Gulliver entertains it. From time to time he perfunctorily acknowledges this discrepancy and vaguely accounts for it (e.g., pp. 43, 111). But for the most part he simply tells his tales, with evident relish and lively humor. There are some dozen of these, all concerned with romantic intrigue, immoral in some degree, the circumstances and conflicts varying briskly from piece to piece. The narrator breaks up one tale, that of Shefinbasto and Deffarhesal, which begins in Chap. II and does not conclude until Chap. IX. The serialized telling gives suspense to the tale and helps unify the work. Different narrators tell the different parts to Gulliver and their widely contrasted interpretations provide a dramatic, if shallow, illustration of the subjective nature of gossip.

In spite of the publisher's emphasis, the amorous intrigues are not the whole gist of the *Memoirs* and in some of the other elements the author achieves a very fair approximation of Swiftian technique. Aside from his taste for gossip, Gulliver rings true. His plaints about court disfavor (pp. 41-43) and his intermittent expressions of homesickness have a familiar ring and gain ironic point in the light of the conclusion to the original *Gulliver*. A particular oddity of the book is an extended scene involving a fantastic mural map designed on complex mathematical principles; the vividly conceived image, its allusive symbolism, and Gulliver's fascinated interest catch something of Swift's manner (pp. 121-42). New characters emerge, sketched with Swiftian economy, labelled with mouth-filling names that, like Swift's, sound genuinely exotic rather than allegorical or anagrammatic. The further descriptions of Lilliputian manners and customs are strange enough to be novel yet English enough to invite comparison, as were Swift's.

Witty and biting social satire marks much of this. Not at all unworthy of a sequel are the ridicule of projectors (pp. 34 ff.), duelling (pp. 48 ff.), the theater (pp. 94 ff.), and legal inequities (Chap. IX). A satire on Lady-authors (pp. 64-71) is in Swift's own vein, especially the aphoristic summation: "Women there set up for Writers, before they have well learned their Alphabet, and Booksellers build fine Houses out of needy Authors Brains" (p. 65). Martin Kallich sees a debt to Swift in the satire on religion (*The Other End of the Egg*, 1970, p. 4, referring to *Memoirs*, pp. 112-19).

Paradoxically, it is in a final point of imitation that the meretriciousness of the *Memoirs*—its vast distance from *Gulliver's Travels*—becomes most evident. Swift, while fundamentally concerned with mankind as a whole, also incorporated personal satire into his work. And so does the author of the *Memoirs*, but in a fashion essentially opposite to Swift's. The author of the *Memoirs*, in largely unmistakable allusions to living public figures, aristocracy, and royalty, reveals scandals of private not public life and, far from being outraged at these, clearly delights at having such unsavory goings-on to report.

Incongruously in a work alleging to be by Swift (presuming that someone who knew about Sympson most certainly would have known who wrote *Gulliver's Travels*), the most blatant passage of all is an attack on Pope. Right at the start, Gulliver utters earnest disclaimers of any personal involvement in the intrigues of which he will tell, citing besides his virtue the practical matter of size. For, writes Gulliver, "the inequality of our Stature rightly consider'd, ought to be for us as full a Security from Slander, as that between Mr. P-pe, and those great Ladies who do nothing without him . . ." (p. 16). The passage then refers to Pope's deformity and accuses him of licentiousness, impotence, vengefulness, and plagiarism. The nature of this attack and its presence in this pseudo-Swiftian work make even more intriguing the already interesting question of who wrote the *Memoirs*.

Pope himself claimed the author was Eliza Haywood and immortalized her with his wrath in *The Dunciad*. The first edition (1728) contains a sequence in which a bare-breasted "Eliza," described as "yon Juno of majestic size,/With cow-like-udders, and with ox-like eyes," is offered as a prize and won by Curll for sending his "stream" higher than his competitor's. The 1729 *Dunciad* in which Pope provided footnotes and appendices for the poem suppressed the detail about the bare "fore-buttocks" but identifies Eliza in a note which reads in part "*Eliza Haywood*] This woman was authoress of those most scandalous books, call'd *The Court of Carimania* <1727>, and *The new Utopia*. <*Memoirs of a certain Island adjacent to the Kingdom of Utopia*, 1725 . . .>"(*The Dunciad*, Book II, n. to l. 149. The material within diagonal brackets is by James Sutherland, ed., *The Dunciad*, The Twickenham edition of the *Poems of Alexander Pope*, Vol. V, 2d ed., 1953, p. 119. The entire poetic attack is *Duncaid* II, 149-82, in the 1729 version.) What is curious here is that Pope does not, in this note, make any mention of the *Memoirs of the Court of Lilliput* which was far more direct and vicious an attack on him than the two books cited; yet his Appendix II, "List of Books, Papers, and Verses, in which Our Author was abused, printed before the Publication of the Dunciad: With the true Names of the Authors" does cite it: "Memoirs of Lilliput, Anon. [Mrs. *Eliz. Haywood.*] 8°. Printed 1727." (*Dunciad, with Notes Variorum* . . . 2d ed., 1729, p. 176; see Sutherland, p. 208).

If the *Memoirs* is really by Mrs. Haywood, there may even be a question of which passage provoked which. If all three of her attacks on Pope and his friends came first, what was her provocation and why does Pope not cite the *Memoirs* in the note to the "Eliza" passage? Or is it possible that Mrs. Haywood heard ahead of time of the role she was to have in *The Dunciad?* Many details about *The Duncaid* were known in London literary circles for months before its publication. Was the *Memoirs* then a case of vengeance in anticipation?

To the casual reader, superficial likenesses between Mrs. Haywood's established works and the *Memoirs* seem to support Pope's identification. But Mrs. Haywood's biographer finds fundamental differences that make him very dubious about Pope's claim (George Whicher, *The Life and Romances of Mrs. Eliza Haywood,* 1915, pp. 119-20).

Whoever the author was, the *Memoirs* clearly holds its share of interest among Gulliveriana, being one of the most perceptive reflections of what Swift was and was not doing in *Gulliver's Travels.* It was fairly popular (Teerink cites three editions). Its Scriblerian associations are several. As a scandal chronicle, it has historic value; in its own right, its style is sprightly and its satire incisive.

Travels into Several Remote Nations of the World by Lemuel Gulliver Vol. III, 1727

ALONGSIDE the *Memoirs, Travels into Several Remote Nations of the World,* Volume III, is a pale affair, whose author had a notably small talent for either imitation or invention. But he did have Grub-Street ingenuity and diligence, a very carefree attitude toward literary honesty, and an excellent sense of timing.

These features aided in turning to profit his inside information about the publication of the original Gulliver. His intimacy with the situation is startling. Not only did he know the role of Sympson long before this was made public, but he seems to have known the contents of the Gulliver-Sympson letter. In his introduction he accuses Sympson of having altered the original text (I, 6), just as Gulliver does in his letter to Sympson. Yet, as was mentioned above, Gulliver's letter was not published until the 1735 Faulkner edition and even there it is dated 2 April 1727, at least a month after *Travels* III went on sale. The source of information may have been hearsay—as the spelling "Simpson" suggests—but it was accurate.

The point is that *Travels* III claimed to be, not just an imitation of the original, but a genuine continuation thereof. With scarcely any concern for real resemblances, its author did interest himself in enough superficial connectives between the works to support his hoax. And his method was a success. Much of the public was evidently fooled. What mattered more, the work sold and endured—out of all proportion to its worth.

To begin with, the title is exactly the same as the one Swift used.

"Volume III" refers to the fact that Swift's work had first appeared in two volumes, Volume I containing Lilliput and Brobdingnag; Volume II, Laputa etc. and the voyage to the Houyhnhnms. Only four months elapsed between the publication of Swift's first edition and this spurious third volume. Anonymous like the first two, it does not carry even a printer's or bookseller's name. In format it matched Vols. I and II, its content being like theirs divided into two parts. The introduction, which in style is the most Swiftian part of the whole book, far from protesting its genuineness carries conviction by simply not raising the question at all.

Further reinforcing its status as a genuine sequel, it was advertised with such phrases as "Sold by Booksellers, Where may be had the two former Volumes" (*Craftsman*, No. XXV). Presumably booksellers found it advantageous to have three volumes to sell instead of only two. Repeatedly the three appeared as a set. Sometimes all were bound together into one hefty volume. Although the Swift had gone into three editions by the time *Travels* III appeared, some of the combined volumes attached the sequel to a first edition of the original; thus, with 1726 on the title page, the whole seemed to have been issued together from the start.

How aware the English publishers were of the imposture is not known. Certainly foreign translators and printers gave it an enthusiastic welcome. French, Dutch, and German versions appeared in 1728. Even more regularly than did the English, continental publishers included it with Swift's original when new editions and translations were issued. Teerink cites more than a dozen such combined sets (see scattered items between nos. 373 and 427).

Making free with Swift's title and reputation was only a part of the fraudulence of this work. Almost three-fourths of *Travels* III comes from Denis Vairasse's *The History of the Sevarites or Sevarambi . . . by one Captain Siden*, 1675. With deceptive openness, *Travels* III carries the subtitle "Part II, A Voyage to Sevarambia" (bound opposite Part I, 118); but nowhere does it say that there was an earlier work by this name. As it was more than fifty years since Vairasse's work had appeared in England, the title would not have been especially familiar at the time of *Travels* III. Furthermore, the borrowings from Vairasse begin half way through Part I, at the end of "A Second Voyage to Brobdingnag" (Part I, 50), not at the beginning of Part II where the title appears. It is questionable how many readers would have known that what they were buying was very much the work of Vairasse and not at all the work of the original author of *Gulliver*.

A comparison of Vairasse's work and *Travels* III is interesting in several respects.

Something of a parallel, in fact or in pretense, is found in the printing histories of the two books. Whether Denis Vairasse wrote first in English or in French has not been established. Though French, he was living in England early 1670s and in 1675 the first part of his work was published in English in London. By 1677 he was back in France and there he issued, in French, a much longer version. The author of *Travels* III likewise published his work first in England, but claims in the introduction (Part I, 6) that he wrote it originally in French.

A comparative study of *Travels* III and *The History of the Sevarites* has not been made (see Philip Gove's rather unduly complicated outline of the problems, *The Imaginary Voyage in Prose Fiction*, 1941, pp. 268-71). But some relationships are readily discernible. The sequence and general content of *Travels* III is that of Vairasse's English text, not the French version, which was greatly amplified. On the other hand, the language of *Travels* III differs from that of the English *History of the Sevarites*. Often its author freely abridged the original. Even where he kept pace with Vairasse, he did not copy the English word for word. A comparison with the French shows that he did not directly translate either. His method was a combination of summary and paraphrase.

Noting what he took from Vairasse and what he omitted reveals how very indifferent the author of *Travels* III was toward Gulliver's style. For he is far more interested in action than in ideas, wild beasts than people, and magic and other exotic phenomena than manners and philosophies of life; and he makes his selection from Vairasse's text accordingly. Every naked dancing girl, every risque or romantic love tale is included, alien though they are to the taste of the original Gulliver. Yet he could capture a Swiftian flavor when he cared to, as in the passage about laws (Part II, 82-84) which is enlarged from the briefest hint in the *History of the Sevarites* (II, 118).

The beginning and end of *Travels* III (Part I, Intro. & Chaps. I-II; and Part II, Chap. VI) are independent of Vairasse and most directly imitate Swift. The introduction links *Travels* III to the original with both circumstantial detail and a very sharply satiric tone. So different is the matter and manner of the introduction from the rest of *Travels* III that it may well have been by another writer, one really appreciative of Swift's work. The idea of returning Gulliver to the land of the Houyhnhnms apparently exhausted the author's invention and obviously he had to borrow. Perhaps he deserves credit in his choice of a work to plagiarize. For Swift himself knew the Vairasse and, while its general interests are rather different from his, he may have taken some inspiration from its general utopian character (Emanuel von der Mühll, *Denis Veiras et son Histoire des Sevarambes 1677-79*, Paris, 1938, pp. 260-62, esp. n. 38). There is no evidence of whether or not the author of *Travels* III realized this. The point is that where Gulliverian elements are discernible in the plagiarized sections, they are thanks to Vairasse, not to the author of *Travels* III.

All in all, this most presumptuous of the Gulliverian imitations is a far cry from the Swift. But it provides a colorful fable illustrating booksellers' venality, public gullibility, and popular taste.

Thanks are due to the Beinecke Rare Book and Manuscript Library of Yale University for permission to use its copies of these two texts for this facsimile edition. We wish to express our gratitude also to the American Philosophical Society and to the Research Committees of C. W. Post College and Saint Francis College for grants which helped finance this work.

JEANNE K. WELCHER

C. W. Post College
Greenvale, New York

GEORGE E. BUSH, JR.

Saint Francis College
Brooklyn, New York
July 1971

[illegible]

[illegible]

[illegible]

[illegible]

[illegible]

TRAVELS

INTO SEVERAL

Remote NATIONS

OF THE

WORLD.

VOL. III.

J: Vandr Gucht Scu
R. Cooper Inv

TRAVELS

INTO SEVERAL

Remote Nations

OF THE

WORLD.

By Capt. LEMUEL GULLIVER.

VOL. III.

Accidit in Puncto, quod non ſperatur in Anno.
Gaudent ſecuri narrare pericula nautæ.

LONDON:
Printed in the Year M.DCC.XXVII.

THE

CONTENTS.

CHAP.

The CONTENTS.

CHAP. II.

The unfortunate Death of Lmnſrimpnmo *and* Trtnmpſnic. *The Author, and his Boat's Crew carried to* Lorbrulgrud. *Made much of by the King and Queen. His Eſcape from thence with his Company. A violent Storm. A* Dutch *Ship Founders at Sea. The Crew ſaved on Board the* Golden Dragon, *and afterwards caſt away upon an unknown Coaſt.*

CHAP. III.

Twelve Men ſent aſhore. The reſt follow. Tents erected, and a Trench thrown up. The Ship pull'd to Pieces, and a Pinnace built. Eight Men imbark in her for Batavia. *The Author choſe Com-*

The CONTENTS.

CHAP. VI.

The Author and his People leave their Camp, and are conducted to Sporunda. *A Description of the* Osparenibon, *and several other Material Passages.*

A

INTRODUCTION.

OUR Underſtanding too oft is made Bawd to our Follies; in every Stage of Life we are playing the Fool: In our Infancy, Rattles and Gewgaws take up all our Time; from thence to Twenty, we think every Year an Age till we arrive at Manhood; and from thence to Forty, we imagine thoſe Hours loſt that are not ſteep'd in Variety of Follies miſcall'd *Pleaſure*; from Forty to Sixty we gradually deſpiſe the Weakneſs of Youth, and not having it in our Power to be as ridiculouſly wicked as we have been, think of Repentance; and if we ſurvive a longer Term of Years, inſenſibly

B creep

creep to a Second Childhood; as *Cato* has it, *Nam quicunque ſenex, ſenſus puerilis in illo eſt:* But no more of this common moralizing Topick.

I AM very much ſurpriz'd, that the merry World will find a Meaning in my former Trifles, when I meant nothing more when I committed them to Paper, but to refreſh my Memory, and look over, with a pleaſing Satisfaction, the many Dangers I had, through the Care of Providence, gone through.

I FEAR my Fate will prove ſomething like that of the famous *Chriſtopher Columbus*, who was ridicul'd for his Notion of a New World, and when he had prov'd what every one thought an idle Chimera, was robb'd of the Honour by *Americus Veſpuſius*, and what the former had diſcovered, the other ran away with the Credit and Name; and I am terribly afraid ſome more fortunate Mortal will tread the Paths I have gone before;

before; new Name the Countries I have discover'd; so I shall, consequently, lose the Honour I have justly deserv'd, and *Gulliver*'s Name be buried in Oblivion.

SOME have been pleas'd to quarrel with my Name; but I can assure them, 'tis the same my Ancestors for Ages have enjoy'd; and I can prove, that many have borne Offices of Trust as well as Credit; and an Acquaintance of mine from *Wales*, has promis'd me to trace my Genealogy a Century before the Flood. Then for slandering me with Politicks, that provokes me with Disdain; for I am so far from fouling my Fingers with any such thing; that I never read any other Part of a New's Paper, but Advertisements; never convers'd with any about St. *James*'s (tho' I have Relations there) or ever shav'd in a Barber's Shop.

B 2 AND

And now I'll give you a Proof of my Honeſty. Though I had a Caſting-Vote in our ſmall Corporation, laſt worrying for Repreſentatives, I gave it freely without any Gratuity; tho' the Gentleman that receiv'd the Benefit, to avoid the heinous Crime of Bribery, offer'd me a long Purſe full of Gold, for one of the Hairs of the good King of *Brobdingnag*'s Beard, which I had happily ſav'd for a Walking-ſtaff, though my Eldeſt Daughter had often begg'd it, inſtead of Whalebone, to furniſh out her Hoop-Petticoat; though a Friend of mine that is going Abroad, would have adviſ'd me to let him ſhew it to ſome curious *Virtuoſi*, and call it the Staff that *Balaam* ſmote his Aſs with; and notwithſtanding, he aſſured me of Succeſs, yet I am too much a Gentleman, to impoſe upon any one.

That for my Honeſty.

Then

THEN for my Religion (though I own I have ſome Scruples now and then, which are eaſily remov'd by our Curate over a Bottle of Prieſts Port) I go to Church twice every Sunday, and ſeldom fail, unleſs by ſome Accident, Dinner is later than uſual; or unhappily my eaſy Chair falls in my Way: Then I am as punctual upon Saints Days and Holidays, *Aſh Wedneſday* only excepted: And this is one very great Reaſon why I never attempt the Acquaintance of thoſe Relations I have about the Court, for fear I ſhould be forc'd into ſome Employment; go to Church once for a Place, and then the Buſineſs of my Poſt follow ſo hard upon me, that I ſhould never have Leiſure to go there again.

BUT ſomething too much of this; as my Friend *Hamlet* ſays.

THE following VOYAGE I wrote Originally in the *French* Tongue, with a Design to have it publish'd at *Paris*; but losing Part of my Fortune in the *Mississippi*, gave me such a Disgust for that Nation, that I have at my leisure Hours, Translated it into our Mother Tongue; which Copy, I should have reposited in my Friend Mr. *Simpson*'s Hands, the Editor of my former Volumes, if I could have had the Opportunity of seeing him; but he avoids me, I suppose, as imagining I am out of Humour with him upon that Affair, for his Omission of several material Passages: Yet I freely forgive him; tho' the Bulk of those Volumes would be considerably increas'd, if he had printed my Course of Sailing, and many Sea-Terms, fit only to be understood by the Marine Race, a Specie of Human Kind I have a great Veneration for; though if I had known of the Printing and Publication of my former Volumes, I should

I should have made as warm a Struggle to have kept them in, as a young Author does Speeches in his *Coup d'Essay*, when the Actors through Understanding and long Experience, can give good Reasons for their Expulsion; yet I must own, every Parent is, or should be, fond of his Issue.

I FIND mention'd in my last Page but Two of my second Volume, that I permitted my Wife to sit at Table with me; but I found so little Satisfaction in her Company, that I soon repented my good Nature, for my Aversion daily increased.

THE Respect to my two Companions in the Stable, augmented daily, and I was never more happy than in their Conversation, for I had with great Pain, Labour and Expence of Time, learn'd them both the *Houyhnhnms* Language, and I soon discover'd in the *Sorrel*, my Elder, a prodigious Genius, and it was eaſy to be perceived what Abhorrence they nouriſh'd for the deſpicable Race of *Yahoohs*. I doubt not but many will eaſily judge I had a hard Task in bringing them to underſtand me, but they ſhould conſider even the *Wild Youth*, can utter ſome Monoſyllables very plain, and his indefatigable Tutors are in great Hopes of making him converſable, and then we may be let into the Secrets of his Life.

I SELDOM convers'd with my Companions, but it put me in Mind of an excellent Speech in the Play of *Mithridates* King of *Pontus**;

——Caſt before your Eyes
The generous Horſe looſe in a Flow'ry Lawn,
With choice of Paſture, and of cryſtal Brooks,
And all his chearful Miſtreſſes about him,
The White, the Brown, the Black, the Shining Bay,
And every Dappled Female of the Field.

Now

Now by the Gods! for ought we know, as Man
Thinks him a Beaſt, Man ſeems a Beaſt to him.

My Sorrel I had nam'd *Lmnſrimpnmo*, which, in the Language of the *Houyhnhnms*, means *full Perfection*; my Bay *Trtpmpſnic*, which I tranſlate, the *Light of Reaſon*: Oh how it gaul'd me to ſee ſix of thoſe noble Creatures tugging a gaudy *Yahooh* in a gilded Chariot! I believe the Thought had robb'd me of my Underſtanding, if on the other Hand I had not ſeen as oft two brawny *Yahoohs* carry one of their own Specie in a *Sedan*; and, I muſt own, I never made Uſe of any other Vehicle, as much out of Spight, as Conveniency, to be reveng'd in Part for the ignominious Treatment the generous *Houyhnhnms* met with.

My Reſpect was doubled for 'em, upon the following Accident; An inſolent

lent *Yahooh* of my Wife's Breed, met me, by Accident, and in a majeſterial Manner reproach'd me with my Conduct to his Siſter, meaning the Creature I had formerly called Wife. I endeavoured to avoid him, but to no Purpoſe, for he ſeiz'd me faſt hold by the Arm, and forc'd me to ſtay: It is hardly poſſible to imagine the Agony I was in at his hateful Touch, and I believe I ſhould have fainted away (for I had never convers'd with a *Yahooh*, ſince my laſt Voyage, nearer than the Length of my Cane) if my lucky Stars had not ſhone on me with their ſtrongeſt Influence: A well proportion'd *Houyhnhnm*, that had ſlipp'd his Neck from the vile Bonds impoſed upon him, came running down the Street, with the amiable Word *Hnhnms*, which, in their Language, ſignifies *Liberty*, and immediately ruſhes in his Courſe againſt this hateful Detainer, and hurled him againſt the Ground, with ſuch Force, that his Bruiſes would not permit him to riſe without

without Help: I was much rejoic'd at this unexpected Release, left my Tormentor upon the Ground, and ran Home, full of grateful Thoughts for the Service done me.

WHEN I came Home, I went to my Companions to relate the Accident; but was surprized to find *Trtpmpsnic* in Tears: I was confounded at the Sight, and it was some Time before I could get him to discover the Cause of his Grief: At last, with broken Sighs, and Tears trickling down his lovely Cheeks, he declar'd, that the insolent Groom had rode upon *Sorrel*, and led him in a Halter to Water, instead of bringing them, according to my Agreement with him, Water in a Brass Pail, provided for their Use.

I WAS confounded with the Greatness of the Crime, especially when I saw what Effect it had upon *Lmnsrimpnmo*, who appeared inconsolable: I ask'd 'em, Why they suffer'd it? they told me, They

they did not know how Refiftance would be taken: Upon that Inftant, I call'd for the culpable Wretch, threw his Wages over the Wall, and commanded him to be gone that Moment, but he anfwer'd, in a fawcy Manner, That he would not ftir 'till he was allow'd Time to provide for himfelf; and when I, with many Words, declar'd he fhould have no further Concern with me, he infolently reply'd, he would! and immediately rufh'd in upon me, feiz'd me by the Throat, got me down, and I believe would have murdered me, had not my Friend *Lmnfrimpnmo* given him fuch a Salute with his Feet, that fell'd him to the Ground, with two of his Ribs broke: He got up, with much Pain, went out curfing me, and my dear Preferver.

I WAS at a great Lofs to think how I fhould get another in his Room, and had fome Thoughts of doing that Office myfelf, but neither of my Companions would

would agree to it: The ſame Day I got one to my Mind, to attend upon 'em, and, for-Fear of any Diſorder for the future, I had our Agreement drawn up in Writing, and he behav'd himſelf ſo well, for ſome Time, that I thought myſelf the happieſt Creature in Life, for he ſeem'd to love my Companions as well as myſelf, though he had not the refin'd Notions of their Underſtanding nor Language, as I had; but, however, he was the only *Yahooh* that I could bear to touch me; for we, poor helpleſs Creatures! can do little of ourſelves, nay, it is ſome Years after our Birth, e'er we can help ourſelves; while the excellent *Houyhnhnms* are no ſooner air'd in this World, but they have the Uſe of all their Faculties, and need no Aſſiſtance; which is enough to convince me they are the nobleſt Specie.

MY *Yahooh* Family became every Day more irkſome to me, and every Action of theirs call'd the Tears into my my Eyes, to think of the agreeable Converſation I had formerly loſt, with thoſe exalted *Houyhnhnms*.

I HAD often mentioned my Thoughts to my Companions, once more to bear the Fatigues of the Sea, with the charming Hope of viſiting that delightful Country, though I would have dropped the Deſign, if they had not readily come into it, for I ſhould not have had the Confidence to attempt ſuch an Undertaking without them, being I was well aſſured from their Friendſhip, to want no Advocates, while they were with me: I was much rejoiced to find them as eager as myſelf. But the Hope of Liberty is a prevailing Argument, though they wanted nothing with me.

ONE Accident in my Family, added Wings to my Deſires: *Lmnſrimpnmo* diſcover'd a criminal Converſation between my Wife and Groom, and their Scene of Guilt the Stable. I muſt own

I

I was at firſt a little diſcompos'd at the Relation; but then again I reflected I was thinking like a *Yahoob*, and reſolv'd to forget the Indignity; but, as I ſaid, it made me put my Deſigns the ſooner in Execution, for I went the very Day to ſeveral Merchants, and inform'd them of my Readineſs to be employ'd in a Voyage to *China*, or any Part of the *Eaſt-Indies*, but had the Mortification to meet with no Encouragement, for a Rumour had ſpread among them that I was out of my Senſes. I had Recourſe to my Friend Mr. *Simpſon*, the only *Yahoob* I had any Dealings with, who did his Endeavour to ſet that idle Report aſide, but to no Purpoſe.

My ill Succeſs had almoſt put an End to my Life, for it threw me into an Illneſs; but I had the good Fortune, if I may call it ſo, to recover, without the Aid of Phyſick, though I once order'd my Groom to prepare me a Drench in the ſame Horn he had bought for my my Companions, which he brought me; but as I was opening my Mouth to receive it, the Fellow let it fall, in a Fright, and crying out, *Nay, now I am ſatisfied of my Maſter's Madneſs*, ran out of the Room, and alarm'd the whole *Yahooh* Neighbourhood with the Story: When I had recover'd my Strength, I made my firſt Viſit to my Companions, who were very much rejoiced at the Sight of me. The firſt Queſtion I ask'd, was, Whether they had received any ill Uſage from the Groom? They declar'd none in the leaſt, which was a very great Satisfaction to me: We condoled each other with the ill Succeſs of my Attempt, but I put them in ſome Heart, when I told them, I was reſolved to make a Voyage for *Oſtend*, and try to get a Command under the *Emperor*. I went accordingly the next Day, and made a Bargain for our Paſſage, and it was late before I came Home.

As

As I was paſſing by our Garden, I heard my Wife's Tongue, with two or three more in hot Diſcourſe: though no Thought about her gave me any Pain, yet; I found, I ſtill retain'd the *Tahooh* in my Mind, and had Curioſity enough to liſten: Said my Wife to one that was with her, *I know no one that keeps a private Mad-houſe. That ſhall be my Care*; reply'd the other, *and the ſooner the better, for who knows but in one of his Fits, he may do you ſome Injury? It's very true* (anſwer'd my Wife) *let it be to Morrow, if it's poſſible, but if we can't finiſh that Affair to Morrow, I beg the Horſes may be diſpos'd of: I am heartily vex'd* (ſhe continu'd) *that I have not parted with them before, for he won't ſuffer any Body to ride them, and I am aſſured he's expenſive enough in their keeping.* What Words can expreſs the Horror I felt at this Diſcourſe! my Hair ſtarted as I had ſeen a Goblin, my Limbs trembled, and all my Frame confeſs'd the wild Sur-

C prize.

prize. I ran into the Stable, when I had recover'd Strength enough to do it, flung myſelf down between my Companions, and had not Power enough to utter one Word, my Heart was ſo full. My two Friends ſeem'd to partake of my Sorrow, and we mingled Tears together: We were interrupted in our ſilent Scene of Grief, by my Groom's Entrance, who, ſobbing, told me, he was almoſt ready to die with Grief, to think of parting with *Jack* and *Dick*, as he call'd my two Companions; for, ſaid he, I know they are to be ſold to Morrow; Yes, ſaid I, I know it is reſolved, but they ſhall ſooner have my Heart, than my Conſent; and therefore I'll remove them to Night, notwithſtanding it is ſo late. I wiſh you would, Maſter, return'd the Groom: It ſhall be done then, ſaid I; let them be carried to ſuch an Inn, and I'll follow you, and give Orders about them. While the Fellow went to prepare himſelf, I broke the Matter to my Companions, though

though with ſome Difficulty, for there is no Words in the *Houyhnhnms*'s Language, to ſignify *Buying*, or *Selling*. They were very diſconſolate at the Information, fearing they ſhould be ſold to Slavery; but I chear'd them as well as I could, in telling them, that ſhould never be while I was alive. When the Groom came, I ordered him to get a *Sedan*, and directed him to go with my Companions juſt before: When we arrived at the Inn, I pick'd out a Stable fit only for two, and order'd my Groom to ſtay at the Inn, 'till next Day. When every thing was ſetled at the Inn, I went Home, and took the whole Night to provide for my Voyage: In the Morning, my Wife was ſurpriz'd to ſee ſo many Trunks and Boxes: ſhe ask'd me, haſtily, Where I was going with them? I told her, I had Intention of going into *Northamptonſhire*, for a Month or two, and bad her enquire no further. This I had done ſeveral Times before in the Summer, and therefore ſhe was willing to believe me now.

I convey'd my Luggage to the Inn, for fear they might have dogg'd me to the Water Side, and by ſome Stratagem, hinder my Voyage. But every thing happen'd according to my Wiſh.

THE next Day I embarked, with my two Companions, having firſt ſent the Groom upon a Sleeveleſs Errand. I muſt own I had ſome Regret in parting with him, for the Affection he ever expreſſed to his Charge, but I knew very well he would not accompany me in my Voyage, therefore I never mentioned it to him.

A

A SECOND VOYAGE TO *BROBDINGNAG.*

CHAP. I.

The Author sets out for Ostend, *where he is made Captain of the* Golden Dragon. *Sets Sail from thence, arrives at* Teneriff, *from thence to St.* Salvadore, *where eight of his Men run away with his Long Boat. The Governor refuses to let him search for them. His Departure from thence, and Landing upon* Brobdingnag.

*Ecember* the 1st. 1721. we set Sail from *Limehouse* on Board the *Two Brothers*, Captain *Smithes* Commander, bound for *Ostend*, where we arrived safe, without any Hazard in our Voyage, on *Christmas-Day*.

I found many Sea Officers of my Acquaintance, who offer'd me their Aſſiſtance; at laſt I agreed with Meſſieurs *Grant* and *Willis*, two *Engliſh* Merchants, of the *Roman* Perſuaſion; and,

APRIL 1. 1721. I went on Board the *GoldenDragon*, as Commander, bound for *Japan* and *China*, in a Trading Voyage. My two Companions were ſtow'd as conveniently as we could, and they ſeemed contented with their Lot, though the firſt three Days of the Voyage, they were terribly Sea-ſick.

APRIL 23. We made the *Pike of Teneriff*, bearing *S, S.W.* diſtant about 14 Leagues, according to my this Day's Obſervation. The next Day, about Noon, we anchor'd in the Port of *Oratava*, ſaluted the Town with ſeven Guns, and had five in return. It is needleſs to deſcribe a Place ſo well known by all the World.

AFTER

AFTER eight Days Stay, to refresh our Men, we set Sail for the Coast of *Brasil*, in Company with two *English*, and one *Dutch* Vessel: In the Night we perceiv'd a Light, which we suppos'd belong'd to some Ship, and in the Grey of the Morning, we discover'd an *Algerine Rover*, who boarded the *Dutch* Vessel, and carry'd her off, though we endeavour'd to come to their Assistance, but to no Purpose, for it growing stark Calm, they took their Prize in Tow, and with the Help of their Oars, soon got her out of Danger.

SOME of my Men were uneasy at my giving Orders to assist the *Dutchman*, telling me, in a surly Manner, they had nothing to do with them, and if we had been in the same State, they would not have loosen'd a Sail to come to our Assistance; and every one agreed we were not in a Condition to engage an Enemy, considering what a long

Voyage we had to make. I inform'd them, That what I had done was out of Humanity (though I muſt now declare it was only to give them an Opinion of my Courage) but, for the future, I would do nothing without a Council-Board: Upon that Inſtant, I drew up the Names of thoſe Perſons who were deſign'd for that Body, gave it to the Sailors to peruſe; who return'd it me, and agreed to what I had wrote, likewiſe begg'd Pardon for what they had ſaid.

I was very well pleaſed I had made them eaſy, being what had happened to me before, often came over my Memory. We made a ſucceſsful Voyage, 'till we came to *St. Salvador* in *Braſil*, where eight of my Men, with the Ship's Long-Boat, deſerted me, and though I intreated the *Governor* to let me make Search, yet he very handſomely refus'd me, telling me it was a a Custom to protect all Persons that took Sanctuary among them.

I BEGAN here to study how I shou'd bring my Affair about, for I was pretty well assured, that my Men would not agree I should land upon the Island of *Houyhnhnms*, if I had the good Fortune to find it.

I WAS very much concern'd I could not converse with my two Friends as usual; but my Affairs would not permit it. I knew pretty well that the *Houyhnhnms* Land was situated between 43 and 46 Degrees of *Southern Latitude*, in the *Indian* Sea; but that was not the Course to Steer for *China*. However, I sounded some of the Officers, and in my Discourse, told them I had formerly been in an Island in such a Latitude, where there was the richest Gold Mines in the Universe, though I did not declare who were the Inhabitants; but told them they were a Nation

Nation of peaceable *Indians* that were fond of Commerce; and though I abhor a Lye, yet I fram'd such a plausible Story that gain'd Belief, and with one Consent, they offer'd to break it to the Men, which was done the same Day, and approv'd by the whole Crew: Accordingly we steer'd our Course for that Latitude, and met with nothing extraordinary till we had pass'd *Madagascar*, in some of our Maps call'd St. *Laurence*. In sight of that Island, we discover'd several Pieces of a wreck'd Vessel, and by the *Lyon* which was broke from the Bow of her, we easily knew her to be *English*-built; about two Leagues farther, we could perceive a Ship's Boat, that made many Signals for our Assistance; we came soon up with them, and took the Men on Board, but in a very miserable Condition, for they had eat nothing for Six Days; they had drawn Lots for their Lives Half an Hour before they discover'd us; but the Wretch that was condemn'd, to sustain

ſuſtain the Lives of their ſtarving Companions, beg'd an Hour to prepare himſelf for another World, and before the Time was expir'd we were in Sight. The Ship they belong'd to, was call'd the *Loyal Ann*, Captain *Smedley* Commander, Homeward bound from *China*, a private Trader; but were Shipwreck'd upon a Barren Iſland within Thirty Leagues of *Madagaſcar*. The Captain and the reſt of the Men, upwards of Thirty, all periſh'd; this I was let into, two or three Days afterwards, when they had recover'd a little Strength.

JUNE the Firſt, between Nine and Ten in the Night, a Storm aroſe, and we were aſſur'd by ſome experienc'd Sailors it would be long and violent, for St. *Helmo*'s Fire was ſeen hovering in many Parts of the Ship. It ſprung up at *N. W.* and continu'd in its utmoſt Violence Two and-twenty Days, ſo that we were oblig'd to ſcud under bare Poles,

Poles, or now and then with a Reev'd Foreſail.

THE 23d of *June*, the Storm ſeem'd to abate ſomething of its Violence, and on the 24th we could hoiſt our Topſails.

THE 25th being very Calm, we mended a Hole in our Starboard Bow, occaſion'd by the Fluke of our Anchor, which, during the Storm, had broke its Laſh and beat againſt the Ship, tho' unperceiv'd, as we ſuppoſe, for ſeveral Days.

THIS Day we Steer'd more to the Weſtward, as imagining we had gone too far North already. On the 28th, a Boy at the Topmaſt-Head, cry'd out Land! Land! We were in general ſurpriz'd, as not expecting it; but, however, we bore *S. S.W.* for the Shore. As we came near, I verily believ'd it was the Iſland of *Houyhnhnms*, and I could not help run-

running down to inform my Companions of what I thought, who were greatly rejoiced; for the Fatigues of the Sea had much impair'd their Health, and they ſtood in need of all their Philoſophy to bear their Hardſhips with Patience.

THE nearer I drew to the Shore, the more I was confirm'd in my Opinion, though I did not make any of the Sailors acquainted with what I thought; neither was there one among them that could tell what Country it was.

WE caſt Anchor in a very good Harbour in Fifty Fathom Water, and though we could not perceive any Inhabitants, yet I was aſſured we were at the Place I ſo long wiſh'd for. Our Men were almoſt afraid to venture on Shore. But I order'd out the Long-Boat that the Shipwreck'd Men were ſav'd in, (which happen'd lucky enough, for I mention'd before how I loſt mine)

I got,

t

I got, with much difficulty, my two Friends in, and with Eight of the Sailors row'd up the River, telling the Crew I would be with them again in two Days.

WE row'd about two Leagues up the Stream, yet ſaw nothing of the Inhabitants, neither *Houyhnhnms*, nor *Yahoohs*, which made me reflect with Melancholy, that I might be miſtaken. However, I reſolv'd to go aſhore the firſt convenient landing Place, which I did, about Half a League farther: I whiſper'd my two Friends to have a little Patience, till we had been up to view the Country.

CHAP.

CHAP. II.

The unfortunate Death of Lmnſrimpnmo *and* Trtnmpſnic. *The Author, and his Boat's Crew carried to* Lorbrulgrud. *Made much of by the King and Queen. His Eſcape from thence with his Company. A violent Storm. A* Dutch *Ship Founders at Sea. The Crew ſaved on Board the* Golden Dragon, *and afterwards caſt away upon an unknown Coaſt.*

WHEN we were landed, we walk'd about, but could not perceive the Foot-ſteps of Man or Beaſt, ſo we with one Conſent, reſolv'd to go to our Boat, and return on board the Ship, with a Deſign to cruize about the Iſland, 'till we found ſome more convenient Place; but we had the Mortification to find, that the Tide had run ſo low, our Boat was aground, paſt our Strength to get off, ſo we were

t

were obliged to make a Virtue of Neceſſity, and wait 'till the Tide came up again : We took our Sails out of the Boat, and with our Oars, *&c.* made a Sort of a Shelter from the Sun, which was exceeding hot, yet notwithſtanding my two Friends, and I, took a Walk further up the Country. We had not gone far, e'er we perceived, a Form of a monſtrous Height, which I preſently knew to be a Native of *Brobdingnag* : As ſoon as ever my two Companions perceived him, Fear overcame their Reaſon, and they fled away in the utmoſt Fright, but I have often wiſhed I had been blind, rather than to have ſeen the Death of two ſuch Friends; for while they were in their Flight, a Couple of Hawks of the Country, as it were, by Conſent, flew down upon them, each ſeizing one in its Talons, and ſoon took their Flight with them : The Sight made me loſe my Senſes, and I fell down in a Swoon : When I came to myſelf, I found I was in the Hand

of

of that *Brobdingnaganian*, who, tho'a poor Fiſherman, yet had ſeen me in the Court of *Lorbrulgrud*, and was very much rejoiced to find me again after ſo long an Abſence. I was inconſolable for the Loſs of my Friends; but the good-natur'd *Brobdingnaganian* gave me ſuch wholeſome Counſel, that I was amaz'd at his Morality. I told him in what Condition I had left my Companions, and he immediately bended his Courſe towards the Water-ſide. As ſoon as ever the Crew perceiv'd him coming, they ran towards the Boat and got into it; but that could little avail them, for the *Brobdingnaganian* took up the Boat, Men and all, and brought them ſafe aſhore under his Arm, and laid them gently on the Ground. I comforted them as much as my Circumſtances would permit me, and by degrees they ſeem'd to come to themſelves.

THE *Brobdingnaganian* carried us all to his Houſe, and provided a Leg of a

D Lark

Lark for our Supper. When we had ſupp'd, he made us a convenient Bed in one of his Childrens Cradles, and the Men ſlept very contentedly. For my own Part, Sorrow kept me awake, but 'twas well for ſome of the Crew I was ſo, for juſt after Sun-riſing, I ſaw a Flea jump upon the Side of the Cradle, in order to bite one of them; but I threw my Shoe with ſuch Force, that I overſet him, and ſo we eſcap'd the Danger; tho' an unfortunate Accident happen'd to one of my Midſhip-men, *George Plummer*, who lay outermoſt, having occaſion for a Chamber-pot, which was the good Woman's Thimble, and ſtooping to reach it, e'er he was well awake, fell out of the Cradle, and came to the Ground with ſuch Force, that he lay for dead; for the Diſtance from the Top of the Cradle to the Floor, was at leaſt four Yards. I heard him fall, but could not get to his Aſſiſtance, by reaſon of the Height; I awaken'd my Companions, and inform'd them of the Miſchance; but all the

Help

Help we could give him, was to look over the Side of the Cradle and pity him. At laſt the *Brobdingnaganian* got up, and help'd us out. I immediately pull'd out my Lancets to let *Plummer* Blood, and in an Hour's time he came to himſelf, though much bruis'd; our Hoſt was very much concern'd at the Miſchance, but told me we ſhould run no more ſuch Hazards for the future, for he would carry us to Court that very Day, it being not above fourteen *Strums* off, which amount to about a Hundred and Fifty of our *Engliſh* Miles.

He immediately provided one of his old Shoes, and ſtuff'd it with ſome of their Thiſtle-down, which is very near as fine and ſoft as our Flocks.

Poor *Plummer* complain'd of a ſtrong Smell that aroſe from his Apartment, that almoſt over-came him. But there was no Remedy.

D 2 When

When we had Breakfaſted upon the Remains of our Supper, our Hoſt ſet out with us in our Boat under his Arm, and *Plummer* in his Hand : Upon the Road, I ask'd him, What was become of *Glumdalclitch*, and whether they had any Notion how I was carried away ? He told me that *Glumdalclitch* had been in priſon ſince my Abſence, tho' every Body was convinc'd, the Loſs of me was more Grief to her, than the Loſs of Liberty. But the King and Queen were ſo much concern'd at my Loſs, that the Court went into Mourning for 8 Days, and I have heard (*ſaid he*) that ſhe, even to this Day, talks about you, with a vaſt deal of Tenderneſs, and took ſuch a Diſtaſte to the *Monkey* that carried you to the Top of the Palace, that ſhe has given it to one of her Maids of Honour, but upon this Condition, never to bring it in her Sight again.

We

We discours'd of several Things in our Journey, and I was very much pleas'd to find I had not lost any of the Language of the Country. I began to think less and less of my Two unfortunate Friends, which is a convincing Proof I was still but a poor *Tahooh*. We had gone about half Way our Journey, when *Plummer* made Signs to speak with me, and call'd me, as he told me; but his Voice being weak, and he so far distant from me, that I could not hear him, for our Host had the Boat upon his Shoulder, and I set in the Head for the Conveniency of Discoursing with him; but the Readers will have a more lively View, if they will call to their Remembrance, a Poulterer with a Dozen of Partridges, or lesser Birds, in his Tray upon his Shoulder.

I desired our Porter to let me speak with the sick Man in his Shoe; but he, imagining we all of us might have something to ſay to him, took the Boat off his Shoulder, kneel'd down upon one Knee, and brought his both Hands together. *Plummer* told me, he was not able to breathe, the Heat of our Hoſt's Hand had ſo overcome him, and begg'd I would give him a Pinch of Snuff. I then deſired him to put *Plummer* into the Boat to us, that he might have the Benefit of the Air, which he conſented to, but firſt asked me what it was I had given to him? When I had inform'd him, he ſeem'd deſirous to take ſome of it, but yet was unwilling to rob me, however, I thought fit to offer it in return of his many Civilities; but his Fingers being ſomewhat too big to put in my Box, I pour'd it all on the Nail of his Fore-Finger, and he apply'd it to his Noſe, as he had ſeen me do it before him, and though it was no more to him, than three Grains to us, yet it made him ſneeze ſo loud, that we had almoſt loſt our Hearing, but what was worſt of all, holding his Noſe over our Boat,

Boat, ſuch an impetuous Hurricane flew from his Noſtrils, that threw us all along upon our Backs; and one *David Mackenzie*, a *Scotchman*, was blown out upon the Ground, and had his Brains daſh'd out againſt a Stone. Our Hoſt was the firſt that found him out, but his Grief for the Accident was equal to ours; he begg'd we would not ſpeak of it at Court, which I made them all promiſe, though there was no Need of any ſuch Conjuration, for none of them knew the Language of the Country but myſelf. Well, ſince you have given me your Word, ſaid he, I'll take it up (meaning poor *Mackenzie*) and having, by chance, his Wife's Needle-Caſe in his Pocket, he put him into it. But ſneezing again, he happened to break Wind, and though the Report was louder than a Cannon, yet it did us no Damage; but the unſavoury Smell that aſcended (for he had replac'd us once more upon his Shoulder) had almoſt killed us

D 4 all:

all: A *Dutch* Sailor that bore it beſt, took one of the Oars, and hitting him upon the Noſe to put us down, for I was ſo overcome with the Stench, I had not Power to ſpeak; he ſaw we were all very much diſorder'd, but did not know the Reaſon, nor I did not think fit to tell him; I only ſaid the Heat of the Sun offended us, which to remedy, he undid the Loop of his Bonnet, and by that Time he had finiſh'd, the ill Savour was gone, and the Flap of his Bonnet prov'd a very good Awning for us, for the Sun, in Reality began to be very powerful. I deſir'd our Conductor, if it were poſſible, to ſtay in ſome Village near the Capital 'till the Dusk of the Evening, that the Citizens might not gaze upon us: He inform'd me, that was what he intended, and that he would eaſily find an Expedient to conceal us.

WHEN we came to dine at our Inn, we were all ſet upon the Table in our Boat;

Boat; our *Dutchman* wanting to untruſs a Point, and getting out of the Boat upon the Table, fell into a Sawcer of Vinegar, and had he not been skilful in Swimming, had certainly been loſt; for though the Liquor was not over his Head, yet the Bottom was ſo ſlippery, he could not ſtand upon his Feet, but he ſwam to the Edge of the Sawcer, and, with much Difficulty, got upon the Table.

THERE had been no Danger, if this Accident had happen'd while our Hoſt had been in the Room; but he was juſt gone in the Kitchen, to give Orders about Dinner, and had lock'd us in the Room; for to prevent any Tydings of us flying to the Court before him, he conceal'd us under his Coat when he came in, even keeping it a Secret from the Woman of the Houſe, who was his Relation by the Mother's Side.

AFTER

AFTER Dinner, we continu'd our Journey as before, and when we came in Sight of the City, he put the Boat under his Watch-Coat, as it was his Cuſtom to do before, whene'er he met any Paſſengers; ſo we got into the Palace, without being ſeen by any one.

WHEN we came to the Gate, the Porter made ſome Scruple of admitting him, which oblig'd our Hoſt to take him in a Corner, and diſcover what he had got under his Coat. As ſoon as the Fellow ſaw me, he knew me, notwithſtanding my Change of Dreſs, it being the ſame Servant that lived there when I was in the Palace; for the *Brobdingnaganians* ſeldom change their Officers, unleſs convicted of Bribery, which very ſeldom happens: This Fellow had no ſooner perceived me, but he ran in, alarm'd the whole Palace, and upon the Inſtant, the good King with his Conſort, roſe from their Supper, and, with

with the utmoſt Impatience, ordered me to be brought in: I ſoon diſcover'd the Pleaſure they received at my Preſence by their Countenances, which Satisfaction was much augmented when they had ſeen Seven more of the ſame Specie.

THE King put us one by one into a Plate upon the Table, and then held us even with his Face to view us more diſtinctly. The Princeſs, who was near-ſighted, took out her Glaſs to obſerve us, and moſt of the Gentlemen and Ladies in waiting, did the ſame according to her Example, for the Courtiers of *Brobdingnag* are ſtrict Followers of the Royal Family.

THE King told me, with a good-natur'd Smile, that the whole Court had grieved for my long Abſence, and therefore was impatient to know what Fortune had befallen me. I informed him in the real Truth of every Thing men-

mentioned before, only added, That when I came into my own Country, I was so much concerned for the Content I had enjoy'd in his Court, and so unluckily lost, that I was never easy 'till I had engaged a Vessel, and many more of my Countrymen, to make the Voyage, in hope to find his Majesty's Dominions again, which we had, beyond Expectation, met with. I thought it proper to say this, that our Reception might be the more favourable.

WHEN I had inform'd his Majesty the Ship that brought us was in the River, he would have sent twelve of his Guards, to bring her to Court that Moment; but I begg'd him to defer it a Day or two, when I would go myself, in order to measure her, that I might give Directions for a Carriage with Wheels to be made, that would transport her without Damage: After a further Conversation about indifferent Matters, I begg'd the Release of *Glumdalclitch*, which was easily granted: But Words

Words cannot expreſs the Joy ſhe felt at the Sight of me; the Reſpect ſhe had for the Court, did not hinder her ſnatching me from the Plate before the King, and clapping me in her Boſom, wept for Joy, to that Degree, that I was as wet, as if I had tumbled into the Sea; but I conſider'd it was her Love that occaſion'd my Misfortune, ſo paſs'd it over.

WHEN ſhe went to Bed, ſhe would have us to lie with her; ſhe plac'd us in a Row upon her Pillow, but ſhe would have me next her, and cover'd us all with her Neck Handkerchief doubled, but I intreated her to lay it ſingle over us, or the Heat would ſtifle us: As my Head was near her Ear, we convers'd ſeveral Hours before we went to ſleep, and ſhe let me into the Hiſtory of the Court ſince my Abſence, as alſo the Sorrow ſhe underwent for my Loſs.

WHEN we awak'd in the Morning, ſhe gather'd us up in her Powder-Box-Lid,

Lid, and carry'd us, according to her Order over Night, into the Queen's Dreſſing-Room; and to divert her, I ordered *John Frampton*, a *Cheſhire* Man, to dance the *Cheſhire-Rounds*, which wonderfully pleas'd the Queen, and all the Ladies: Her Majeſty asked me, if I could not do as much; I told her, that only was a Dance perform'd by the *Shalloms* of our Country, (which, in their Language, ſignifies *Peaſant*) but, to pleaſe her, I danc'd a *Minuet* upon her Busk, which lay upon her Toylet: She thank'd me, but I eaſily ſaw ſhe lik'd *Frampton*'s Performance much better than mine, and ſhe did not ſcruple telling me ſo; but ſhe laugh'd when I told her there was Abundance of People in *Europe* got handſome Livelyhoods, and ſome Eſtates, by learning the Inhabitants how to walk.

WHEN the King came in, which he forbore to do 'till the Queen was dreſs'd, he told me there were People provided

to

†

to attend us to our Ship, and the Carpenter would go with us. I had forgot to mention a Conſultation we had among ourſelves, when we were in Bed, while *Glumdalclitch* was undreſſing : The Reſult was, if poſſible, to make our Eſcape, which we could never compaſs if any of the *Brobdingnaganians* went with us; therefore I told the King, if he pleaſed, we would take no other Attendance, than the Perſon that brought us to Court, and this was the Reaſon I gave his Majeſty for it; Our People might be frighted to ſee ſo many Figures of ſuch a large Size; and that I fear'd ſome would not be willing to come by fair Means; but if his Majeſty would leave it to me, I would manage it ſo, that every thing ſhould be done without Diſturbance ; for, added I, the *Engliſh* are fond of their Liberty, and will ſpend the laſt drop of their Blood to defend it; the King fell into a great Fit of Laughter, and told me he would leave

leave it all to my wiſe Conduct; for, ſaid he, I won't endanger my Subjects ſo far, as to ſend them againſt ſuch a terrible People as your Countrymen are. *Glumdalclitch* would fain have gone with us, but I would not ſuffer it: The Hoſt that brought us to Court, in the ſame Manner, carried us back again: When we were arrived at his Houſe, I deſir'd he would bring us to the Water Side, which he comply'd with. When our Boat was afloat, I bid him good Day, and deſir'd he would be at the ſame Place at that Time on the Morrow; he ſtood looking at us for about half a League, and then a high Point of Land hid him from our Sight; By good Fortune we had the Tide with us, ſo we got on Board our Ship, in leſs than an Hour.

As ſoon as ever we were up the Side, I order'd the Anchors to be weigh'd, and before Night we were out of ſight of Land. Then my Men began to recover

cover their Fright, and, consequently, out of Danger of the *Brobdingnaganians*; I mean those that were with me on Shore, for we were so eager to get out of their Power, we had not the Leisure to talk much. But when we related what we had seen on Shore, they imagined we had eat of some infectious Root, which had robb'd us of our Understanding, and it was with much Difficulty, we persuaded the wisest Sort to believe us; but many of the ignorant Wretches thought we were all Bewitch'd, and ever continu'd in that Opinion.

WE Steer'd *S. S. E.* which Course we did not doubt wou'd bring us to some Part of *China*, in less than Twenty Days.

I had not now so strong an Inclination for the Country of the *Houyhnhnms* as I had before I lost my two Friends, tho' I cou'd not think of them for some

E time

time without Tears; then on the other ſide, my Officers and Seamen began to be leſs diſtaſteful, for within a Week, I condeſcended to dine with my Lieutenant; ſo apt is evil Converſation to corrupt a poor weak Mortal, whoſe Frailties increaſe with his Years.

WE continued our Courſe One-and-twenty Days without diſcovering Land, which began to cauſe an Uneaſineſs, for the Weather was ſo Hazy, we could not make an Obſervation to know what Latitude we were in. The next Day we ſpy'd a Sail, and about Noon came up with her: It prov'd a *Dutch* Ship from *Batavia*, bound for *New Holland*, and that Morning ſprung a Leak; the Water gain'd ſo faſt upon their Pumps, there was no Hopes of Safety. They had got out their Boats, in order to their laſt Reſort, but as ſoon as ſhe diſcover'd us, they made Signals of Diſtreſs, and while we were drawing near them, they fill'd their Boats with Proviſion and

and their richeſt Goods. As ſoon as they had acquainted us with their Condition, we gave them all the Aſſiſtance lay in our Power, and before Night we had got every thing of Value out of her, and left her to the devouring Waves. We were very much crowded for Room, inſomuch that ſome Brutes aboard began to murmur at what was done.

ABOUT Midnight a violent Storm aroſe from the *North*, and we were oblig'd to bear away due *South*, for we ſhip'd ſo much Water upon a Wind, we were afraid of Foundering; ſo we ſcudded under a Mizen all Night, and in the Morning ſuch a thick Fog aroſe, that we cou'd not ſee twice the Length of the Ship; however a ſtark Calm enſu'd, and the Ship only drove by the Current; but at eight o'Clock we perceiv'd ſhe ſtuck faſt: This renew'd the Terrors of the Night, and all our Hopes of Safety vaniſh'd; I muſt confeſs I

E 2 more

more than once repented of aſſiſting the *Dutchmen*, for ſome Women they had on Board, ſcream'd ſo violently, and were ſo troubleſome, they almoſt confounded us. Our Fears increas'd, till the Sun diſſipated the Fog, and then we found our Ship was ſtuck faſt upon a Sand, about Half a League from the Shoar; but whether it was an Iſland, or the Continent, we could not tell, however, we began to recover our Spirits, and let it be what it would, we thought our Condition much happier than ſome Hours before, when we expected every Moment to be buried in the Sea.

ABOUT Noon we had a clear and warm Sky; we immediately reſolv'd to land all our Lading, and explore our New Diſcovery; but firſt we thought it adviſable to ſend Twelve of our ſtouteſt Men well arm'd, to ſee what they could diſcover on Shore.

CHAP.

CHAP. III.

Twelve Men ſent a Shore. The reſt follow. Tents erected, and a Trench thrown up. The Ship pull'd to Pieces, and a Pinnace built. Eight Men imbark in her for Batavia. *The Author choſe Commander in Chief of all the Forces. The Names of his inferior Officers. With many other Paſſages.*

AS ſoon as the Men were landed, they cautiouſly view'd the Country from a riſing Ground; but could not ſee either Houſes or Inhabitants, and thinking it dangerous to go farther, without more Strength, return'd on Board. The next Morning, we doubled the Number, with Orders to ſend the Boat back, to land our People and Goods by degrees, for there was no ſtaying on Board. Before Night we had landed our Proviſion, and the moſt valuable Part of our Goods, threw up a large Tent to ſhelter us from the Inclemency of the Weather, and near it were erected ſmall ones for the Crew.

WHEN we had a little ſettled our Things, we call'd a Council, to debate what way we ſhould take for our Preſervation, and we came to this Reſolution, That one Half of our People ſhould throw up a Trench round our Tents, to prevent any ſudden Aſſaults by Man or Beaſt, and the other to go in ſeveral Parties to diſcover the Country, and to fetch us in Fuel, and what other Conveniencies ſhould come in their way.

THE Twelve Men that were left on Board, had Orders to ſearch her, and give us an Account of her Condition, and in the Evening of the next Day after our going on Shoar, they brought us Word, her Back was broke, and if we could find the Means to get her off, ſhe would be of no Service to us, ſo ſo it was reſolv'd in another Council, to pull her to Pieces, and with the Materials build us a Boat that would bear the Sea, in order to ſend to *Batavia* for Aſſiſtance, which was allowed to be the firſt Port belonging to the *Europeans*.

OUR Reſolves were immediately put in Execution, and every Perſon that was ſerviceable, I order'd to Work. The Parties that diſcover'd the Shore on each Side our Camp, found ſeveral Sorts of Shell-fiſh, which were very Palatable, and the Sea abounded with Variety of other Fiſh, therefore we put our Nets in order, to take them.

TO ſpare our Sea-Proviſions, we liv'd with what we caught by Fiſhing, but we were put to it for Water, tho' we had dug a Well within our Trenches, but it prov'd Brackiſh.

OUR Diſcoverers went every Day farther and farther up in the Country, but could meet no Inhabitants, nor any other living Creature, but Snakes like thoſe in *Europe*, *Rats* as big as *Rabbets*, and a Fowl ſomething like our *Wood-Pidgeons*. Some of our Men ventur'd to dreſs the Rats, and found them excellent Meat, as alſo the Birds, and, bating their Whiteneſs, their Taſte reſembled that of a Chicken.

We had mounted our Guns, but our Neceſſity made us ſlight our Fortification, for we dreaded no Enemy but that of Famine. In fourteen Days, our Workmen had finiſh'd a Boat with a Deck, and Conveniencies to hold Eight Men with Six Weeks Proviſion, which was what we could ill ſpare, as being oblig'd to take it out of our Sea Stores. When every thing was provided for the Voyage, great Debates enſu'd among the Men, about who ſhould go in her; for we found no one was willing to venture upon ſo hazardous an Undertaking; but to prevent all Diſputes, we ſubmitted

mitted to Lots, firſt ſigning a Paper I drew up for that Purpoſe.

THE Lots fell upon Two of my Crew, and Six of thoſe we had ſav'd from Shipwreck, the Maſter being one; When they found it was their Deſtiny, they reſign'd themſelves to the Will of Heaven, and with chearful Hearts ſet out the 20th Day after our Shipwreck, having firſt agreed, if we ſhould remove our Quarters, to leave Directions where to find us: We follow'd them with our Eyes and Wiſhes, as far as we could ſee them, and ſent up Prayers to Heaven for their good Succeſs. After they were out of Sight, we call'd a Council to debate upon a Manner of Government, where I was unanimouſly choſe their Leader.

I then drew up the following Articles;

I. *THAT*

I. *THAT every one of the Company (Women excepted) ſhould take an Oath to Obey what I and the Council ſhould reſolve, upon Pain of ſuch Puniſhments as we ſhould think fit to inflict upon them.*

II. *THAT I ſhould have the Privilege alone of chuſing my proper Officers, though if they committed any Miſdemeanor, to be cenſur'd by the Council.*

III. *THAT I might be allowed a double Vote in Council.*

THESE Articles were readily agreed to, and ſign'd by every Body; and the ſame Day, I had a Tent erected in the Middle of our little City, larger than the reſt.

ON the next, a Counſel was conven'd, where I choſe my Officers. Mr. *Van Nuit* of *Dutch* Extraction, I made Intendant of the Proviſion; *Swart*, an an Engineer of *Batavia*, Maſter of the Artillery, *Blondel Morrice*, a very able Seaman, Admiral of our Fleet, which conſiſted of our Long-boat, Yawl and a Pinnace, that was upon the Stocks, rais'd from the Ruins of our Ship. Mr. *Brown*, my firſt Mate, I preferr'd to the Poſt of *Major General*; *Morton*, ſecond Mate, born at *Bath*, Captain of my firſt Company; *De Haes*, a *Frenchman*, a very active Man, and one that underſtood military Diſcipline, Captain of the ſecond Company; *Van Schelder*, born at the *Briel*, Captain of the third Company, and *Du Broſch*, a *Norman*, Captain of the fourth. I gave all theſe Gentlemen leave to chooſe their inferior Officers, and the Buſineſs was done without any Diſputes or Uneaſineſs.

WHEN we had choſe our Officers, we number'd our People; we had Three hundred and Seven Men, Seventy-four Women, and Three Boys, all in a good State of Health; though when we firſt landed,

landed, we had ſeveral indiſpos'd, but they ſoon recover'd, which was a Proof of the Healthineſs of the Country. The whole Company I divided into four Parts, Mr. *Morrice* choſe Six-and-twenty of the beſt Sailors, and three Boys to Man our Fleet; *Swart* Thirty for managing the Artillery; Two hundred more form'd our four Companies, Fifty in each Band; Mr. *Van Nuit* had the Remainder at his Command, to bring in Forage for our little Camp: Among the reſt, we had two Trumpeters, one I gave *Van Nuit*, and the other I kept for myſelf.

OUR Affairs thus ſettled, the ſame Evening I ſummon'd the Officers, and declar'd it our beſt Way to ſet out for a Diſcovery of the Country, before our Proviſions were too far ſpent, and, if poſſible, to find a more convenient Place for a Camp, for every thing about us would ſoon grow ſcarce; and another Reaſon I gave them for a Removal, was the

the Badneſs of our Water. They all came in readily to my Advice, and ſet themſelves with great Alacrity to put it in Execution.

ADMIRAL *Morrice* received Orders in Writing, to get ready his two Boats, and to arm his Sailors; one was to coaſt to the Weſt of our Camp, with Captain *Morton*, and Twenty Soldiers, to wait their Motions on Land; the other, which was commanded by the Admiral to go to the South, and myſelf, with a Party of 40 Soldiers, on the Shore to attend them; Captain *De Hays*, with 30 of his Company, to penetrate in the Heart of the Country: The reſt of the Officers and Men were left to guard our Camp.

THE next Day, we all filed off, well arm'd with Powder and Ball, Cutlaſſes, Half-Pikes, and three Days Proviſion. I commanded *Morton*, if it was practicable, to meet the Boat every Night,

Night, as I intended to do the ſame with *Morrice*. The Sea was very calm, and not a Breath of Air ſtirring, which render'd it warm walking. For Ten Miles together, the Country round us was much the ſame as that of our Camp, nothing growing but Buſhes and Thorns, neither could we find either Brook or Spring. We join'd our Boat at a little Opening, and took ſome Refreſhment. After Dinner, we purſu'd our Journey, and before we had got Five Miles, we could perceive the Country to be a little uneven, gently riſing in ſmall Hills, and about two Miles farther, our Van came to a ſmall Brook of delicious Water: they halted, and ſent one to tell us the agreeable News; upon each Side, were ſmall Trees, which render'd a pleaſing Shade; under theſe Trees we halted, and made Signals for our Boat to come to us.

AFTER taking a ſlender Repaſt, we ſent our Boat up this little River, and fol-

follow'd leiſurely, intending to reſt ourſelves all Night, if we found a convenient Place, or otherwiſe to repoſe in our Boat. But e'er they had row'd a Mile, they met with a charming Cluſter of lofty green Trees, where we pitch'd our Camp. *Morrice* had provided Fiſh for our Supper, of a very delicious Taſte, though unlike any thing our Rivers yield, beſides very large Oyſters, and other Shell-fiſh.

We ſurrounded our Fire with green Boughs, to prevent its being ſeen at a Diſtance, and after placing Centinels, went to Reſt.

In the Morning, I ſent five Men farther up by the Brook Side, to diſcover more of the Country, but they came back in an Hour, informing us, that a Mile farther, the Country round them, was much the ſame as our Camp, ſo by Conſent of every one, we croſs'd the little River in our Boat, and purſu'd farther

farther on, keeping the Boat in View. The farther we went, the more unequal the Country appear'd, and at five Miles diſtance, as we gueſs'd, we diſcover'd a Wood of very high Trees, that ſtood on a Promontory, running in the Sea. We refreſh'd ourſelves, and were reſolv'd to go there, if no Impediment ſtood in our Way. We reach'd the Wood in two Hours, and found the Trees very lofty, without any Underwood, which made our March eaſy in it. I thought it highly proper to double our firſt File, for fear of an Attack either from Man or Beaſt. In this cautious Manner we march'd in a direct Line, ſtrewing Branches as we paſt along, that we might the more readily find our Way back. When we came to the other Side of the Wood, we diſcover'd the Sea again, and Trees of a great Height about ſix Miles farther; then we were aſſured this was a large Bay between two Capes or Headlands.

THE

THE Proſpect gave us a vaſt Pleaſure, and we all of us wiſh'd it had prov'd our Fortune to have been caſt away near it. We had left our Boat on the other Side of the Wood; but I diſpatch'd three of our Men, with Orders for *Morris* to double the Cape with the utmoſt Expedition. Another Party I ſent to the Sea-ſide, for Diſcovery, and they quickly return'd laden with very good Oyſters, with ſuch Shell-fiſh as we found the Night before; others I ſent to look out for freſh Water, but they went two Miles e'er they found any, yet their Trouble was recompenſed by the Goodneſs of it, for they found the Situation ſo pleaſant, that they diſpatch'd ſome of their Number to acquaint us with it. Others that I had ſent farther Inland, return'd with ſome Deer they had kill'd near a Brook upon the Skirts of the Wood. The Sight of ſuch good Fortune animated our jaded Spirits.

F WE

WE left this Place, and directed our Course for the Brook of Water our Men had found out. When we arriv'd, I was so well pleas'd with the Place, that I resolv'd to stay there all Night, and not expecting or desiring a pleasanter Situation, resolv'd to remove our People there from our first Camp.

OUR Men kindled a Fire, and dress'd their Venison: Before it was ready, all our Company came together, and we supp'd with as much Satisfaction, as if we had been every one at his own Home.

THE next Day, the Boat's Crew carry'd me to our old Camp, leaving the rest of my Men under *Morrice*'s Command: We arrived there before Sun-set, and were received with many Expressions of Joy.

MORTON

MORTON and *De Hayes* arrived about two Hours before me: *Morton* inform'd us he had gone two Days to the *West*, consorting with the People in the Boat every Night; but met with a barren, sandy Country. The first Day they were much distress'd for want of Water, because the Boat could not come to Shore in many Places; but the Second, they came to the Banks of a large River, that was brackish near the Sea; but two or three Miles farther up, it prov'd fresh; yet they were much frighted at two Crocodiles that came out of the River to attack them; but the Report of their Fire arms scar'd them away; but finding the Country much the same, their Provisions almost gone, and their Men wore out as well in the Boat as ashore, they return'd to the Camp.

DE HAYES, who march'd in the middle of the Country, was as unsuccessful

cessful as *Morton*, for he met with nothing but a standing Pool, four or five Miles over, and many Water-foul flying about the Banks, but they could take none: Behind this Lake they could perceive a large Ridge of Mountains trending *East* and *West*, as far as they could see, yet, fearing the Want of Provision, return'd. Their Informations made every Body willing to go to the Place I had discover'd.

THE next Morning we agreed in Counsel, to remove to the *Verdant Vale* (as I call'd it) with all Expedition practicable. Our Pinnace was not quite finish'd; so we us'd our other two Boats to remove our Goods, sending our Labourers and Tools with the first Load: Mr. *Morrice* accompany'd the first Party, *de Hayes* the Second, and myself the last in our new Pinnace, with our Guns and Ammunition.

CHAP.

CHAP. IV.

Removal from their first Camp. A new Town founded. A Tyger kill'd by their Hunters. The Women cause many Disorders among them. A Criminal try'd before the Author. One of the Sailors devour'd by a Shark. The Women divided among the Men. The Admiral returns from his Discoveries with a Native of the Place.

IN my Absence, our People nam'd our New Settlement after my own Name. Our Men had built them Huts by the Brook Side, and every one seem'd contented with their Fortune, and we might have liv'd as happily here, as in our native Countries; but

Nescio qua natale solum dulcedine cunctos
Ducit, & immemores non sinit esse sui.

F 3 WE

WE had Venison and Fish in such Plenty, that had our Number been trebled, we were in no danger of starving; though at first we were in great Fears, for want of Salt; but our Admiral, among the rest of his Discoveries, found a sufficient Quantity to serve us Ages, if we could find no Means of getting away. It was naturally made by the Spray of the Sea driving upon Holes in the Rocks, and then crusted by the Heat of the Sun. Our greatest Fear was want of Powder, for that wasted every Day (though we had a large Quantity) yet I gave Orders to be as sparing as possible: We likewise foresaw our Cloaths would not last for ever nor even our Boats and Tackling, yet I had so often experienc'd the Providence of God, that I was assur'd of his divine Assistance.

WE continu'd salting Venison and Turtle, and curing Fish, in order to augment

ment our Sea Provision. Having several Casks of Pease, and some Beans, we resolv'd to sow some of each, to see how they would improve: In order to it, we cut down several Trees, grubbing up the Bushes and Under-wood, which was burnt upon the Place to fatten the Earth: We then sowed, or rather planted the Pulse, and left it to the Care of him that gives the Increase.

OUR Huntsmen going farther in the Wood one Day than usual, kill'd such a Number of Deer, it was not in their Power to bring them Home, so they hung a Couple of them upon the Bough of a Tree, in order to secure them for another time; but going the next Day to fetch them, they saw a large Tyger upon the Tree feeding upon the Deer: Our Men were so surpriz'd at the Sight, that they could not tell whether it was best to go backward or forward. They absconded behind the Trees some time, to observe the Creature; but two of the

Hunters taking Aim both together, fir'd, and brought him down: He roar'd terribly at firſt, but being ſhot in two Places, could not riſe, and in a little time expir'd. They ſtripp'd him of his ſpotted Skin, and with the two Deer brought it to our Camp in Triumph: We were pleas'd with their Succeſs, yet I was invaded with new Fears, for it ſoon ſtruck to my Imagination, there were many others of the ſame Kind, if not Variety of Species, and it was to be fear'd, they might, one time or other, invade us in our Camp: I mention'd this to the Council the ſame Day, and it was reſolv'd, without any delay, to fortify ourſelves. We went to Work the next Morning, and in Ten Days time, our Camp was Palliſado'd round, ſo ſtrong, to defy any Attempt from Man or Beaſt.

AN Order was given to the Huntſmen, not to go ſo far into the Woods for the future,

future, which Order was willingly obey'd in regard to themſelves.

I have mention'd before, that we had Women among us, ſome having Husbands with them, and others unmarried, but moſt of them came from *Batavia* to ſettle in *New Holland*, drawn away by the advantagious Propoſals made by the *Dutch*, though we may juſtly imagine, they had left the beſt Part of their Virtue behind them. While we were fatigued and in want, there was little Notice taken of them; but when Plenty, Eaſe and Idleneſs crept among us, the Females thought it was time for them to begin. At firſt they were cautious in their Interviews with the Men, taking Advantage of the Night, which was ſoon diſcover'd, for the Centinels finding them out in their ſtollen Pleaſures, were for putting in to be Sharers, which generally ended in Quarrels. One I ſhall mention here: One Woman by her Wiles, had drawn to her Lure two of our Men,

Men, though unknown to each other: One of them, according to his uſual Cuſtom, coming to viſit her, ſhe deny'd him Entrance, which caus'd in him a jealous Suſpicion, and watching his Opportunity, he found his Rival in the Embraces of his Miſtreſs: Rage at the Sight ſo far overcame his Reaſon, that he plung'd his Sword through the Bodies of them both, and made his Eſcape without being diſcover'd. The wounded Pair were found out by their Cries, in the ſame Poſture the Man had left them, and were carried to the Surgeon's. When I heard of the unfortunate Story, I aſſembled the Council, that we might determine how to detect the Author of the Deed, and put an End to ſuch Actions for the future. We examin'd the wounded Man, but he declar'd he had never injur'd any of the Community, nor the Woman either could not, or would not diſcover it.

The

THE next Day, I took this Method to find out the Criminal: I order'd every Man to Muſter before us, and found him out by the Loſs of his Sword; we brought him to his Tryal immediately. The firſt Queſtion I put to him was, to know the Reaſon of his coming without his Sword? He anſwer'd me boldly, he had lent it to one that was gone upon an Expedition with the Admiral. When I heard him ſay this, I order'd the Sword to be produced, and demanded of him, if he knew it: Yes, ſaid he, 'tis the Sword I lent laſt Night to the Perſon I mention'd: This is the Sword, ſaid I, that was found in the Bodies of the wounded Perſons, therefore upon ſuch a Proof of your Guilt, we ſuppoſe you will confeſs your Crime. Dear General, the Man reply'd, it does not follow, that I committed the Act, becauſe it is my Sword; it is as probable that the Perſon who borrow'd it of me, did it on purpoſe to conceal the Crime.

The

The Tryal lafted Half an Hour, and the Fellow was fo fubtle in his Replies, we were oblig'd to defer it till *Morrice*'s Arrival, who was gone to difcover farther to the *South*. In the mean time, News was brought us, that one of his Men, in fwimming over from one Rock to another, was devour'd by a ravenous Fifh, which coming to the Criminal's Ears, he fix'd upon that Man for the Perfon he had lent his Sword to, and gave fo good a Defcription of his Perfon and Cloaths (which he had cunningly gather'd from People that came to fee him) that we could have no farther Proof againft him: So finding the Perfons likely to recover, I order'd his Releafe, but every one allow'd him Guilty; and what was a Proof, the Woman, when fhe recover'd, openly declared it, by telling fhe was the Caufe of his Misfortunes, expreffing the greateft Love imaginable to him; though fome reported, her Kindnefs increas'd from the Strength of his Body, having never been

been hurt as the other was; but I took that only as a Suppoſition from thoſe who had not all the Regard for the fair Sex. However, this Accident taught us, as long as we had Women among us, it would create farther Diſorders, if ſome Method was not taken to prevent it, by allowing the Uſe of them in a decent Manner: But having no more than Seventy-four Women, and ſome of them married, and upwards of Three hundred Men, we could not give every one a Wife. We allow'd every principal Officer one to himſelf, and the Liberty of chuſing according to their Rank; the reſt we diſtributed into ſeveral Diviſions, allowing every Man under Fifty, to aſſociate with his Woman every fifth Night: For my own Part, I had no Inclination that way, and Seventeen or Eighteen, near my own Age, gave up their Right to the Young and Able.

FOUR Women that had Husbands in *New Holland*, were not of the Number,

ber, but profeſs'd Chaſtity a great while: Theſe Four kept together, and ſeem'd very Reſerv'd ſome time, but at laſt, finding no Hopes of ever ſeeing their Maſters, they became a little uneaſy, and by broad Signs, give us to underſtand, Society was as pleaſing to them as their Neighbours, ſo we took their Neceſſities into Conſideration, and order'd them Conſolation.

FROM ſuch ſmall Beginnings, Empires have been founded, and *Rome*, the Miſtreſs of the World, began with Raviſhment, though our Damſels were willing enough.

THE Time was come we expected Relief from *Batavia*, if our Pinnace had eſcap'd the Danger of the Sea. I therefore commanded our Men to chuſe in the Foreſt, a tall and ſtreight Tree, which I had fix'd upon the Brow of the Cape, with a white Sail, the largeſt we had, that it might be diſtinguiſhable, and

and in the Night I caus'd Fires to be kindled, to direct them if they ſhould come in the Dark; but Providence had order'd it otherwiſe.

FOR three Weeks together there fell abundance of Rain, with violent Winds, and we could perceive great Storms at Sea, though our Bay felt little of it.

OUR *Peaſe* and *Beans* throve very well, with Promiſes of a plentiful Crop, and when they were ripe, we found one Buſhel would yield Three hundred; yet our good Fortune in this, could not hinder another Dread falling upon us: Our Hunters had ſo frighted the Game, that they became ſo ſhie, we could not kill the fourth Part of the Quantity we had formerly done; therefore I gave out an Order, fleſh Meat ſhould be eat but Thrice a Week, and Fiſh the other four Days, for we had Plenty of that. Our Hunters had been out ſeveral Days, and return'd without Succeſs, and, conſequently,

ſequently, our Fears for the want of fleſh Meat increas'd; however, we reſolv'd to ſend our Boat out, to Coaſt along the Shore, with their utmoſt Endeavours to find ſome other Part of the Country, where the Beaſts reſorted, and by Providence, they came Home in three Days, their Boat laden with Deer, and another Beaſt reſembling our *European* Hogs, but of a more delicious Taſte. This rais'd the ſinking Spirits of our Men, and their Joy was as extravagant as their Fear. *Morrice* inform'd us in his laſt Diſcovery, he had found out an Iſland about five Leagues in Circumference, where the Deer ſwam over to, from the Continent; when they landed firſt, they found many Thouſands in a Herd, and great Numbers of Fawns, which convinc'd him that was the Place they reſorted to in Rutting-time. *Morrice* having ſuch good Succeſs in his Diſcoveries, deſir'd he might take another Voyage to the *S. E.* for he was aſſur'd there was a River from that Part of the Country. Accordingly he ſet out with

with Twelve Men, and a Week's Provision. We pray'd for his happy Success, went upon the Affairs of our Colony, till his Return, and several Laws were instituted for the Good of our new Commonwealth.

FOUR Days being past, the limited Time of his Stay, we began to fear for him, every one imagining he had met with some Disaster. We durst not venture our Long-boat to go in quest of him, for fear she should meet with the like Misfortune, and then we should all suffer; for by means of our Boats we could provide Subsistance.

SEVERAL of our Hunters had made a new Plantation on the other Side of the Bay, but without the Boat that *Morrice* had with him, could not assist each other. This gave us much Uneasiness again, and our Spirits were once more sunk to the last degree of Dejection: Our People walk'd about the Settlement like Men that had lost their Tongues, and

Deſpair was lively written in their Faces.

ON the 12th Day of *Morrice*'s Abſence, caſting a longing Look towards the Sea, I perceiv'd three Boats making towards the Shore, one of them we all knew to be that of *Morrice*'s, which occaſion'd ſuch Acclamations among the Men, our Ears were of no Uſe to us. We much wonder'd at the other Boats that came along with him, but looking farther Seaward, we diſcover'd Ten Sail more, which unexpected Sight, once more gave a Damp to our Joys, and now we began to have Fears for our Liberties and Lives. I commanded every Man to his Arms, and got our Cannon in order, to oppoſe them if they ſhould attempt any thing: But they all came to Anchor ſhort of the Shore, and only *Morrice*'s Boat advanc'd: When he came within hearing, he call'd to us to lay by our Fears, and deſir'd we would ſend the Boat to fetch him on Shore, which we did. When the Boats were joyn'd, joyn'd, he ſtept into it with one of his Men, and handed down a grave tall Perſon in a black Gown, a Hat on his Head, with a Flag of Truce in his Hand, and immediately row'd to the Shore where our Men ſtood. When I ſaw this Stranger, I went to the Water-ſide to receive him. *Maurice* told us in few Words, this Perſon was diſpatch'd from the Governor of a City, about Twenty Leagues up the Bay, where he had been very amicably received. When we heard he came as a Friend, we all bow'd to him, in token of Gratitude, which he return'd in the ſame Manner, and ſtretching his Hands towards Heaven, cry'd in very good *French*, *May the eternal Power that rules the World, bleſs you; the Sun his great Miniſter, and our glorious Monarch, ſhine upon you their happieſt Influence.* *Maurice* informing him I was the Chief, he took me kindly by the Hand, which I offer'd to kiſs, but he would not ſuffer it, embracing me, and kiſſing my Forehead, deſiring we would lead him to our Camp. When we came

G 2 there,

there, he obſerv'd our Fortification, and ſeem'd to approve of what we had done to defend ourſelves. When he had ſufficiently view'd the Diſpoſition of our Settlement, he turn'd to me; Sir, ſaid he, I have been inform'd by your Officer of your Adventures and Misfortunes, which induced me to venture myſelf in your Power, without fearing any Indignity offer'd my Perſon; therefore if you will give me leave, I will retire into one of your Tents, and repoſe myſelf, while you hear from Mr. *Morrice* what has befel him ſince his Abſence.

WHEN he had done ſpeaking, I led him into my Tent, and went to *Morrice* with ſome Impatience to hear his Story.

CHAP.

CHAP. V.

Morrice *relates the Particulars of his Voyage.*

MY noble Partners in Misfortunes (ſaid *Morrice*) when I ſet out with the Licence of my worthy Chief, and the reſt of the Council, I ſteer'd *S. E.* the firſt Day, and met with a River that runs into the Bay, where for that Night we caſt Anchor, early in the Morning weigh'd, purſu'd our Voyage up the Stream, and when we were ſail'd about Three Leagues, we perceiv'd the Land open by degrees, which form'd a ſmooth Lake of Water ſo far widening, as we ſail'd along, that the Land was no more to be ſeen; we ſail'd on with a ſmooth Gale that hardly ruffled the Water, till we diſcover'd ſeveral ſmall Iſlands in the Lake, deck'd with Trees of a delightful Verdure.

At Night we caſt Anchor again between two of theſe Iſlands about Half a League aſunder, with an Intention of going aſhore as ſoon as it was Light.

WE paſt Half the Night in Diſcourſes of theſe new Diſcoveries, and our good or evil Fortune, and then went to Repoſe as fearing no Enemy: But at Dawn of Day, when we got up to put our laſt Night's Determination in Execution, I'll leave you to gueſs our Surprize, when we found ourſelves ſurrounded with twelve Veſſels, without Hope of eſcaping. The Loſs of Liberty, was the leaſt we expected; however we reſolv'd to fight it to the laſt, and therefore got ready for an Eagagement. While we were in this Confuſion, one of the Boats advanced with a Perſon who had a Flag of Truce waving about his Head, and as he came nearer us, he bow'd his Body, and told us in *Spaniſh*, to caſt off our Fear, for he meant us no Harm: I order'd one of the Men, who interpreted for us, to aſk him the Reaſon of their

their gathering about us? and he replied, with no other Intention than to give us what Aſſiſtance we might ſtand in need of. He then proceeded to ask us concerning our Voyage, and how we came there in ſo ſmall a Veſſel; to which Queſtions we gave him ſuitable Anſwers.. When he heard what ill Luck had befel us, he gave us Comfort, by telling us Fortune was ever variable, and that great Minds ſhould be above her Frowns. There appear'd in him an open Heart, and ſo many Marks of Sincerity, that we were all pleas'd with his manner of expreſſing himſelf, and finding by our Interpreter, that I was their Leader, and an *Engliſhman*, he addreſs'd me in that Tongue, which ſomething ſurpriz'd me: He ask'd me if we were all that were ſav'd, and I told him we were. I thought it Prudence to tell him ſo, till I found what Treatment we ſhould receive from them. Come, ſaid he, don't deſpair, you are fallen into a Country where you will find every thing to ſatisfy a moderate Man. I beg'd him to tell me the

Name of this hoſpitable Land. In our Language (ſaid he) 'tis call'd *Sporunda*, and the Natives *Sporvi*: Tributary to the opulent Country of the *Sevarambe's*, whoſe Capital was call'd *Sevarinda*; but the City where we intend to carry you, is call'd *Sporunda*, not above five Leagues off. Perceiving ſome Alterations in our Countenances at his laſt Words, he went on, Gentlemen, I adviſ'd you at firſt not to entertain any Notions of Fear, for no Ill will happen to you among us, unleſs you deſerve it by your Miſtruſt or Temerity. We are no Barbarians, as you, perhaps, may imagin; and farther, you ſee our Numbers could eaſily compel you to ſubmit, who are as perfect in the Art of War, as any of your *European* Nations, which you will find to your Coſt, ſhould you provoke us: however, you ſhall be compell'd to nothing, and if you don't approve of going with us, take your Fortune in the Name of God: I'll retire to give you time to conſult among your ſelves, and Heaven direct your Councils for the beſt;

beſt; thus ending, he went to the Head of our Boat, to one of his Companions. We ſoon came to a Reſolution, which he perceiving, met us in the Middle, and ask'd us what we had determin'd? To take your courteous Advice, Sir, (ſaid I) and follow as you ſhall direct. We are a Set of unfortunate Wretches, fitter to excite Pity than Anger.

GENTLEMEN, ſaid he, I am pleas'd with your Reſolves, upon your own Accounts, and we ſhall bring you into a Country of Wonders.

Upon this, he made a Signal to the reſt of the Boats, who came in good Order, and ſtop'd on each Side of us, we were immediately ſupply'd by them with freſh Proviſions of various Sorts, all of an excellent Taſte, as alſo a delicious Wine, the Product of the Country. During our Repaſt, he told me his Name was *Caſhida*, and that of his Companion *Banoſcar*: They were two graceful Perſons, and Habited ſomething like the Noblemen of *Venice*: I beg'd beg'd him to inform me how he came ſo perfect in our *European* Language: That, ſaid he, I ſhall inform you more at leiſure, for now we muſt make the beſt of our Way, that we may reach *Sporunda* before Night. He then ſpoke to the Men in his Veſſel, in the Language of his Country, who immediately came a Head of us, faſten'd a Rope to our Boat and ply'd their Oars, leaving the reſt of their Fleet at Anchor. They tow'd us upon this Salt Lake till about Two in the Afternoon, then it leſſen'd by degrees, and we diſcover'd a pleaſing Country on each Side of us, and a League farther, we came into a River of freſh Water, having a Wall built on each Side in the Form of our Caſtles. Between theſe Walls we paſt till we came to the City of *Sporunda*, ſituated ſomething like * *Coblentz*, upon the

---

* *Coblentz* is a ſtrong and populous City, ſeated upon the Confluence of the River *Rhine*, and *Moſelle* in *Germany*: It was formerly an Imperial free Town; but now is ſubject to the Elector of *Triers*, who generally keeps his Court there.

Con-

Confluence of two Rivers. We ſtopp'd at the Key, where were a vaſt Concourſe of People to attend our coming, having Notice of our Arrival by a ſmall Boat ſent before. *Caſhida* landed firſt, where he diſcours'd ſome time with ſeveral grave Perſons in Black, and then made a Sign to *Bonaſcar* to bring us aſhore. When we were landed, we made our Obeiſance to the Men in Black, and the Chief of them embrac'd me, kiſs'd me on the Forehead, and bid us welcome to *Sporunda*.

WHEN we were all landed, they conducted us through a noble Arch, and we paſs'd a ſpacious Street till we came to an auguſt Building, with Piazza's on both Sides, fill'd up with a Green, border'd with Trees, of a different Growth, than what we had ſeen before. We aſcended ſeveral Marble Steps that brought us within a beautiful Hall, where were ſeveral Tables cover'd with Carpets, far exceeding thoſe of *Perſia*. Near the Tables were ſeveral grave

grave Perſonages, dreſs'd in the ſame Habit as our Friend *Caſbida* wore. We were ask'd many Queſtions by an Interpreter, which I took upon me to anſwer according to our preſent Circumſtances; we were then led into another handſome Apartment, where we found a magnificent Supper, dreſt after the *European* Manner. *Sermodas* (the Perſon that is now in the General's Tent) caus'd us to be ask'd, if we had any Stomachs to our Supper? I told him it was ſo long ſince we had ſeen ſuch a noble Preparation, there would be little doubt of the Goodneſs of our Appetites. He ſmil'd at my Anſwer, and led me to the Table at the Head of the Room, where he and the other grave Men ſat down with me: *Caſbida* and *Bonaſcar*, accompany'd my Men at the other Table. After a plentiful Supper, we were led into Chambers, where my Men lay Two together in one Bed: But *Sermodas* and the others, brought me into a Room with one Bed in it, left me, and wiſh'd me a good Repoſe. Before I

went

went to ſleep, *Caſbida* came to me, and inform'd me, he would come in the Morning to give me Inſtructions how to behave before *Albicormas*, Governor of *Sporunda*, who had given Order for us to be brought before him the next Day.

ABOUT Six a Clock the next Morning I was awak'd by the ringing of a Bell, and an Hour paſs'd away in ruminating on the oddneſs of our ſtrange Fortune; about Seven *Caſbida* and *Bonaſcar* came in, and wiſh'd me good Morrow, enquiring whether I wanted any thing. I would have got up and dreſs'd myſelf; but he forbid it, telling me there were other Cloaths preparing for me, and preſently after, came in ſeveral People, with Linnen and Woollen Habits made after the Manner of the Country: Other Attendants brought in a Veſſel of warm Water for me to Bathe in, before I dreſs'd myſelf. When every thing was laid before me, they went out and left me with one Servant, who gave me Directions how to waſh myſelf, which

I

I did with his Aſſiſtance. When I was dry, I put on a Cotton Shirt and Drawers, with Stockings of the ſame. I had alſo a new black Hat, Shoes, a Gown of ſeveral Colours, which was tied with a black Saſh round my Waiſt.

WHEN I was dreſs'd, the Servant went out, taking my old Cloaths along with him; aſſoon as he was gone, *Caſhida* came in, gave me Directions how to behave myſelf before *Albacormas* and his Council, then led me into the Court-yard, where my Men waited for me, dreſs'd after the ſame Manner, though not quite ſo rich, only they had Caps inſtead of Hats on their Heads. After ſtaying ſome time, *Sermodas* came and pay'd me the Compliments of the Day: Finding us in Readineſs, he led me by the Hand into the Street, follow'd by my Men two by two, led by *Caſhida*, and *Bonaſcar* bringing up the Rear. We march'd in this Order through ſeveral ſpacious Streets, till we came to the Front of a noble Palace, built with white and

and black Marble, so well polish'd, that we all thought it new, though we were inform'd it had been built many Years. In the Front, stood a noble Gate, adorn'd with several Brazen Statues of excellent Workmanship, and on each Side, two long Files of Musqueteers, in blue Coats down to their Ancles. When we had pass'd the Gate, we march'd thro' another File, all cloath'd in Red, with Spears in their Hands; in that Court we halted near a Quarter of an Hour, and all the Time we staid, the Sound of Trumpets, and other warlike Instruments were heard, that yielded a pleasing Harmony: From thence we proceeded thro' another Gate, and enter'd a Court compos'd all of black, shining Marble, with several well-finish'd Statues plac'd in Niches of the Building. In this Court stood a Hundred Men in black Habits, more advanc'd in Years than the former we had seen. After we had halted some Time, two grave Men dress'd like the rest, only with this Difference, of a gold-colour'd Silk hanging

over

†

over their Shoulders, in the Manner of Scarfs for a Funeral in *Europe*. These Persons order'd *Sermodas* to bring us before the Governor. We ascended the Marble Steps, with Ballisters on each Side, richly gilt, which brought us into a noble Hall hung with Paintings of admirable Workmanship; from thence to a Second and Third, each exceeding the other in Richness of Furniture. In the last was plac'd a Throne, with a grave, venerable Person seated on it, and from each Side were several Persons sitting like so many Statues, in a profound Silence. The Governor was cloath'd in Purple, and his Council, as we suppos'd them that sat on each Hand, were dress'd like the Two that usher'd us in. We bow'd (as directed) Three times, the first a gentle Inclination of the Body when we enter'd; the second something lower, when we were in the Middle of the Hall, and the third quite to the Ground when we came to the gilded Rail before the Throne. The Compliment was return'd by the Council, by a little bending of their

their Bodies, but the Governor only gently nodded his Head. *Sermodas* went up cloſe to the Balluſter, leading me by the Hand, and gave the Governor an Account of us, in his own Language, which ſounded ſomething like the corrupted *Greek* in the *Morea*, as it is at preſent ſpoke there. When *Sermodas* had ended his Speech, *Caſbida* was brought forward, who gave the Governor an Account of their firſt Meeting with us, which *Bonaſcar* interpreted to me as he ſpoke: The Subſtance was, that going upon the Iſlands ſituated in the Lake, to celebrate a yearly Feſtival, they ſaw us from the Shore about the Dusk of the Evening, on which Diſcovery, they launch'd out their Boats, and ſurrounded us in the Middle of the Night, to prevent our eſcaping; for they are cautious of being diſcover'd by any *European*, well knowing the Corruption of their Manners might poſſibly diſturb that Tranquillity and even Virtue enjoy'd by the *Sporvi*.

WHEN *Caſbida* had finiſhed his Relation, *Albicormas* roſe from his Seat, and bid us welcome, in his own Language, aſſuring me we ſhould be diverted with all the Innocent Pleaſures the Country afforded, giving order, at the ſame Time, to *Sermodas*, to be our Guide and Guard, while we were at *Sporunda*; in the mean Time, a Meſſenger was diſpatch'd to *Sevarinda*, to know the King's Pleaſure concerning us, or, as they call'd him, *The Sun's Vice-Roy*: *Albicormas* was a Man of a good Preſence, though very crooked; and I was ſomething ſurpriz'd to find Abundance of the great Men that had the ſame natural Defect, tho' for the Generality, both Male and Female were very handſome, well proportion'd People. I ask'd my Friend *Caſhida* whether that Deformity was owing to one particular Race, or ſome Accident in Education? He told me thoſe that I ſaw with any Deformity of Body, were born at *Sevarinda*, and ſent to *Sporunda*, becauſe the Laws of that Country ſtrictly forbid any Perſon living among them, that were mark'd with the leaſt Blemiſh in Body or Mind; thoſe Perſons were ſent to *Sporunda* (which, in

their

their Language, ſignifies the Defective) if Nature had not compos'd them in the pureſt Mould, while thoſe that were corrupted from the Principles of Virtue, were ſent to another Place.

WHEN we were diſmiſs'd from the Preſence of *Albicormas*, we went to our Lodging in the ſame Order as we came. We ſtaid at Home 'till Evening, by Reaſon of the Heat of the Day; but then our Conductors took us out to ſhew us the City, which was very Magnificent in the Building, far ſurpaſſing any of thoſe I had ſeen in *Europe*, for the ſtately Structures, admirable Antiquities, as alſo Arts and Sciences. When we return'd, we found Supper as ready as our Stomachs; an Hour after we had ſupp'd, we were led into another Room, where we ſaw ſeveral Women neatly dreſs'd, all very handſome, their Hair hung over their naked Breaſts in amorous Ringlets too tempting to behold: We were much amaz'd to ſee ſo

H 2 many

many fair Women ſtanding in a Row; but *Sermodas* brought us out of our Surprize, by the following Speech. " I
" perceive your Wonder by your Looks,
" and your Imaginations are confound-
" ed, to find ſo many Women dreſs'd
" differently from the Mode of the
" Country: But every Nation has its
" peculiar Cuſtom, ſome pernicious
" in their own Nature, while others
" ſeem ſo thro' the Prejudice of Man;
" Theſe Women are our Slaves, provi-
" ded for your Uſe. The moderate Uſe
" of theſe Things, appointed by Nature
" for Human Race, are good; Immo-
" deration turns to the Deſtruction of
" Human Kind; therefore every Man's
" Mind contains his Good or Ill: A-
" mong the good Things mentioned,
" two are of the greateſt Importance,
" the Propagation and Preſervation of
" the Specie, and theſe are the eternal
" Laws of God in Nature, and theſe
" two Ends, together with the Pleaſure
" we take, in the Means through which
" we may juſtly attain to them, are
" not only lawful and neceſſary, but
" lau-

“ laudable, and commanded : Beſides
“ theſe two great Concerns, there is a
“ Third ; that is, Human Society, with-
“ out which, no Common-Wealth can
“ ſubſiſt : Our Wiſe Law-giver *Seva-*
“ *riminas*, whoſe glorious and immortal
“ Name be ever Rever'd, founded his
“ Government on the Laws of Nature,
“ eſtabliſh'd by Reaſon, carefully avoid-
“ ing to forbid any Thing that is good
“ in itſelf, allowing the Uſe of them in
“ Moderation, to all his Followers ; a-
“ mong the reſt of his Inſtitutions, one
“ is, *That all Youth ſhould marry at ſuch an*
“ *Age* ; which Law is punctually ob-
“ ſerved among us : But as we are obli-
“ ged to Travel into ſeveral Parts of the
“ Kingdom upon our Affairs, and leave
“ our Wives at Home ; ſo a Traveller,
“ where-ever he goes, is provided with
“ a Female Companion, as well as all
“ other Neceſſaries of Life, by the Go-
“ vernor of the Place, where his Buſi-
“ neſs calls him to ; therefore being rea-
“ dy to uſe you with the ſame Indul-
“ gence we do our own Countrymen ,
“ we have ordered theſe Women to at-

" tend you, if you think fit to make " Uſe of them. " There needed but little Rhetorick to prevail on us to accept their Offer, and moſt of us allow'd the Cuſtom of their Country: to be far better than ours, and we return'd him Thanks for the Civilities we met with ſo unexpectedly: Well, ſaid *Sermodas*, I'll leave you to agree among yourſelves in your Choice, ſo left us. When he was gone, two Men came to us, who bid us welcome to *Sporunda*, in *French*; one was a Phyſician, and the other a Surgeon to the Government, who was to examine us for fear we might be ſubject to ſome unclean Diſtemper; We are ſent, ſaid the two Perſons, to know the State of your Bodies, therefore freely declare, if any of you are afflicted with any Diſeaſe; if you are candid in your Declarations, you will meet with Reſpect for dealing uprightly, otherwiſe, Contempt will follow the Concealment: We all told him, That we were ſound and wholeſome Men; however, we were examin'd, one by one, in private, and prov'd to be what we ſaid, which much rejoyc'd the

the two Gentlemen, who left us to proceed in the Choice of our Females. I had my first Choice, my two Mates the next, the rest of the Men drew Lots, and every one was satisfied: As soon as the Choice was made, we were eager to go to Bed; I lay in the same Room I had done before, but my Men were plac'd in another Gallery, in little Cells, something like those I have seen in Monastries abroad. You may guess how we pass'd the Night, for my own Part, I should have lain longer in Bed, but my Paramour left me when the Morning Bell rung, and *Casbida* enter'd to tell me it, was Time to rise, he told me *Bonascar* was gone to release my Men from Fetters, (meaning the Embraces of their Mistresses) when I was dress'd, I enter'd the Hall, where I found my Men waiting for me; after Breakfast, our Guides took us out to shew us the Work-Houses of the City, where Men and Women were employ'd in all the Manufactures of the Country.

WE liv'd in this delightful Manner, 'till the Return of the Messenger that was ſent to *Sevarminas* : In a few Days, he came back, with an Order from the King, we ſhould be brought to the Capital of the *Sevarambians*, that he might ſee us ; I then began to repent I had conceal'd the Truth ſo long, of your being at the Camp ; but conſidering the Virtue of the *Sporvi*, and the Knowledge they had of the Frailties incident to Humanity, I did not doubt his Pardon : therefore I waited on *Sermodas*, and ſpoke to him in the following Manner ; Sir, I know not how I ſhall gain Forgiveneſs for the Offence I have committed, in concealing from you the Truth of every Thing; but when you will conſider, we are born of a Race more liable to Weakneſſes than the Natives of this happy Country, I hope you will forgive us : I then related to him the Hiſtory of what had befel us, which he ſeem'd pleas'd with, and immediately acquainted the Governor, who ſoon excus'd us, when he was told the Motives that caus'd me to conceal it : He inſtantly diſpatch'd another Meſſenger to *Sevarminas*, and we had Orders to ſtay in *Sporunda* 'till he came back

back, where we liv'd in all the Content imaginable; when he return'd, a Mandate was brought, that order'd our whole Number before the King, where we were aſſured, our Uſage ſhould be much nobler, according to the Goodneſs and Magnificence of their Glorious Monarch. This is the Sum of all our Adventures, ſince my Abſence, and this Fleet, you ſee, is come to convey us all to *Sporunda*, in order to our further Journey.

CHAP. VI.

The Author and his People leave their Camp, and are conducted to Sporunda. *A Deſcription of the* Oſparenibon, *and ſeveral other Material Paſſages.*

WE were very well pleas'd with *Maurice*'s Relation, and thought ourſelves happy in our Misfortunes, to be thrown among ſuch Hoſpitable People, where we little expected any Inhabitants; our Men came in Crouds about the Hut, to know our Reſolutions (for thoſe that accompanied *Maurice*, had related to them their

their Adventures) we ſoon determin'd to wait upon *Sermodas*, and truſt to theſe generous Natives our future Fortune. One Thing I muſt own a little dampt my Joy, and that was, if any Succour ſhould arrive from *Batavia*, not finding us where we had appointed them, they would of Courſe imagine we were all cut off by ſome Diſaſter. But *Maurice* remov'd even that Fear, telling me the *Sevarambians* had Veſſels that traded to ſeveral Parts of the World, and if we did not approve of ſtaying among them, he aſſured us there would be no Difficulty in having Leave for a Veſſel to tranſport us where we ſhould think fit. This, ſaid *Maurice*, is what I learnt, when I was among them; for enquiring of *Caſhida*, how they came to underſtand ſo many of our *European* Languages, he anſwer'd, they ſent People for that Purpoſe yearly, to all the Courts of *Europe*, not only to trade, but to learn the Language, Cuſtoms, and Manners of each particular Nation. The good Inſtitutions were put in Practice, by an Order of Council, and the bad were recorded in their

their Archives, to be read on particular Days, that the Natives might learn their own Happineſs, in poſſeſſing the Good, and ſhunning the Bad: The Knowledge of this wip'd away from our Minds the Terrors we had imbib'd, concerning our Loſs of Liberty, and every one prepar'd to remove from this Place, with the ſame Joy, as if we were on our Voyage Home. I went to wait on *Sermodas*, to pay him my Reſpects, who came to meet me with a chearful Countenance; Well, ſaid he, in *French*, How do you like the Deſcription your Officer has given you of our Country? So well, Sir, ſaid I, that we have all of us a longing Deſire to be there, if you'll pleaſe to conduct us: 'Twas for that Purpoſe I came, reply'd *Sermodas*, and though you have, by your Induſtry, made your Camp a Place not to be deſpis'd, yet you will find our Cities and Towns ſo well furniſh'd with every Thing needful for Human Life, you will not regret the Loſs of it. When we had made a ſlender Repaſt, we imbark'd our People and Goods on Board the Veſſels *Srrmodas* had brought with

with him; our Admiral, in one of them, was ſent to fetch our Men from our new Plantation, on the other Side of the Bay, and the third Day after our leaving the new Settlement, we arrived at *Sporunda*. Our Reception was much the ſame deſcrib'd before by *Maurice*, only *De Hayes* and I, had more Attendance and Reſpect paid us: *Albicormas* roſe from his Seat, when I was brought before him, and very tenderly embraced me; bidding me Welcome; we had ſeveral Diſcourſes, by an Interpreter, concerning the Affairs of *Europe*, and I was much ſurprized, notwithſtanding what I had learn'd from *Maurice*, to find a Perſon ſo well read in the Policy of our Nations, he underſtood *Latin* and *Greek* to Perfection, and ever afterwards we convers'd in one or other of thoſe Languages; from this generous Governor, I was inform'd in every Thing that was curious of their Country.

WHEN all our People were arrived, they were cloathed in the ſame Manner as *Maurice*'s Men were before; but there aroſe

arose some Difficulty concerning our Women; for, in our Camp five Men were allow'd the Use of but one Woman, and only the Officers had the Privilege of having a Woman to themselves. *Sermodas*, and the rest of the *Sporvi*, were very much displeas'd at the Plurality of Men to one Woman, declaring it would not be suffer'd in their Country: We had no Excuse for it, but our Necessity, which he admitted of, and order'd a List of our Men and Women, that a Number of the latter might be provided for those that wanted Companions. The next Day, every Man had his Mate, and Beds with other Conveniencies; We soon found a great deal of Discontent in those Women we brought with us, being not so well serv'd, as when they had five Men for their Recreation; but it was to no Purpose to repine, those of the Number that prov'd with Child, were oblig'd to chuse one of the Five, for the Father, though I can't say with what Justice, yet there was no other Way to decide it: But there were but few found pregnant, that had to do with

with more than one Woman; which proves, that Ground too much till'd bears the leaſt Corn.

THE fifth Day after our Arrival, *Sermodas* informed me, we ſhould prepare to go to the Temple, where the *Oſparenibon* (or Marriage Rites) were ſolemnized, it being the Grand Feſtival, and perform'd four Times a Year: I and my Principal Officers, were dreſs'd in new Cloaths, the Habits of the Country, and the reſt of the Men that were not cloathed before, were furniſhed: We went with our Conductors, *Caſhida* and *Benoſcar*, to the Governor's Palace, from thence to the Temple, a Noble Structure: In one of the Iſles ſtood a Row of beautiful young Men, and Women: The Men with Garlands of green Boughs on their Heads; the Women with Chaplets of odoriferous Flowers of different Colours. The back Part of the Temple was hid from our Sight, by the Interpoſition of a Silk Curtain. We ſtaid viewing the Curioſities of the Place, ſome Time, before any one elſe came

in;

in; but at laſt our Ears were charm'd with the Sound of ſeveral melodious Inſtruments; while the Muſick was playing, the Windows of the Temple were darkned, but ſo many Wax Tapers were plac'd every where, that the Light formed a new Day; Then the Curtain was drawn, and expos'd to our View the High Altar of curious Workmanſhip, inlaid with Flowers of Gold, and in the Centre hung a Globe of Cryſtal, that illumined the Place: In the Extremity of the Altar, was plac'd the Figure of a Woman, with many Breaſts, giving ſuck to as many Infants: The Muſick we heard came nearer, and, at laſt enter'd the Temple, follow'd by *Albicormas*, and the whole Senate of *Sporunda* in magnificent Habits: In the Middle of the Temple, he was met by ſeveral Prieſts with Cenſors in their Hands, ſinging very agreeably, they bow'd to him three Times, then led him to the High Altar, where every one bowed thrice, and retir'd to their Seats.

THE

THE Governor plac'd me at the Foot of his Throne, and the reſt of my Officers and Men were rang'd over againſt us on the other Side. After ſome other ſhort Ceremonies, the Prieſts beckon'd the young People I mention'd before, who approach'd the Altar, the Men on the Right, and the Virgins on the Left. The High Prieſt aſcended a little Throne, and made a ſhort Oration; immediately after enter'd ſeveral Prieſts, with Fire in a Cenſor, kindled, as we were inform'd, by the Sun Beams. *Albicormas* approach'd it with the utmoſt Reverence, kneel'd and made a ſhort Prayer, which ended, the Prieſts began another Song, accompany'd with the Inſtruments.

WHEN the Symphony was ended, the High Prieſt ask'd the firſt of the Range of Virgins, *If ſhe would be Married?* She bow'd, bluſh'd and anſwer'd *Yes.* He then proceeded to ask the ſame Queſtion thro' the whole Range, while another did the ſame by the young Men. When that Part of the Ceremony was over,

over, the Prieſt took the firſt young Woman by the Hand, led her to the Men on the other Side, and bid her chuſe her Husband; when ſhe had fix'd upon the Perſon ſhe lik'd, ſhe ſtopp'd, and demanded of him, *If he was willing to be her Lord and faithful Husband?* The young Man readily anſwer'd *Yes, if ſhe would promiſe to be his true and loyal Wife:* She reply'd, *till Death.* The Bridegroom then took her by the Hand, kiſs'd her Forehead and Lips, then led her to the lower End of the Temple. This was the Marriage Ceremony, all the reſt doing the ſame, marching out of the Temple by Couples, with the Muſick ſounding before them.

I can't but admire this Inſtitution, being there's no danger of forc'd Marriages, for the Man may refuſe when he's ask'd, if he does not approve of the Maiden, which does ſometimes happen; and if a Virgin is diſappointed thrice, ſhe has the liberty of chuſing any marry'd Senator, who never refuſes to take the Perſon for one of his Wives, for *Polygamy* is

I allow'd

allow'd among them. The rest of the Day was wasted in Feasting and Mirth, tho' in so large a Place, there was not the least Disorder committed thro' Excess.

THE next Day we were carry'd to the Temple, to see another Ceremony, the Sequel of the former. All the young Men walk'd in Triumph, preceded by Musick as before, with the green Boughs, their Wives Garlands, and, according to the Custom of the *East*, Tokens of their Wives Virginity in their Hands. They approach'd the Altar, and Consecrating these Tokens, with their Wreaths, to the Supreme Being, the Sun, the King and their Country; then retir'd in the same Manner they enter'd. The Solemnities continu'd three whole Days.

OUR Time of leaving *Sporunda* was come, therefore I went with my Officers to return *Albicormes* the Thanks which were due from his Civilities. You are now going, said he, to a Place that exceeds this as far as the radiant Beams of the Sun excel the faint Glimmerings of the

the Moon; *Sermodes* at my Requeſt will be your Guide, therefore I ſhall deſire you for your own Sakes, to obſerve his Inſtructions. So tenderly embracing us, he bid us Farewel, wiſhing us a good Journey. The next Day we embark'd on board ſeveral curious painted Barges on the weſtern River, which gave us a delightful Proſpect of the Country on each Side. We reach'd a ſmall City that Night, call'd *Sporuma*, in the Territories of *Sporunda*. We were very well received by the Chief of the Place, and the Governor, who had Notice of our Arrival, had provided every thing that was neceſſary for our Accomodation, and bid us Welcome. We ſaw nothing Remarkable here; but the Puniſhment of Fourteen Malefactors. There were three Claſſes of them, the firſt were Six Men, one for Murder, the other Five for Adultery; the ſecond, Five young Women, Two to be puniſh'd as the Husbands thought fit, for being falſe to their Beds, the other three Females, for having given up their Virginity before Marriage; the laſt, were the Three young Men that Debauch'd them, who were to ſuffer three Years Impriſonment with them, and, the Time expir'd, to wed them. The Criminals were brought before the Gate of the Council-Houſe, and ſtript of all their Cloaths to their Waiſt. One of the Women that had wrong'd her Husband, was the loveliest Creature that e'er my Eyes beheld, and her Dejection ſeem'd more to heighten her Charms; ſhe was about Two-and-twenty, lovely brown Hair, and ſuch round poliſh'd Breaſts, as ever Nature fram'd. I was oblig'd to muſter up all my Fortitude, to reſolve to behold the Executioner do his Duty: I believe the ſame Emotion as affected me, ran through the whole Crowd, for every one look'd as thoroughly concern'd as myſelf. The Officer was juſt lifting up his Scourge to fall upon that lovely Body, when her Husband preſs'd through the Crow'd, and cry'd, Hold! hold! The Man ſuſpended the Blow, to hear what he had to ſay. Sir, ſaid he, I am that unfortunate Woman's Husband, therefore beg to have the Liberty of ſpeaking two

two or three Words to her, e'er you proceed in your Chaſtiſement. He then approach'd his Wife, and wiping away ſome Tears that fell from his Eyes, in broken Accents, ſpoke to her as follows; *You know*, Ulisba, *with what Affection I have regarded you from the firſt Moment of our Marriage to that of your Crime, you ſtand now to be puniſh'd for, and till that fatal Moment, I flatter'd myſelf with a reciprocal Affection: Even now my eaſy Heart tells me I have ſome Share in yours. I am no Stranger to the Wiles us'd by the Deſtroyer of your Honour, and my Peace; and I am convinc'd, if he had not given you many convincing Circumſtances (though falſe) of a criminal Converſation between his Wife and me, you would have ſtill been innocent. Theſe Tranſactions I have been inform'd of within theſe Three Hours; if I had known this before, I would have ſooner put an End to my own Being, than have ſuffer'd you to come to this; and if you have ſtill that Tenderneſs in your Heart, which once you gave me Reaſon to believe (as the Law muſt be ſatisfy'd) the impending Stroaks ſhall fall upon me, to ſave that precious Fleſh, more dear to me than my own*

own Eyes. Here he paus'd, to expect her Reply. The fair Criminal stood some time silent, while the Tears bedew'd her lovely Cheeks; at last she spoke; *Turn thy Eyes, my dear* Bramista, *from an Object that ought to move no other Passion than Indignation. Whatever Motive induc'd me, I am guilty, though my Heart never consented; but be assur'd, I have long ago sincerely repented of my Crime, and I would this Moment part with Life to convince you of it.* The tender Scene lasted some time, and the Result was, the Husband received the Stripes which were due to his Wife, with a chearful Countenance, while the lovely Offender seem'd at the Gates of Death at his generous Sufferings. This Custom is allow'd any Malefactor of this Nature, for another Person to receive their Punishment, if any one is willing to undergo it.

AFTER the Ceremony, we went to our Lodgings full of melanchollly Thoughts at what we had seen; The next Morning we imbark'd upon the same River, but the Stream growing stronger,

ſtronger, we were oblig'd to make uſe of Horſes to Tow us along; we could perceive, at a great Diſtance, vaſt high Mountains, which *De Hays* aſſur'd me by their Situation, were thoſe he had diſcover'd, when he ſet out from our old Camp, to explore the Country. The next Day, we left the River on the *Weſt*, and purſu'd our Journey on Land to the *South*, in Chariots for the Officers, and the reſt of the People in a Vehicle like our Caravans, only neater made; we made but a ſmall Journey before we din'd, for the Ground riſing by degrees, made it hard Labour for our Cattle. At Night we gain'd the Baſe of the high Mountains, and ſtopt at a Town very handſomely built, call'd *Sporogunda*, and were candidly receiv'd by *Aſtorbas* the Governor, a Perſon well skill'd in the Dead Languages. Here we reſted three Days, but ſaw nothing different from the other Cities of the *Sparvi* (for they are all built alike) but vaſt Canals made by Art, to water the adjacent Plains; ſuch a ſtupendous Work would have coſt Fifty Millions of Livres in *Europe*;

but

but here was finiſh'd without any Expence, every one lending a helping Hand, having no current Coin; but bartering one thing for another: Yet they have the richeſt Mines in the Univerſe, but they only uſe the Oar for Utenſils of the Houſe, or to adorn their Temples.

HERE I ſhall end my firſt Part, that my Pen may reſt, till we get over the Mountains of *Severambe*; where we ſhall deſcribe the Cuſtoms, Manners, Policy and Religion of a Nation, the Envy, when known, of all the other Parts of the World.

End of the Firſt Part.

TRAVELS

INTO SEVERAL

Remote NATIONS

OF THE

WORLD.

By *Captain* LEMUEL GULLIVER.

VOL. III. PART II.

A Voyage to SEVARAMBIA, &c.

LONDON:

Printed in the Year MDCCXXVII.

THE

CONTENTS.

CHAP. I.

THE Author, and Company, leave Sporunda, *and arrive at the Mountains; their Journey over 'em describ'd; a terrible Rencounter with several Wild Beasts,*

A 2

CHAP. II.

CHAP. III.

CHAP.

CONTENTS.

TRAVELS.

TRAVELS.

PART II.

A VOYAGE *to* SEVARAMBIA.

CHAP. I.

The Author, and Company, leave Sporumba, *and arrive at the Mountains; their Journey over 'em deſcrib'd; a terrible Rencounter with ſeveral Wild Beaſts, in which the Author was in danger of Death.*

T the Baſe of theſe great Mountains, which were the Confines of *Sevarambia*, we repos'd our ſelves three whole Days, in a Town call'd *Cola*, which in the *Sevarambian* Language, means, *Delightful Prospect*: Water'd by three Fertile Rivers, *Banon*, *Caru* and *Silkar*. The Earth along the verge of this Ridge of Mountains is extremely Fruitful, even beyond Imagination. The Induſtrious Tillager reaping four Crops every Year, being the Glebe wants neither Heat, nor Moiſture.

THE Climate of *Sevarambia*, and its Borders, is the moſt benign in the Univerſe, and the Seaſons are more diſtinguiſh'd by the Sun and Stars, drawing nearer and farther from the Poles, than the Inclemency of the Weather.

THE chief Reaſon of our Stay here, was occaſion'd by *Sermodas*, who had many Acquaintance, and particularly a Female Friend, who ingroſs'd the beſt part of his Time: However, he gave us all the Diverſion the Place afforded, by ordering to be ſhewn us the delightful

lightful Gardens and Seats upon the Rivers, that far exceeded, both in Situation and Grandeur, any I had ſeen in our Parts of the World. But the hunting the Oſtriche, was what moſt delighted our Men, which was after this Manner.

THE Beagles, not unlike thoſe of *Europe*, are brought coupled into the Park where the Oſtriches are kept, and at a Signal of a Wind-Inſtrument are unloos'd; when they have got ſight of their Quarry, they purſue different Ways, 'till at length they ſurround the Chaſe, who only continues running, for their Wings are too ſmall for Flight. When they come within Reach, the Creature with its Bill, and ſtump'd Feet, lays about like a Stag at Bay; and tho' no Stroke it gives deſtroys the Dogs, yet it occaſions great Confuſion among 'em, by tumbling 'em up and down. When the Creature is thoroughly tir'd, it endeavours to fly, for the Dogs ſo embarraſs her Feet, there's no hopes of her Running. The Efforts ſhe makes, ſtill weaken her the more, 'till ſhe drops down for want of Strength, and then the Dogs ſeize her; but ſhe is immediately reſcu'd by the Huntſmen from their Rage, and put in a Cage, 'till ſhe recovers her uſual Strength, and then ſhe is ſet at Liberty again. This Diverſion gave me the more Delight, from its Innocency; becauſe the Purſu'd, nor Purſuers, came to any great Hurt. For I muſt own, when I have been hunting in my Native Country, and heard the Horns ſound the Death of the Stag, my Mind has been over-clouded with Melancholy. I have pitied the Fate of the noble Beaſt. I have often reflected with Concern upon the Barbarity of Man, to chuſe for Diverſion a thing that ends in Death; therefore my Sentiments are, never to oppoſe any thing that does not firſt oppoſe me.

THIS

THIS Town of *Cola* was the laſt in the Precincts of *Sporunda*, and that is the Reaſon Travellers ſtay here ſome time to enjoy themſelves with the fair Sex; for that Privilege is deny'd 'em whenever they enter the *Sevarambian* Dominions. For ſuch Delights agree not with the rigid Virtue of the Inhabitants, or the Nature of the Air. For at the firſt Tincture of inordinate Deſires, the whole Body undergoes a Revolution; their Skin appears Languid and Sallow, Boils and Blotches poſſeſs their Faces, eſpecially the Noſe, that Correſpondent to the nobler Members.

IN ſhort, all manner of vicious Thoughts inſtantly appear on the outward Form, and diſgrace the Entertainer. I have often thought, if ſuch a Change were made in my own Country, what frightful Wretches would even the beſt of us appear.

AFTER three Days Refreshment at *Cola*, *Sermodas* provided Carriages to convey us over the Mountains, where our Desires had been long before.

THE Beasts we rode on were very like the *Unicorn*, pictur'd as one of the Supporters of the Arms of *England*; a Creature swift, and sure of Foot, and as docible (thro' the Industry of the Inhabitants) as any of our well-temper'd Horses.

INSTEAD of a Bridle, a Cord of Silk was fasten'd to its Horn, which answer'd that end; for by different Pulls as we were directed to make, the Creature would go swifter, slower, stop short, or turn, just as we wou'd have it.

AFTER Dinner we took leave of our Friends in *Cola*, and some of us with Regret, as not being thoroughly fix'd in the Principles of Virtue.

WE

We ſaw ſeveral fierce Beaſts down in the wild Vales below us, where we were often diverted at the Sight of ſeveral dreadful Combats among 'em, about their Prey; but the Pleaſure I receiv'd was to think I was out of the reach of their Teeth and Claws, tho' even the terrible Yells they made ſometimes took off that Satisfaction.

One Battel held near half an Hour, which we halted to ſee. Two Bears had ſurpriz'd an ill-fated Deer in the Buſhes before us; and before they had wounded her to Death, a furious Lion flew in, to force from them their Prey. One of the Beaſts encounter'd him, while the other held faſt the dying Victim; but ſeeing his Companion almoſt worſted, ran in to his Aſſiſtance, and attack'd the Lion ſo vigorouſly, that the kingly Beaſt gave way to their Aſſaults, and retir'd; but the laſt Bear followed him (for the other was ſo wounded in his Legs, he was forc'd to remain on the Field of Battel, tho' no Conqueror) which the Lion perceiving, ruſh'd upon him ſo furiouſly, that he was forc'd to ſeek for Safety by Flight. Upon which the Lion return'd, and fed upon the Deer, in Sight of the wounded Bear, who found himſelf too weak for another Tryal: Yet the flying Bear returning immediately, the other rous'd himſelf as well as he cou'd, and both together gave the Lion another Aſſault, which obliged him to run off with a Piece of the Deer in his Mouth; then the Bears fell too, and devour'd all but the Guts.

BEFORE Night we came to vaſt high Mountains nam'd *Sporakas*, whoſe Tops exceeded the famous *Pike* of *Tenneriff* for Height; and, tho' a warm Climate, are ever cover'd with Snow.

As

As we proceeded in our Journey, my Ears, as I thought, were ſaluted with the Sound of Trumpets, and ſeveral Wind muſical Inſtruments, which made me ſay to *Sermodas*, I hop'd there was no Danger of being attack'd by an Enemy. My Fears made *Sermodas* and the *Sporvi* ſmile. No, ſaid he, we are in no Danger, no Oppreſſion or Violence ever come from humane Kind in our Land, ſince the Flood, of which we may boaſt a better Account than any *European* can give. Indeed, ſome Attempts have been made upon our Borders, but without ſucceeding. We have not the Paſſions and irregular Deſires of other Mortals; but if at any time ſuch things ſhould ariſe among us, the Aggreſſor is immediately baniſh'd the Kingdom, never to return. Then he inform'd me the Sound I heard, came from a fall of Waters that was near us. At Night we reſted in a natural Rock, that had ſeveral convenient Chambers

Chambers work'd by the ſame Hand, but one ſo refulgent, that I imagin'd at firſt I was viewing the Retiring-Room of the Sun.

WHILE Supper was preparing, *Sermodas* led us to view this Profuſeneſs of Nature's Handy-work; and one wou'd have imagin'd by the Luſtre, it was one intire Diamond, but he told us it was nothing but Ice chryſtaliz'd by Time, and ſo hard, the Beams of the Sun had now no more Power on it.

AFTER viewing ſufficiently this glorious Sight, we went to Supper; but were diſturb'd, by a Leopard purſu'd by a wild Maſtiff, that had taken Shelter in one of the inner Rooms to reſt themſelves, but were rous'd by the Noiſe of our People. We had ſtopp'd the Entrances of our Lodgings with our Baggage, ſo that the Beaſts could not get out; which ſo allarm'd me, and

and our Men, we ran for our Arms to diſpatch 'em; fearing they ſhould take it into their Heads to attack us: Shake off your Fear, ſaid *Sermodas*, ſit ſtill, and you'll ſee ſome Diverſion. Before he had done ſpeaking, the two Beaſts began to grin at one another, and at laſt fell to the Aſſault; ſometimes the Leopard ſeem'd to have the Maſtery, and then again the Maſtiff. The Engagement wou'd not have ended but with the Death of one by the other, or both, if *Sermodas* had not order'd two of our Men to diſcharge their Pieces on 'em; the Leopard was kill'd upon the Place, but the Maſtiff retreated into one of the inner Rooms, where we gave him leave to ſtay till Morning, firſt ſecuring the Entrance.

At Dawn of Day we roſe, took our Barricado's from the Mouths of our Cells, and by throwing wild Fire, the Maſtiff came running out, but he ſoon met with the Fate of his Antagoniſt. As

As ſoon as it was broad Day, we went to view once more thoſe Rarities of Nature; but I ſhall forbear deſcribing 'em, leſt they ſhould ſeem ſo incredible to the Reader, he might be apt to cenſure the Truth of the whole.

When the *Sporvi* that have any Blemiſh by Nature arrive at this Place, they waſh themſelves in a Fountain of Water, of a yellowiſh Colour, which not only cleanſes the Body, but waſhes away all baſe Deſires, and prepares them for the Converſation of thoſe virtuous Inhabitants on the other Side of the Mountains.

All the *Europeans* likewiſe waſh'd here; and I muſt own for my own part, I felt my ſelf a new Creature in my Inclination, and every Man of my Company declar'd the ſame.

When

When we were ready to purſue our Journey, we were ſtopp'd by the following Accident. A *Jaccal* came in ſight of our *Unicorns*, which is a Creature they have the ſame Antipathy to, as a *Grehound* has to a *Hare*; nothing cou'd hinder their Purſuit, and we were oblig'd to ſtay 'till they had hunted him down, and devour'd him; when they had ended, we purſu'd our Journey, and before Noon we had a Proſpect of the delightful City of *Sevarambi*, whoſe tow'ring Pinnacles ſeem'd to reach the Sky. The Sight charm'd us all, and the pleaſing Satisfaction we felt, wou'd but faintly be deſcrib'd by Words.

As we journey'd on, *Sermodas* gave us the following Advice as to our Behaviour, when we came amongſt the *Sevarambi*. You muſt be ſure (ſaid he) not to be Over-loquacious, for if they

5 find,

find, by a Multiplicity of Words, any Indiſcretion, they will deſpiſe you, and not think you worthy to dwell among 'em. Take great care you are not ſingular in your Behaviour; never ſwear; and if you are ever admoniſh'd by any of 'em, be ſure to reform; follow their Advice, and imitate 'em in all their Actions; then they will reſpect and love you. Uſe the Benefits Nature beſtows upon this happy Country with Moderation. If any one offers you Preſents (for as they are generous, you will have many) never reject 'em, for they take it as a great Slight to have their Gifts refus'd. For other Advice, I ſhall give it you as things occur, and be always ready to ſerve you.

WHEN he had ended, we return'd him Thanks, with a general Promiſe to have a ſtrict Regard to his wholeſome Counſel.

WE

We came at laſt to the bottom of the Mountain, where flow'd a noble River, broader much than the *Thames* at *Rotherhith*. *Sermodas* told us this Stream almoſt encompaſs'd the Kingdom of *Sevarambi*. It was the ſetting of the Sun by that time we came to the River, therefore we were obliged to wait 'till the next Day, 'ere we could croſs it; for the *Sevarambians* have no Bridges over, becauſe they will not admit of ſuch eaſie Acceſs into their Dominions.

They fear two things from Strangers, their Vices, and Diſeaſes; therefore all Paſſages to 'em are well guarded. We repos'd our ſelves 'till Morning in fragrant Bowers of *Jeſſamine* and *Roſes*, purpoſely planted for the Conveniency of the *Sporvi*, when they come about any Buſineſs to *Sevarambi*; for the Boat that wafts over, does always remain on the other ſide of the River.

The

THE Calmneſs of the Evening invited us to walk by the Banks of the Stream; where we were entertain'd with a Conſort of harmonious Birds, the Inhabitants of thoſe delightful Groves, compos'd of Variety of Trees, ſome peculiar to the Climate, and others ſuch as we have in *Europe*.

WE were ſo well pleas'd with our Situation, our Thoughts cou'd not form to us a Place more glorious, or pleaſant; but *Sermodas* told us we ſhou'd be of another Mind on the Morrow.

I ASK'D *Sermodas* how this Country, ſo excellent in every thing, cou'd ſo long be conceal'd from thoſe of *Europe*, ſo fam'd for their Diſcoveries in Navigation? That, ſaid *Sermodas*, requires a long Diſcourſe to inform you; however I will not leave you entirely in the dark; according to our Tradition, which

which, we may without boasting, declare, exceeds any thing of yours.

ADAM, your first Parent, for his Disobedience, was banish'd *Paradise*; they had Liberty of possessing the circumjacent Parts, but no Hopes of ever entring there again. When the Flood came upon the Face of the Earth, it drove it to another Chaos, remov'd Mountains and Vallies, and at last form'd by its violent Workings another World, less fair than the former; but *Paradise*, that was at first seated in *Asia*, was remov'd intire here with the Hands of Angels, by the Command of the Omnipotent Power; and because there was none of the Race of *Noah*, worthy to inhabit this Place of Perfection; a Couple were form'd, not of the slimy Earth, but of the refin'd Metals, which makes their Bodies clearer, and their Flesh purer, free from those gross Matters that compose the other Parts of the World.

THIS Pair was call'd *Chericus* and *Salmoda*; and from their Loins have proceeded the *Sevarambian* Race. They had a hundred Sons, and the ſame Number of Daughters. His eldeſt Son was call'd *Sevarias*, the Founder of our pure Law, and from whence we derive our Name; who when he paid the Tribute of Nature, after living two thouſand Years, was entomb'd in the City he built.

WHILE he reign'd, ſome of the Offspring of *Noah* were drove by a violent Storm on our Coaſt; one of their Chiefs meeting with a beautiful Virgin nam'd *Seriſſa*, raviſh'd her; the Effects of his Guilt, produc'd Twins; the Boy was call'd *Babo*, and the Girl *Chreſtona*.

THIS Couple being deform'd of Body, cou'd make no Alliances with the *Sevarambians*, who deſpis'd 'em; therefore

fore they match'd together, and increas'd to a numerous People. Our holy Law-giver obſerving their Number, wou'd not out of his Humanity deſtroy 'em, neither wou'd he ſuffer 'em to mingle with the *Sevarambians*, but ſent 'em to build the City of *Sporunda*; and from this Beginning proceeds our Crookedneſs.

FOR this reaſon, as I ſaid, they will not permit us to marry among 'em, tho' they love us as Brothers; but their Humanity is ſuch, they eſteem all the Race of Mankind.

SEVARIAS knowing the Weakneſs of our Nature, granted us many Privileges, which he wou'd not permit the pure Race that ſprung from him to enjoy, neither did they deſire it, from the Strength of their Virtue. But if they ſhou'd be ſo far led by wild Deſires, as to forget their great Founder's Laws; the very Crime

C 2 wou'd

wou'd be their Puniſhment, for their Guilt would appear in their Countenances, by viſible Tokens in their Faces, of Boils, and Sores; there would need no other Tryal for their Conviction. And to puniſh ſuch as fall from the Purity of their Manners, they are inſtantly baniſh'd this earthly *Paradiſe*, and confin'd to live upon the Borders on the other Side of the River, where they often repent their paſt Crimes, and ſink to the Grave in Penitence for degenerating from their Race.

BUT I ſhall enlarge farther in deſcribing the Cuſtoms and Manners of theſe excellent People, when we come among 'em; for they never venture on this ſide the River, for fear the Purity of their Manners ſhou'd be corrupted by the Converſation of Strangers.

OUR Diſcourſe was interrupted by the Yelling and Approach of ſeveral wild Beaſts, of whom we ſoon had a View.

View. A Party of Jaccals, follow'd in the Rear by two old Lyons, and ſeveral young ones, in queſt of their Prey, came furiouſly upon us; they were ſoon join'd by many other wild Beaſts, who came in upon the Cry of the Jaccals; we had no other Remedy but Flight, for fearing no Danger, we had left our Weapons behind us. We ran with what haſte we cou'd to gain our Lodgment for Security, and the common Axiom of *Fear adds Wings*, had like to have been ſpoil'd; for my own part, I muſt freely own the Danger robb'd me of my Strength.

One of the foremoſt Leopards caught *Maurice* by the Skirt of his Habit, which he tore off, and devoured; this Stay gave him Time to eſcape: Another ſeiz'd me by the Buttocks, and held me ſo hard, I gave over all Thoughts of Life; for the reſt of our People had got far before me. However the Terrors of Death appear'd to me, I was resolv'd to defend my self as well as I cou'd. I seiz'd fast hold of one of the Ears of the Beast, and thrust my Finger into his Eye, which caus'd him to roar out, and loose his first hold; but he immediately sprung on me again with his open Jaws, which I perceiving ran my Hand down his Throat, held fast his Tongue, and with our Struggling, tore it up by the Root. In this time, several other Beasts had surrounded me; but I flung the Tongue among 'em, and there ensu'd a terrible Fight for it, which gave me an Opportunity of getting several paces before 'em, follow'd only by an old Bear. My Haste, and often looking behind me, made me stumble over a Stump that lay in my way, and the Bear in his furious Career ran over me, before he cou'd stop himself.

Now I thought all means of Escape were lost, therefore I recommended my self to Heaven, and expected my fatal

fatal End. But through Providence divine, the Men at our Lodgment hearing the firſt Roaring of thoſe wild Creatures, came running out to defend us with their Arms, and met the Bear, ere he had leiſure to turn about upon me.

THIS gave me Strength and Opportunity to riſe, and ſnatching a Sword from one that had a Gun to defend himſelf, I aſſaulted the Bear, and at laſt plung'd my Weapon in his Heart.

THE reſt of the Company had kill'd upwards of a hundred, of different Sorts. Among 'em was the Beaſt *Suſa*, more formidable than any of the others, having ſix Horns reſembling that of a Bull, and little inferior to that Animal in Strength.

SEVERAL of the *Sporvi* were wounded in this Encounter, which were inſtantly dreſs'd, none of their Hurts proving mortal. We all return'd Thanks to Heaven for our wonderful Eſcape, every one according to his own way of Worſhip; and then refreſh'd our ſelves with a Repaſt prepar'd for us.

WE ſpent the reſt of the Evening in Diſcourſes of each other's Danger. Then the hurt men were dreſs'd again, and by applying a Bark of a Tree that grew by the River Side to our Wounds, we found immediate Eaſe, and went to repoſe our ſelves 'till Morning. When we aroſe, we found our ſelves intirely heal'd by the Vertue of this Bark; and happy for us it was ſo, otherwiſe we cou'd not have paſs'd that River, the *Sevarambians* ſuffering none to land with any Wound unheal'd.

CHAP.

CHAP. II.

The Author and Company cross the River, and arrive in Sevarambia. *A Description of their Journey to the Capital City, and their Reception there.*

THE Boat that was ready to carry us over, was built something like our Horse-ferry Boats, only much handsomer, and four times as large. *Kibbas* was the Commander's Name. He went to visit *Sermodas* in his Lodgment. After some private Discourse together, he came and kiss'd me on the Forehead, embrac'd me, and told me we were all welcome to their Confines, condoling at the same time with us for our Misfortunes.

WHILE

WHILE our Baggage and Unicorns were imbarking, we ſtripp'd the wild Beaſts we had kill'd the Day before of their Skins, which we were inform'd was the moſt acceptable Preſent we cou'd make to the *Sevarambian* King, the *Severites* preferring thoſe Furrs before Gold or Jewels.

BUT the Plenty of thoſe things made 'em of little Regard, for no Country in the World yielded more Mines, or a purer Sort, than thoſe of the *Sevarambians.*

KIBBAS, when every thing was ready, ordered us all to bathe in a Fountain of Water at the back of our Lodgment, which we had not ſeen before. Its Virtues were ſuch, it cleans'd the Body of all manner of Scurfs, and Diſeaſes of the Skin.

AFTER

After we were dreſs'd again, and underwent ſome other Ceremonies in order to our Purification, we went into the Boat, and were conducted on the other ſide of the River.

Its Borders were lin'd with ſeveral of the moſt beautiful Men and Women Imagination cou'd create; and tho' mine had been active in forming Deſcriptions of 'em, yet they far exceeded my Thoughts.

As ſoon as we were landed, we had each of us a Gown of Green, with Buttons of a Stone reſembling a *Jaſper*, made after the manner of a *Turkiſh* Veſt, with Loops on each Side, ſome of Gold, and others of Silk and Silver, according to the Dignity of the Perſon.

When we march'd a little way from the River, with Crowds of thoſe charming People on each Side, bidding us wellcome,

come, we were met by a grave Perſon, that commanded Reſpect from the Majeſty of his Countenance. He was attended by ſix of his Sons, and four Daughters, that exceeded in Beauty, even thoſe we had ſeen before; His Name was *Zidi Marabet*, the Chief of the firſt Town. He graciouſly ſaluted us, and told us in very good *French*, their King had given Orders to entertain us kindly.

After a ſhort Conference with *Sermodas*, he led us to his Palace, which was a noble Building of black and white Marble, but more Uniform than any I had ſeen at *Sporunda*.

The Town was ſeated upon the Banks of the River, and was compos'd of ſix large uniform Streets that led to the Water-ſide; moſt of the Houſes built with Marble, and ſlated with a ſort of Slate that reſembled burniſh'd Gold, eſpecially when the Sun ſhone

4 upon

upon 'em. Tho' the Buildings were all beautiful, yet *Zidi Marabet's* exceeded 'em all in Grandeur. Before his Portal was a beautiful row of Trees, of a different Growth from what I had ſeen, that yielded a moſt delightful Odour. Round his Houſe and Garden were Canals cut, that receiv'd the River, well ſtor'd with ſeveral ſorts of Fiſh.

THE Inſide of the Palace anſwer'd the Grandeur of the Out, all furniſh'd with Tapeſtry wrought with Gold into ſeveral delightful Landskips, and all other Branches of Painting.

AT this Place we ſtaid ſeven Days, in Expectation of an Anſwer from the *Sevarambian* King; for as yet we had no Orders to proceed any further.

DURING our ſhort Stay, we were Partakers of all the Pleaſure imaginable; ſometimes Hunting, Fiſhing or Fowling,

Fowling, and at other times with Consorts of charming Musick; in short, we pass'd our Time in all the innocent Delights our Senses cou'd require.

WHEN the Order came, we had Advice to prepare for our Journey, and accordingly we set out with our Guide.

WE travell'd thro' a Country of the most delightful Prospect in the Universe; and tho' Nature had been profuse with her Blessing, yet her Handmaid Art often lent her Assistance.

AS we pass'd along, we saw several Beasts of the most wild Kind, but here so Tame as to fear nothing from their Approach. Our Appetites were exuberantly feasted with Food of the finest Relish; and the Juice of the Grape, tho' of the noblest Flavour, had no intoxicating Quality.

WE

We pass'd many Cities and Towns in our Way, which gave us a surprizing Pleasure in their View, and the Courtesy of the charming Inhabitants exceeded our Belief.

The Fields and Meadows were water'd with running Streams, that glided along in various Meanders, as sporting with their delightful Banks.

The pleasing Thought of my Happiness grew upon me so fast, that I wish'd the River we had pass'd to come into this Country had been the River of Oblivion, that I might have forgot all I had known before: The only Fear that possess'd me, was, the Thought of not being a continu'd Inhabiter among 'em; and that perhaps we should be oblig'd to leave it in less time than we had resided among 'em. Yet Hope was ready with its Flattery to persuade me the Clemency of the *Sevarambian* King wou'd wou'd grant us any Privilege we ſhou'd require.

IN every Town we came thro', we had Muſick to attend us 'till we were paſt its Juriſdiction; and we *Europeans* were ſurpriz'd to ſee the Performers ſo young, that it always put me in mind of the Angelick Choir. But *Serniodas* told me, the Natives ſtudied *Philoſophy, Mathematicks, Aſtronomy* and *Muſick* from their Infancy. *Phyſick* they are ignorant of, as having no uſe for the Virtues of Drugs or Simples; their purity of Manners prevents their contracting any Diſeaſes, and Death ſeldom pays 'em any Viſits but by Accident, or length of Years. In ſhort, never were People better fitted for ſuch a delightful Climate. The Men were bleſt with all the maſculine Beauty of the fineſt Statue of *Angelo*; and the Women (tho' to compare 'em to any thing but Angels wou'd injure 'em) lovely beyond Imagination, carry ſuch

ſuch a Sweetneſs, Majeſty, and Virtue in their Looks, rouze no unclean Deſires, but rather a pleaſing Admiration of their majeſtick Form.

We beheld ſeveral Birds of Prey, as we thought, as *Eagles*, *Vultures*, &c. but *Sermodas* inform'd us, they prey'd on nothing but Inſects. Neither were they in Fear of any hurtful Creature in the Air, Earth or Water, having no ſuch thing in their whole Country, nor ever heard of 'em but from the Accounts of Strangers; and when we have told 'em Stories of Perſons being aſſaulted by any voracious Creature, they would reply, Sure the Divine Being was much incens'd againſt 'em, by permitting ſuch dreadful Creatures to have Power over 'em.

They have many Mines of Metals, as I ſaid before, but they only form 'em into Utenſils, or to adorn their Buildings. Precious-ſtones and Pearls are more common here than elſewhere; but they have no Traffick with 'em, nor ſend any Abroad, unleſs for Preſents to great People by thoſe *Sporvi* that go into other Countries; for they have learnt by thoſe Perſons, there's no approaching a ſordid great Man of *Europe*, (as they have Reaſon to believe 'em all ſo) without ſuch Credentials.

IF our Merchants had the Liberty to trade here, they might eaſily gain more Riches than the *Spaniards* at firſt got from *America*.

IF one Perſon ſtands in need of what another has, they barter ſomething; but if any thing is wanting, and the Perſon has nothing to give in exchange, he is ſure to have wherewith to ſupply his Neceſſity, from their Love and Eſteem of one another; ſo that Poverty and Want are utter Strangers to 'em. And for Hoſpitality, no Age in the World can parallel. An Example of this fell out our firſt Day's Journey. TEN

TEN of the Chief of the Place civily contended to entertain us that Night; and to pleaſe them all, *Sermodas* thought fit to divide our Number into ten equal Parts, ſo that they were all well ſatisfy'd, but endeavoured to outvie one another in our Reception.

WE were ſix Days in our Journey to *Sevarinda*, the Capital of the Country, and Reſidence of their Kings, who all take the Name of *Severias*, or *Severminas*, their firſt Founder.

D 2 CHAP.

CHAP. III.

An Account of the Provinces of the Ambitious, Adulterers, Fornicators, Knaves, and Fools. The Author and Company come before the Sevarambian *King; their Reception. Their Laws, Religion, Customs and Manners.*

WHEN we arriv'd at the Palace, allotted for our Reſidence, ſeveral of thoſe amiable People came in to viſit us, with Preſents of Fruit and Flowers, as alſo a Band of their Muſick. One of 'em made us a Speech in the *Sevarambian* Language, which *Sermodas* interpreted for us, being to this Effect. " Well-" come, moſt illuſtrious Strangers, " to our City of *Sevarinda*. Baniſh " all Thoughts of your paſt Misfor-" tunes. Your Loſſes will be recom-" penſed.

" pensed. We rejoyce to have an Op-
" portunity of imitating the great Cre-
" ator of all things, in shewing our
" Bounty to Strangers of another Li-
" neage."

When he had ended his Speech, he bow'd very low, nodded to his Companions, and begun their Consort, which consisted of such harmonious Airs, we thought we were listning to Celestial Musick. A Banquet was prepar'd for us, where we tasted of more delicious Wine, if possible, than we had before. It has that Effect upon those that drink it, that it brightens the Countenance, and makes 'em look young, in defiance to Nature. Nay indeed, Age there is only distinguish'd by white Hair and Beards, which they are forbid to cut off, by the Laws of their Land. And one would Imagine *Hebe*, the Goddess of Youth, had her constant Dwelling among 'em.

THE ſame Evening *Sermodas* waited upon the King, and return'd to us with a Wellcome from him into his Dominions, with Advice, he deſign'd to ſee us on the Morrow, being very impatient 'till that Time came.

AFTER Supper, I beg'd *Sermodas* to give me ſome Account of this King, and his Dominions; which he comply'd with, as follows.

OUR Wiſe and Potent Monarch is lineally deſcended from our great Lawgiver; he is the ſeven thouſand five hundred and ninth King that has govern'd this preſent Monarchy. He has threeſcore and five Principalities in his Dominions, ſurrounded by the River you croſs'd over; Theſe are govern'd by four Vice-Roys, choſe every three Years, out of the Chief of the Kingdom, celebrated for their Wiſdom and Virtues.

BESIDES

Besides theſe, there are ſeveral Provinces without the River, as ours of *Sporunda*, which is the only one that regard the Manners of the *Sevarambians*. The others are inhabited by baniſh'd Perſons for ſeveral Enormities, and are never to enter on this ſide the River again.

The Province next to us, is that of *Adulterers* and *Fornicators*, that carry the Marks of their Crimes in their Countenances, and thro' Shame, never ſhow their Faces among perfect People. They have no ſettled Habitation, but roam about thro' the Woods like the ancient *Tartars*; the Men and Women mingling as their inordinate Deſires prompt 'em.

They are govern'd by a Woman, whoſe Principles correſpond with her Subjects; her Name *Bruſtana*, (or *foul Deſire*, in the *Sevarambian* Language.)

The Country they poſſeſs, yields every thing for the Support of Man, which they enjoy in Common, as they do one another; tho' often, by their irregular Deſires, they are involv'd in Feuds, which ſeldom end but in Death.

THE next Country is inhabited by Knaves, commanded by *Marabo-* (or, *Infernal Cunning*.) In this Province they are never at Peace, ever broaching new Plots and Contrivances, endeavouring to Deceive, and Circumvent one another.

THESE People had another Country formerly allotted 'em, poſſeſs'd by covetous Perſons, who had made great Improvements, which the *Maraboians* underſtanding, drove 'em out, and ſettled in their Room, forcing them into a barren Country, where they have lived ever ſince.

THE next Province is poſſeſs'd by the Turbulent and Ambitious: Theſe are

are the moſt dangerous of all, often endeavouring to breed Commotions among the *Sevarambians*, but ever fruſtrated in their wicked Intentions. Near their Borders, *Severeminas* keeps a conſtant Guard, to prevent their Motions. There are thirteen Provinces more, compos'd of Perſons of irregular Lives; theſe and the Reſt formerly promoted a Rebellion againſt the *Sevarambians*, being with much Difficulty repuls'd, and have ſince been rigorouſly guarded within their own Confines, by Forts and Caſtles built for that Purpoſe on their Borders.

Another Province I had almoſt forgot to mention, which is that of Idiots; this is an Iſland to the South of *Sevarinda* call'd *Cracos*, (or the Iſland of Folly) where they poſſeſs every thing that is needful for Life, without any Trouble. For 'tis incumbent on Fortune to take care of Fools, while Knaves have Cunning enough to provide for themſelves.

If

IF you have any Curiosity, I believe I can prevail upon our wise King to give us leave to visit some of these Countries, with a sufficient Guard to secure us from any Insults; for tho' our happy Climate ever enjoys Peace and Tranquility, yet upon our Borders and adjacent Islands, there's as much Tumult as in any of your northern Parts of the World, disturb'd by airy Dæmons, that slily creep into the Minds of Men: Here we have but few, being the fragrant Smell of an *Aromatic* Tree ascends into the Region of the Air, and drives them from us. Besides, we have holy Charmers, that bind these Spirits, if ever they are caught among us, to one of these Trees, and scourge 'em with Rods made of the Bark, so that we are very seldom troubled with 'em.

SERMODAS gave us a farther Description of many things in this celestial

lestial Country, which fill'd us with amazing Delight and Satisfaction.

He told us the King's Revenue was always certain, as well as his Expences, and he had never Occasion to demand any additional Supplies. Tho' the meanest of his Subjects would think themselves honour'd, if he wou'd accept of all their Substance.

Our present Monarch is about Forty Years of Age, tho' his Looks declare him much younger. He has reign'd over us upwards of two and Twenty Years, and in that time he has not given the least Cause to wish his Soveraignty shorter, but we pray for his Length of Years as our greatest Happiness.

After this pleasing Discourse, we were led to our Apartments, all furnish'd with the richest Cloth of Gold, and Embroidery. Our Beds were of the

the fineſt Down, in which we took the ſweeteſt Repoſe imaginable.

WE were wak'd by a Concert of charming Muſick in an adjacent Room, about ſix a Clock in the Morning; for my part, all I ſaw and heard, ſometimes perſuaded me I was in a pleaſing Dream.

AFTER the Muſick had play'd ſome time, *Sermodas* enter'd my Chamber, attended by a Perſon with an intire new Change of Dreſs, ſent me by the King's Order. He begg'd me to be very expeditious in preparing my ſelf, for the King intended to give us Audience before Dinner.

WHEN we were all ready, we ſet forward, attended by the moſt illuſtrious of the whole City: As we paſs'd along, the Streets and Windows were lin'd with the Inhabitants to gaze upon us; for Strangers are ſeldom ſeen in their capital City. Our Senſes were fill'd fill'd with the Wonders we beheld, as we paſs'd along. The Auguſt Buildings, the beautiful Inhabitants, and rich Dreſſes, ſeem'd as if we were beholding the exuberant Fancy of an excellent Painter.

ALL Arts and Sciences ſeem'd here to have their firſt Source, and I was aſham'd to think they excell'd us as much in thoſe things, as they did in Beauty and Virtue. Our Wonder was increas'd, when we came in Sight of the King's Palace; it ſtood upon an Eminence ſurrounded with a River, over which was a Draw-bridge of Silver, with Chains of Gold. Within the Bridge were three Walls, each exceeding the other in the Richneſs of Compoſition, the laſt having Grains of Gold, Silver, and other Metals mixt in the Cement, ſo that the Brightneſs of its Luſtre reflected by the Beams of the Sun were too glorious for our weak Eyes to look upon. In the vacant

Places between each Wall, were planted Trees of a charming Verdure. The Palace was built within the third Wall, but before it were Figures cut by the beſt Artiſts, of all manner of Men, as well as Beaſts of different Kinds, that gave the Beholder a vaſt Pleaſure in looking on 'em.

THE Palace was orbicular, with four Galleries, and as many Gates that reach from Side to Side.

THE King ſat under a Throne adorn'd with many coſtly Jewels which form'd a Sun, and the radiant Luſtre it gave, hinder'd the Eye from fixing upon it any long Time. Upon the ſix Steps that were rais'd before it, were plac'd twelve Lyons, ſix on each Side, of a reddiſh Stone, with large Saphires for Eyes, that as a Perſon look'd upon 'em, they ſeem'd to rowl in their Heads.

WHEN

WHEN We came within four Paces of the Bottom of the Throne (preceded by twelve Noblemen who ſeparated on each Side as we advanc'd) we kneel'd down as we were inſtructed, and bow'd our Bodies to the Pavement: At the Sound of ſeveral Inſtruments, we ſtood up. I then, with a low Inclination of the Body, made him the following Speech in *French*, being a Language his Majeſty underſtood perfectly well. "Moſt Potent and Illuſtrious Mo-"narch, you ſee before your Throne "a Company of unhappy Men, ſhip-"wreck'd upon your Dominions. We "come here before your Majeſty by "your gracious Command, to render "our poor Thanks for the many and "ſignal Favours we have receiv'd from "your Subjects, whoſe only Bliſs is to "have ſuch a glorious Prince deſtin'd "by Fate to command 'em. Your "Clemency, your Wiſdom, and all "thoſe

"those Virtues your Soul inherits, "shall be the eternal Theme of all the "northern World, if we ever set Foot "upon our native Shores, tho' the Ac- "count of this glorious Land will al- "most seem fabulous to those that have "not been Eye-witnesses of the extra- "ordinary things found in your Majesty's "Dominions." The King smil'd, and with a gentle Nod of his Head spoke to us in very good *French*, "I am too "much a Lover of Justice to think of "injuring you. I sent for you, to learn "the Custom and Manners of a part of "the World, famous for their Under- "standing and Discoveries; and to do "you all the good Offices that lie in "my Power. Your Losses shall be "made good to you, so that I hope "what you at first counted a Misfor- "tune, shall turn to your Benefit, "and Content. You shall, if you ap- "prove of it, see all the Countries of "my Dominion; that you may, at "your Return, tell the Wonders of

"a

" a Kingdom ſecreted from the reſt " of the habitable World; and farther- " more, thro' your means, I wou'd " promote a Trade with your northern " Nations; and I ſhall, with the Advice " of my Council, chuſe out ſome Iſland " in the Pacific Sea under my Domi- " nions for the Advantage of that " Commerce; for the Laws of my " Kingdom will not allow of Strangers " ſettling among us.

He then proceeded to aſk me the State of *Europe*, our Government, Laws, Religion and Politicks: To which Queſtions I anſwer'd to the beſt of my Underſtanding. When our Converſation was ended, he made me and my Officers a Preſent of a ſmall Caſket of Jewels each, and a Collar of Gold and Amber-greece, which he will'd us to wear while we were in his Dominions, as a Token of his Friendſhip and Favour.

HE then order'd *Zidi Parabas*, the Maſter of the Ceremonies, to provide us Apartments in his Palace; and *Zidi Marobat*, his Chancellor and chief Miniſter, to have Conference with us concerning Trade, and how to promote it. I acquainted the Chancellor with our Art of Navigation, and our Secrets of Traffic; deſcribing our Merchandizes, and the Productions of *Europe*, eſpecially *England*. He ſeem'd very well pleas'd with the Account I had given him, but inform'd me they expected no diſhoneſt and ſharping Men to carry on the Commerce, and that none ſhou'd come nearer than *Sporunda*, unleſs an Ambaſſador, or upon ſome very extraordinary Occaſion.

WHEN We had made an End of our firſt Conference, he led us to ſhow us the Rarities of the Palace, which Deſcription wou'd exceed all Belief; and therefore I ſhall leave it to the Imagination

nation of the Reader, and he that has the ſtrongeſt, will fall ſhort of what it is.

As we return'd from viewing the Rarities of this Earthly Paradiſe, we met the King coming back from Hunting. Their Method is quite different from ours in *Europe*. They hunt with tame Foxes (far exceeding all Dogs in Swiftneſs) the Hare, Deer, Rabbet, &c. They have alſo tame *Leopards*, to hunt larger Beaſts.

When the King has an Inclination to take this Diverſion, the grand Huntſman prepares a ſufficient Number of tame *Leopards*. The wild *Bear*, or *Lyon*, or what other wild Creature the King deſigns to hunt, is let looſe in a Park, a League from the Palace. As ſoon as ever the train'd *Leopards* perceive their Game, they endeavour to ſurround him; when he finds himſelf over-power'd, he preſently ſeeks for

E 2 Safety

Safety by Flight, but they purſue him, and the Creature ſoon falls a Victim to their Rage.

THE King and his Nobles (for no other is admitted to partake of the Sport) are all mounted on *Mules* richly capariſon'd, their Furniture moſt of 'em adorn'd with Jewels.

THE King when he came from hunting, went into his Palace, follow'd by his Courtiers and menial Servants, moſt of 'em bidding us welcome, in *Latin*, *Spaniſh*, *French*, or *Italian*. We enter'd a Hall three hundred Foot long, where Preparations were made for Dinner.

THE King with his Queen, three of his Sons, and ſix of his Daughters, ſat at a Table at one End of the Hall, under a Canopy of State. The Courſes were ſerv'd in at the Sound of muſical Inſtruments plac'd in the Galleries above us.

WE

We ſat down with *Zidi Parabas*, *Sermodas*, and ſeveral Noblemen, at the long Table.

It would fill up a larger Volume than this, even to deſcribe the Rarities we ſaw in this Palace. Some of the Courtiers obſerving we were very well pleas'd with our Treatment, ask'd us if we had ſuch Pleaſures in *Europe*. I anſwer'd, we had many and various kinds of Diverſions, but none like what we ſaw there, which far exceeded ours, from their Simplicity and Innocence. Another at the Table propos'd ſeveral Queſtions in *Latin*, of Natural Cauſes, and handled the Argument ſo judiciouſly, that it was eaſy to perceive they exceeded us as much in profound Knowledge, as in other things. We were very well pleas'd with their Diſcourſe, it being a Cuſtom, as well as among the ancient *Greeks*, to handle ſuch Subjects in time of Repaſt.

E 3 After

AFTER Dinner, *Zidi Parabas*, by his Majeſty's Command, brought us near the King, who was ſitting on a Throne, with *Larida* his Queen on his Right Hand, and his Children on the Left. His Majeſty convers'd with us in *Spaniſh*, to pleaſe his Conſort, who underſtood that Language. And when he diſmiſs'd us, made us each, another valuable Preſent.

AFTER Dinner, we were conducted to view the Rarities of the City, their Temples, public Halls, &c. Their Court of Judicature was pav'd with tranſparent Stones of a ſingular Beauty. On both Sides were their Lawyers Cells, or Priſons, for they are not ſuffered to walk up and down the City, for fear they ſhou'd by their Quirks and Devices infect the Inhabitants.

As ſoon as we enter'd, they flock'd about us, in Hopes of Buſineſs; but finding

finding that Curioſity only had brought us thither, they ſlunk back into their Cells, vex'd at their Diſappointment.

While we were looking about us, the Judge went into his Seat at the Sound of the Trumpet. Immediately after a Company of *Sevarambians* came into the Hall, with a young Man and Woman, that had forgot the Virtues of their Race, having had criminal Converſation together. They had both large Wens, or excreſcences of Fleſh upon their Noſes and Foreheads, that appear'd even in the very acting their Crime, as *Sermodas* told us it ever did. Lord! thought I, if the Inhabitants of my Country were inflicted with the ſame Puniſhment, what a bottle-nos'd Generation ſhould we be?

Upon the Inſtant came out the Lawyers, Serjeants, and the whole Train of Pettyfoggers, ready to be employ'd. *Sermodas* told me they had a

Hall of Juſtice in every Capital of a Province; but they were only look'd upon as Butchers and Executioners, having no ſuch Honours conferr'd on 'em as thoſe of their Fraternity in *Europe*; being not permitted to converſe with any one but Criminals, and thoſe in Publick.

THERE was no extenuating the Crime of the unhappy Pair, the Marks declared 'em Guilty. But the Confuſion in their Countenances was ſo viſible, that I pity'd their Fall from Virtue.

THE Lawyers were for having 'em put to Death, being they had receiv'd no Fees from 'em. The Male Offender would have pleaded the Wens in his Face proceeded from another Cauſe, but the Judge ſoon convinc'd him to the contrary, and the criminal Couple were immediately baniſh'd to the Province govern'd by *Bruſtana*.

I

I MUST own, I was very uneaſy in this Hell in the midſt of Paradiſe, therefore expreſs'd a Deſire of going; but another Offender being brought, my Curioſity overcame my Uneaſineſs, and I was reſolv'd to ſtay this Tryal.

THE Lawyers pleaded in *Latin*, by receiving a Fee from *Sermodas*, only to oblige me; and their Debates were ſo cunning and wide from the Purpoſe, I thought my ſelf in *Weſtminſter-Hall*. This Criminal was accus'd of Theft, a Crime very rare among 'em; tho' there was no Proof by outward Marks, as in the other's Crime, yet the Fellow had enough in his Countenance to convict him.

AFTER the Tryal he was Baniſh'd to the Province of *Marabo*. I told *Sermodas*, I wonder'd the Excellent Government of the *Sevarambians* would allow ſuch a peſtiferous People

7 as

Allegory

as thoſe Lawyers among 'em, where even in *Europe* they ſeldom meet with Eſteem. Why, ſaid he, they are neceſſary Evils, and perhaps, Virtuous as we are, we ſhould find ſome among us, that Fear, as well as Shame, keeps Honeſt. Theſe Lawyers are provided for by the Publick in all their Wants; and if one of 'em ſhou'd prove Honeſt, (as very rarely happens) they would be thruſt out of their Society, nor ever ſuffer'd to plead.

THE Judge upon the Bench was one of theſe, whom the King honour'd with that Poſt for his Integrity, but the Lawyers all hate him, for he has cramp'd them in their Practice very much.

WHEN the laſt Tryal was over, and the Lawyers lock'd up in their Dens, we took our Farewel of this deteſtable Place. We came before their chief Temple, which gave me a great Deſire of of ſeeing the Inſide. *Zidi Parabas* made ſeveral Scruples in letting us go in, but *Sermodas* remov'd 'em.

It was built in form of an Amphitheatre, but open at the Top; yet ſo adorn'd with Gold and Jewels, that dazled our Eyes to look on't.

The Reaſon that *Zidi Parabas* gave for his Scruple in admitting us, was, he fear'd we worſhip'd Images, a thing abhorr'd among the *Sevarambians*.

We adore (ſaid he) the great and glorious Being, that is not to be repreſented by Pencil, nor liken'd to any thing viſible to the Eye. He then led us to one of the Prieſts, who being aſſur'd we were not guilty of worſhipping Images, wellcom'd us, and freely talk'd of their way of Worſhip.

We acknowledge (ſaid the Prieſt) but one Power Omnipotent, Creator of

Heaven

Heaven and Earth. Twice a Week, we have Publick Days of Worſhip, where none are exempted from their Duty, unleſs ſome Illneſs be upon 'em, which ſeldom happens. We then ſing Praiſes to Him, and give Him Thanks for his unbounded Goodneſs; as alſo offer up Prayers for the Proſperity of our King and Country: and that none ſhould be ignorant of their Duty, we have publick Schools to inſtruct our Youth in the paths of Virtue and Religion. And to maintain thoſe Schools, every *Sevarambian* once every Year preſents ſomething for that Purpoſe; and as the Gifts far exceed that Charge, the Reſidue is employ'd in pious Uſes, and Neceſſaries for the Prieſts.

WE have Books compos'd by our great Law-giver, that inſtruct us in the minuteſt Action of Life, and to theſe wiſe Precepts we chiefly owe our Virtue.

THERE

THERE is ſuch an excellent Harmony among us, that what happens of Ill every Day among the Inhabitants of *Europe*, and moſt of the other Parts of the World, is ſeldom heard of here.

AFTER Death, we are taught to believe, we aſcend to the Glorious Region of the Bleſs'd for a Term of Years, and then our Souls take Poſſeſſion of our Bodies again.

OUR Corpſe after Death does not putrifie as yours of *Europe*, but I can ſhew Bodies entire, whoſe Souls have left 'em upwards of two thouſand Years.

WE alſo believe, when our Souls have join'd our Bodies again, we ſhall mix with the other Parts of the World; and thoſe that are good, after their ſecond Diſſolution, will enter the heavenly Beings along with us; but for thoſe

thoſe that are not worthy that Happineſs, they will be caſt into the Sea.

EVEN thoſe of our own Race, that have ſwerv'd from the Rules of Virtue, and live in Baniſhment, if they bear their Puniſhment with Reſignation, and repent of their Crimes, will, when Death overtakes 'em, be happy after a Purgation by Fire, thro' which we all paſs in the middle Region of the Air, with this Difference; thoſe that have liv'd up to the Rules of our great Law-giver, will paſs thoſe Impediments without feeling any Heat, while the others are ſtop'd to be purify'd, and afterwards aſcend.

WHILE he was giving us this Relation, he was interrupted by the Corpſe of a *Sevarambian*, that was brought to be interr'd. He excus'd himſelf for not waiting on us any longer, tho' he told us he had much more to ſay on the ſame Subject. He went from us to open

open the Cells of the Dead, who lay intomb'd in Coffins made of Ivory and Gold. I was glad of the Opportunity of ſeeing their manner of Interment, therefore attended with a great deal of Satisfaction.

At the Portal of the Temple, ſtood above a thouſand People with the Friends and Relations of the Deceas'd. One of the latter ſtood before the Corpſe, and ſpoke to the Prieſt after this Manner; "Holy Sir, we have "brought you the Corpſe of our good "Friend *Suffarali*, a Perſon that ne-"ver walk'd out of the Rules of Vir-"tue and Honour; one that never "neglected his Devotion in this ſa-"cred Temple; we beg he may be re-"poſited with thoſe illuſtrious Dead, "that once were as we are now."

When *Ziribabdas* the Prieſt had ask'd many Queſtions about the Manners and Behaviour of the Defunct, and received ceiv'd ſufficient Anſwers, he order'd the Corpſe to be put on a Table of Porphyry that ſtood in the Midſt of the Temple, and anointed it all over with Oyl of *Bo-tamine*, (or Uncorruption) which is of that Quality to preſerve from Impurity the Body that is anointed with it for a hundred Years. This Oyl is a Chymical Preparation, drawn from ſeveral Herbs, Flowers, and Roots, by the Prieſts, who underſtand that Art to Perfection. At the end of a Century, the Bodies of the Dead are waſh'd over again with this Oyl.

WE went with the Corpſe into the Sepulchres, which were ſo large, there was no ſeeing to the End of 'em, tho' it was as Light as the open Day.

AFTER we had ſatisfy'd our Curio-ſity in this ſolemn Place, we were ad-mitted into the Sepulchres of their Monarchs, where we ſtaid ſeveral Hours, admiring the Bodies of thoſe illuſtrious

illuſtrious Deceas'd; each of 'em was in his Coronation Robes, adorn'd with Jewels of ſuch Value, that I verily believ'd all the Riches of the Eaſt wou'd prove but a private Treaſury to this.

THE Lectures that were read upon ſome of the moſt noted for Arts and Sciences, would fill a Volume larger than this.

WE were then carried to view their Room of Rarities, which were ſo many and various, they would take up an Age in Contemplation.

THERE we were ſhown ſeveral *Taliſmans* of ſuch Virtue, that they wou'd give Life to any Creature expiring at a Mile's Diſtance; a Perſon well skill'd in the Uſe of 'em cou'd do whatever his Imagination prompted him to, and we had many Relations of humorous Actions done by the Virtue of one of thoſe *Taliſmans*.

They told us so many diverting Stories, that I beg'd *Ziribabdas* to let us see some of its Power; with much Importunity he fetch'd out a grave Person from one of the Closets, where he was following his Studies. As he approach'd me, he saluted me in *Greek*, then took me by the Hand, and led me into a Stone Balcony that over-look'd the Country. When we had been there some time, he enter'd with a Globe of Chrystal, as I thought, that had several Cavities in it. I look'd into one of 'em, and could perceive many kind of Birds tho' without Motion, 'till the *Philosopher*, by a secret Charm, set 'em to Work, and upon the Instant we were entertain'd with their different Notes that was very grateful to the Ear: But what more surpriz'd us, was the Approach of all Manner of feather'd Fowl, that perch'd upon the Balconies; when they had settled some small Time, by another Movement, he compell'd 'em to dance

dance to the Sounds of Musick in Pairs according to their Specie. When he had diverted us a full Hour, he dismiss'd 'em.

He then took the Image of a humane Figure in Wax, and repeated these Words, *Bromalock ki kostrabah abrolakar Bourabous, Brinskika Brovaro Birkabu.* Upon that Instant several Men and Women came naked into the Green, and danc'd before us, playing several merry Gambols; neither had they power to stir while the Image was held there. Tho' they were naked, they were all Modest in their Actions, nor knew they their own Shame 'till the Figure was taken from before 'em, and then they ran away in the utmost Confusion. Such is the Power of these *Talismans* over the Minds of Men, as well as Bodies of Birds and Beasts.

I often wish'd the *Talismanic* Art was known in *Europe*; but then the

F 2 Igno-

Ignorant would think the wonderful Effects it had, proceeded from magical Causes. After we had satisfy'd our Curiosity with many more wonderful Effects of this *Talismanic* Power, we took our Leaves of the *Philosopher*, and *Ziribabdas* the Priest, and went to our Apartments for that Day, full of the many Wonders we had seen, which gave a never-dying Birth to Conversation among our selves. *Sermodas* told us he wou'd show us things more wonderful the next Day, than what we had seen yet; But we had seen so many things extraordinary, we thought that cou'd hardly be. When we had refresh'd our selves with Supper, and moderately drinking some of the delicious Wine of the Country, we were told there was a Sight worth beholding in the Air. We all ran into the Gallery of our Apartments, where we were much surpriz'd to see fiery Dragons, Griffons, and flying Serpents fighting in the Air. The first Sight of such

ſuch a terrible Appearance made us all run in again; but *Sermodas* calm'd our Spirits, by telling us what we ſaw was by a *Taliſman*, form'd to divert us by order of the King. We then beheld their Rencounters with Satisfaction.

WHEN this Sport was over, we retir'd to Reſt, but my Imagination kept me ſome time waking. I thought the Divine Being had wiſely confin'd ſo excellent a Knowledge with ſuch a virtuous People; for if ſuch a noble Art was ever known in our vicious Parts of the World, it would certainly be made a wrong Uſe of, not to preſerve, but to deſtroy Mankind.

CHAP. IV.

The Author and Companions ſet out with the Sevarambian *King, in a Progreſs. The wonderful Account of what they ſaw. The Puniſhment of a wicked Stateſman; and their Return to* Sevarambia.

THE next Morning *Sermodas* came to tell us, the King intended to take us with him to ride out of the City. When we were told his Majeſty was ready, we were all mounted upon a Beaſt exactly reſembling a *Camel* in every thing but its Ears, which were of ſuch a Length, we made uſe of 'em inſtead of a Bridle, being thinner than a Glove, and join'd at the Extremity by a ſmall claſp of Silver, or Gold. I was in ſome Fear, when I was firſt mounted on on the Creature, from its Swiftneſs of Motion, and Height from the Ground; but it's the ſureſt-footed Beaſt in the Univerſe, and will travel a hundred Miles a Day.

WHEN we came to the King's Palace, we diſmounted, to pay our Obedience to his Majeſty, who ask'd us of our Welfare, alſo if we wanted any thing; we return'd him Thanks for his Goodneſs ſhewn to us poor Strangers, and that we were in no Fear of wanting among ſuch an excellent People as his Subjects, where Virtue was their only Aim. He bid us mount our Camels, for he intended to ſhow us ſome of his Country, if we thought we were able to bear the Fatigue of our Journey. We anſwer'd, we were proud of the Honour done us by the greateſt Monarch of the World; and for our Health and Strength, we were never better in our Lives, nor more able to

F 4 go

go through any Fatigue, tho' we were aſſur'd we ſhould meet with none.

IN about an Hour we came to a Town call'd *Magnandi*, about two Leagues to the Southward of the Capital, where were ſeveral *Philoſophers* with their *Taliſmans*, waiting to entertain us with their Art, by order of his Majeſty. One of 'em caught a Fly in our Preſence, and by Degrees it ſwell'd up to the Size of one of our Camels.

THE Philoſopher mounted this new made Creature, who perform'd the Journey with as much Vigour as any of our real Camels. Another of 'em out of a Flea form'd a Camel ſo like the King's, which was white, (and the only one of that Colour among us) that no one Perſon could tell the Difference. I muſt own, notwithſtanding what I knew of the Virtue of theſe People, I cou'd not help fancying I ſaw a couple of Conjurers,

Conjurers, or Devils in the Shapes of Men. *Sermodas*, who ſaw my Imagination by my Countenance, told me, none but Perſons fam'd for their refin'd Notions of Virtue and Learning were capable of performing ſuch extraordinary things as we ſaw.

ANOTHER of 'em having an Image of a Woman in his Hand, he held it on high, and pronounc'd ſeveral Words in a loud Voice; upon which all the young Women of the Village came out of their Dwellings, ſtript themſelves ſtark naked, and jumpt about like ſo many *Bacchanalians*. The Sight of ſuch a number of naked Beauties made me condemn the Philoſopher, for forcing 'em to put off their Modeſty with their Cloaths; but *Sermodas* inform'd me, the *Sevarambians* never are aſham'd to expoſe thoſe Parts to public View; adding, it was no Blot upon Modeſty, but to thoſe People who are vicious by Nature. When they had danc'd about a a confiderable while, the Philofopher covered the Image with a Cloth; the young Women went immediately and put on their Cloaths, retiring with much Satisfaction, to think they had diverted their King, whom they honour as a Power Divine.

ANOTHER of thefe wife Men took a Cat out of one of the neighbouring Houfes, and apply'd a pair of Bellows with his *Talifman* to its Pofteriors, 'till the Creature grew as large as a *Flanders* Mare. When he had made an end of blowing, he took the Cat, and by preffing gently its Sides, the Wind came out the fame way it was put in, but in fuch harmonious Sounds, that gave all the Hearers a vaft Delight. And tho' coming from fuch a Place, yet the Air was all perfum'd round us.

OUR Journey was the moft delightful imaginable. Never were People fo rejoyc'd as the *Sevarambians* were at the

the Sight of their Prince. In ev'ry City we came thro', Presents were made to all that attended him; every private Man in my Company return'd with Ingots of Gold worth a Thousand Pound, and the Officers in Proportion; for my own part, the Riches of this World had but few Charms for me, tho' I could not refuse many noble Presents that were made me in Jewels, for if I had, I shou'd have affronted the Givers very much.

AT the Entrance of one of the Cities, I observ'd two Statues in Gold almost covered over with Garlands of sweet-smelling Flowers. I ask'd *Sermodas* the Reason of it, for they seem'd to me as if they were worshipp'd by the People; a thing, we were told, of the utmost Abhorrence among 'em.

THOSE two Images, said *Sermodas*, are the Figures of two unfortunate Lovers, formerly Inhabitants of this City.

ty. Their Parents were averſe to the Match, and the Puniſhment that attends a vicious Love prevented any criminal Converſation, but however they were reſolv'd to continue their Affections to each other, while they had Beings in this World; all other Proffers they deſpis'd.

THEY liv'd in this Platonic Manner 'till they were upwards of thirty Years old, often meeting by Stealth to bewail their Fates, and the Stubbornneſs of their Parents.

THEIR Paſſion increas'd with their Years, and grew at laſt to that Violence, they determin'd to depart the Kingdom, and in ſome other Climate tie the connubial Knot. Tho' this Reſolution was difficult to put in Execution, by reaſon the Borders were ſo ſtrictly guarded. While their Reſolutions were wavering between Hope and Fear, one of thoſe airy *Dæmons* that ſometimes

ſometimes lurk up and down ſeeking whom they might deceive, appear'd to *Ziricus* the Male Lover in the Form of a *Sevarambian*, and promis'd to aſſiſt him in carrying him and his belov'd Miſtreſs, to an Iſland out of the *Sevarambian* Dominions.

ZIRICUS, and *Malimna* his Beloved, agreed to meet at the Mouth of the River *Rocara*, where the Ship waited for 'em. When they came to the Water-ſide, there was no Boat to carry 'em on Board, but the *Dæmon* told 'em it was ſhallow all the way to the very Ship, and that ſhe rode with her Side ſo near the ſhallow Part, that he being a tall Man cou'd put her on Board, without any Damage. Their Loves were too paſſionate to make any Difficulty, and it was agreed, the Lady ſhou'd be tranſported firſt. As ſoon as the execrable *Dæmon* had got her into the middle of the Stream, he plung'd her in, and held her under Water

Water 'till ſhe expir'd. Her Lover hearing her Shrieks, was in the utmoſt Deſpair; and notwithſtanding his Ignorance in ſwimming, yet plung'd into the Waves to ſave the Darling of his Soul. He ſwam to the Body, and brought it lifeleſs to the Shore. His Grief and Sorrow were inſupportable, and the Intreaties of his Friends (who had purſu'd 'em, and came to the fatal Place, where they found him lamenting his unhappy Fate) had not Force enough to make him think of living. He found ſo much Breath as to relate the unfortunate Story, and when he had ended, plung'd his Dagger within his Breaſt, and expir'd upon the breathleſs Body of his Miſtreſs.

IN Memory of theſe conſtant Lovers, the Citizens of *Burino* have erected theſe two Figures, which upon the Day of their unhappy Fate, they crown with freſh Garlands of Flowers.

WHEN

WHEN Dinner was ſerved in, a large white Rat appear'd upon the Table, ſtaring the King full in the Face. The King was ſomething ſurpriz'd at the Boldneſs of the Creature, and order'd his Attendants to drive it away; but the Rat having the Gift of Speech, thro' the Power of the *Taliſmanic* Art, told the King he wou'd not ſtir, 'till he had ſatisfy'd his Appetite. The Speech of the Creature ſoon declar'd it was influenced by one of the Philoſophers; therefore the King enter'd into a Dialogue with him, which being ſhort, and common Sentences, I had learnt enough of the *Sevarambian* Language to underſtand it. The Rat made free with all the Diſhes at the Table, but at laſt fixt upon that the King was at; the King ſeeing him ſo eager, ſpoke to him.

King. Pr'ythee honeſt Rat, be gone.

Rat. I like my Company too well, to leave it ſo ſoon.

King. Your Worſhip will eat all.

Rat.

Rat. There's enough in the Kingdom for you and me too.

King. Who taught you to be thus impertinent?

Rat. My Maſter.

There was a longer Dialogue between his Majeſty and the Rat, but as there was no very great Wit in it, I ſhall ſay no more about it. 'Tis no doubt, the Rat was a Rat of Parts, and in ſome Courts wou'd have found Words enough to be Satyrical; nay even in that virtuous Aſſembly, there was enough ſaid to make the Company merry at the Expence of ſome one among 'em, tho' in Terms too plain, to give any Satisfaction to me; but I was inform'd by *Zidi Parabas*, there was no two Words in their Language to mean the ſame thing. A *double Entendre*, tho' there might be ſome Wit in it, was a ſtrange way of ſpeaking among the *Sevarambians*; and a Lady of the moſt rigid Virtue might hear thoſe Words, we *Europæans* repeat often with Shame, without the leaſt Offence to Modeſty.

WHEN

WHEN Dinner was over, we ſet out for the City of *Tiftani*, the ſecond in the Kingdom for its Riches, pleaſant Situation, and glorious Buildings. The Prince *Moriski*, Governor of the Place, met the King with a numerous Attendance, all beautifully habited; he gave him the Keys of the City, a Cuſtom here, as well as in *Europe*, which the King return'd him again.

THE next Day we embark'd in ſeveral beautiful Boats for an Iſland in the River, about two Leagues over, call'd *Criſtako*, or, *the Iſland of Foxes*, a Place where the King had a noble Palace; here we ſtaid fourteen Days, fiſhing, fowling and hunting; it being the chief Place for thoſe Diverſions in the King's Dominions.

WE left this delightful Place fatigu'd with Pleaſure, but not ſated; and took our Journey towards another City, that

Sevaraminas did me the Honour to tell me, he had ſome ſecret Affairs to tranſact, that even his Council were as yet ignorant of.

MAVRICE and my ſelf rode this Day's Journey on each Side of the King, who convers'd with us upon the Subject of Trade, enquiring into the Nature of our Traffick, and the Conſtitution of our Government, expreſſing a great deal of Satisfaction at the Inſight I gave him into our Laws. He often told us he cou'd not have imagin'd there was ſuch an excellent Government in any of the States of *Europe*, having heard to the contrary from thoſe of his Subjects that had been there. Sir, ſaid I, no Government in the World is more excellent than ours, if follow'd according to their Inſtitution; but ſometimes an ill Miniſter, or violent Parties pervert 'em, and even make the Laws ſubſervient to their Guilt. Parties, return'd the King, what are

thoſe?

thoſe? I deſcrib'd 'em to him as well as I cou'd. Why, ſaid the King, is there no way to prevent ſuch Wranglings? I told him in my Sentiments there was none, for I was pretty well aſſur'd the preſent People in Power wou'd be envy'd by thoſe that had no Power at all, and the greateſt Parties were thoſe *in*, and thoſe *out* of Employments, whether thoſe that had the Power deſerv'd it no. That muſt certainly be owing (reply'd the King) to a Meanneſs of Temper, Pride, or Ill-nature; ſome Perſons muſt be Stateſmen, or there wou'd be no Government. When we came upon the Topic of Religion, I told him our Religious had better than a ſixth part of the Value of the Nation; he anſwer'd, Sure they muſt take a great deal of Pains for it. When I related ſome Paſſages in private Families concerning conjugal Matters, he was aſſur'd we muſt be a People very deform'd and nauſeous to the Eye, intimating the Marks he ſuppos'd that appear'd in the Countenances of thoſe that were that way guilty. But, added his Majeſty, I am pleas'd there are ſome Virtuous in ſo wicked a Nation; for neither you, nor any of your Men, have been Faulty that way. I ſmil'd to my ſelf at his Notions, yet did not think it proper to undeceive him. Our Converſation laſted 'till we arriv'd at the Gates of the City of *Timpanius*. The Governor met the King with a great Attendance, but I obſerv'd his Majeſty's Looks were but cool upon him. His Government was the richeſt of the Kingdom; his Name was *Suriamnas*, and deſcended from a Branch of the Royal Family, but ſwerv'd from their Virtue and Honour, which was a greater Wonder than Winters Thunder with us.

As ſoon as we enter'd the Gate of this magnificent City, our Ears were alarm'd with the Sounds of *Marabi! Marabi!* that is in the Language of the Country, *Juſtice! Juſtice!* The injur'd Inhabitants, by the Oppreſſion of their

their Tyrant Governor, groan'd under a heavy Bondage, and had privately complain'd to the King by their Emiſſaries, which was the chief Reaſon of his Majeſty's taking this Progreſs, tho' it was given out he did it only to ſhow us Strangers the Grandeur of his Dominions.

At the Cry of Juſtice, the Governor's Countenance began to change, as little expecting any ſuch thing; however, he compos'd himſelf in the beſt Manner, and addreſs'd the King, who ask'd him with a firm Voice, the Meaning of thoſe Exclamations. But before he cou'd reply thro' his Confuſion, an illuſtrious *Sevarite*, an Inhabitant of that City, (and the Perſon who had given the King Notice of his deteſtable Proceedings) with a great Train behind him, fell at the King's Feet, and beg'd leave to be heard. His Majeſty bid him riſe, and declare his Thoughts freely, which he did as follows.

"Most Renown'd and Glorious "Monarch, We your Loyal Subjects "have suffer'd long and cruel Hard- "ships from the Inhumanity, Avarice, "and Lust of the Prince *Suriamnas*, "who murder'd many of our Friends "and Relations, confiscated our Estates "without Law or Reason, ravish'd "our Wives and Daughters, with many "other abhor'd Crimes, would make us "Guilty but to name 'em; and when "any of your Liege Subjects admo- "nish'd him, they were sure to suffer "Stripes, if nothing worse. And if "your Majesty had not, through the "Direction of Providence, made this "Progress (from whom we are assur'd "of Justice) we must, in Regard to our "selves, have gone to seek for Safety "and Contentment in some more ho- "spitable Climate, this being made "hateful to us from the Injustice of "our Governor." Before the Speech was ended, the Governor fainted a- way,

way, and lay ſenſeleſs on the Earth. But the King order'd his Servants to take care of him.

His Tryal was deferr'd 'till next Day, and the King had ſuch an Abhorrence for the Crimes he had committed, he would not lodge in his Palace, but went out of the City to one of his own about two Leagues off, follow'd almoſt by all the City with joyful Acclamations. His Majeſty ask'd me what form of Juſtice we had in *Europe* againſt ſuch Capital Offenders? I told his Majeſty the manner of our Proceedings in ſuch Caſes, which very much pleas'd him; but I added, Tho' Juſtice was painted Blind, yet ſhe had her other Senſes the Stronger, eſpecially that of Feeling; and being often Crazy, ſhe found nothing gave her ſo much Relief, as a golden Cordial, of ſuch an intoxicating Quality, as ſhe often prov'd beſide her ſelf. The King cou'd not well underſtand the Allegory; for, as I ſaid before, they have no Double Meanings in their Language, therefore I was oblig'd to explain my ſelf. Tho' I aſſur'd him we had ſome Miniſters of Juſtice that were above contaminating their Fingers with baſe Bribes.

THE next Morning early he repair'd to the City, and aſcended the Seat of Juſtice, erected for him in the Market-place. The Place was fill'd immediately with the Accuſers of the Governor, and the Allegations made plain againſt him for ſuch monſtrous Crimes, that would appear ſo in any *European* Court of Juſtice. He was brought to the Bar, but had nothing to ſay in Vindication of himſelf: Tho' theſe Proofs, ſufficient enough in any other Country, could not condemn him. I whiſper'd *Sermodas* in the Ear, and told him, if Puniſhment did not follow ſuch plain Proofs, Juſtice was deficient in *Sevarambia*. *Sermodas* bid me wait with Patience, and obſerve the Iſſue.

THE

THE Governor, base as he was, found a Pleader, I suppose of his own Stamp, that made a very elaborate Speech in Defence of his Innocence. He told his Majesty his Accusers were out of their Senses, and that some wicked *Dæmon* of the Air had possess'd 'em; for if he was guilty of those Crimes he was accus'd of, the Proof would outwardly appear, as in other Criminals, in visible Tokens on the Body.

HE said so much, that those who were Strangers to his Actions began to stagger in their Opinion. But one of the Philosophers whisper'd the King, who immediately order'd the Governor to be strip'd naked, which was done, but no Marks could be seen on his Body, as Proofs of those Crimes alledg'd against him. The King turn'd to the Philosopher, and after some Talk, order'd Vessels of Water to be brought. where

where the Governor was plung'd in, and waſh'd, but when he was taken out again, I never ſaw ſuch a horrid Figure. There was not one Place upon his Body free from the moſt odious Wens and Tumours, Imagination could form. His Guilt was then too plain.

TO prevent theſe Marks from being viſible, a Philoſopher had given him a *Taliſman* of ſuch Force, (for it could not be call'd Virtue) that with the Help of a *Taliſmanic* Paint, had the Power to keep down thoſe outward Workings.

THE Set of wiſe Men about his Majeſty were very much ſcandaliz'd to find there was ſuch an ill Man among 'em, that would proſtitute his Art to conceal ſuch horrid Crimes; therefore, with one Conſent, they went to work, in order to find him out. Their Charms were too powerful for the other, and he he was ſoon compell'd to come before 'em. They beg'd leave of the King to proceed againſt him themſelves, as alſo to puniſh him as they thought fit, which the King granted. After they had examin'd him in Private, tho' in the Sight of all the People, we were ſurpriz'd to ſee him hurl'd up in the Air, as ſwift as an Arrow out of a Bow, then deſcend with the ſame Rapidity, and daſh'd to Pieces on the Pavement. The King ſeem'd diſpleas'd at their Revenge, but he was ſoon pacify'd, when they told him there was no other way to prevent his doing Ill for the Future, but this violent Death.

The Lawyer that pleaded in the Defence of the Governor was baniſh'd to the Iſland of Knaves, as not being worthy (after ſuch a vile Undertaking, in endeavouring to varniſh Crimes) to have a Being among People of ſuch Virtue.

The

THE Governor was left to the Punishment of the offended People, who whip'd him thro' the Streets of the City, then bath'd him in Honey, and afterwards fix'd him upon a high Pillar without the City, where in two Days he was devour'd by the Insects of the Air, all but his Bones; which were taken down and burnt to Ashes, afterwards scatter'd in the Sea, not allowing even his Dust to remain among 'em.

Cruelty

WHEN this Affair was over, the King set himself to reform the Abuses of the late Governor, and conferred his Place upon his Son *Suricolis*, a Youth of excellent Parts, and as good as his Sire was bad. The young Gentleman out of his Humanity could not help shedding Tears at the Fate of his Father, tho' he knew it was Just, and abhorred his Actions. The King gave him the following Advice, when he conferred his Father's Honours upon him.

" THOU

“ THOU haſt been an Eye-witneſs of “ the Juſtice of an offended Monarch “ upon an undeſerving Miniſter, there- “ fore I doubt not, but the Example “ will be ever before thy Eyes. His “ Guilt might give me a Pretence to “ deſtroy his whole Race; but the In- “ nocent ſhould never ſuffer for the “ Crimes of their Family. I am aſſur'd “ from the Principles of Virtue rooted “ in thy Soul, thou wilt be as ready to “ do Good, as he was prone to Ill; “ therefore I confer thy Father's Dig- “ nities, which he unjuſtly bore, upon “ thee, with this Remembrance, *There's* “ *Rewards for Virtue, as well as Pu-* “ *niſhments for Vice.*

WE left this City after ſtaying there three Days, and return'd to *Sevaram-bia* another Way, full as delightful as the former. Within a League of the City, we were met by ſuch Numbers of People, that our Entry was impe-ded

ded ſeveral Hours. The Inhabitants ſeem'd diſtracted with Joy at the Return of their Monarch, he never having been ſo long from 'em ſince his Coronation.

CHAP.

CHAP. V.

Maurice *falls in Love with a Lady of the Country. A Story of a* Dutch *Lady.*

WHILE we ſtaid at *Sevarambia*, *Maurice* contracted a Friendſhip with a young Widow Lady, which Friendſhip ſoon roſe up to an ardent Paſſion on both Sides; but their Grief was unutterable, well knowing the ſtrict Laws of the *Sevarambians* wou'd not permit 'em to join in Wedlock. He imparted his Paſſion to me, and begg'd my Aſſiſtance, at the ſame time telling me, he very much fear'd his Virtue wou'd not hold Proof againſt the Aſſaults

Aſſaults of her Charms, and he believ'd her Paſſion was ſo ſtrong for him, ſhe wou'd not deny him even the laſt Favour. I begg'd him to ſtand up againſt ſuch a Frailty, that muſt of courſe turn to his Prejudice, and make us all hateful to the virtuous Inhabitants. Nay, there was no knowing what wou'd be the End of their Reſentments; the beſt that cou'd be expected, was to be ſent to the Adulterous Iſland, without the leaſt Hope of eſcaping. *Maurice* told me he wou'd defend himſelf with all his Force againſt the Aſſaults of vicious Thoughts, but he farther aſſur'd me, if he cou'd not be happy with that Lady, he muſt be forc'd to put an end to his Life, to finiſh his Miſery. He ſpoke thoſe Words in ſuch a melancholy Tone, with Tears in his Eyes, that forc'd me to pity him. I told him he might be aſſur'd I wou'd ſerve him to the utmoſt of my Power, and to make a Beginning, I wou'd break it to our Friends at Court that very Day, not in the leaſt doubting

doubting the King's Compliance to every thing, without breaking the Laws of the Land; and to encourage him, I farther told him, if his Majeſty cou'd not comply with his Requeſt of marrying the Lady in his Dominions, yet (if ſhe wou'd conſent to go with him to *England*) I was well aſſur'd the King wou'd not deny him that Favour.

THAT, ſaid *Maurice*, I know ſhe will agree to with Joy, for ſhe has more than once told me ſhe wou'd follow me the World over, and run all Fortunes, rather than be ſeparated.

I MUST own this Affair gave me a great deal of Uneaſineſs, for I knew the Conſequence wou'd be, we ſhou'd be oblig'd to leave this delightful Place, the only Climate in the World I ſhou'd have deſir'd to end my Days in. But rather than have any one that belong'd to me offend in any Degree againſt the wiſe Laws of the *Sevarambians*, I was resolv'd to be contented, and set my self in the best manner I cou'd to gain *Maurice* his Desires.

I WENT to wait upon *Sermodas*, and disclos'd the Affair to him. He seem'd to give me little Hopes of the King's Compliance; however we both waited on *Zidi Marabat*, who promis'd to move it to the King the same Evening in Council. I went to my Apartment with some Discontent, for fear we shou'd not succeed, tho' I kept my Sentiments from *Maurice*, who was of a Temper that cou'd not brook Opposition.

SERMODAS came immediately after me, and seeing in my Looks the Agitation of my Thoughts, wou'd not let me be alone, but desir'd I wou'd take a Walk with him to divert my Melancholy. We went out without any more Company. When we were come to the Borders of the River near the Palace, he made

made a Stand. General, ſaid he, (*for* all the *Sevarambians* gave me that Title) I know the Anxiety you are under for fear our Monarch ſhou'd not agree with your Deſires, neither am I certain whether he will or no, it being what was never practis'd in this Country, and things you know without a Precedent, are difficult to obtain; however, if you ſhou'd fail, there is but one way to make your Friend eaſie, and that is this, I am aſſur'd I can convey him and his Miſtreſs to *Sporunda*, without any blame from *Sevaraminas*, where he ſhall want nothing that is in my Power to grant: If he and you will comply with a Requeſt of mine. I told him, whatever became of us, I believ'd there was nothing in either of our Powers, he might not freely command. At this he made a Pauſe, and a conſcious Bluſh overſpread his Countenance. It was ſome time before he ſpoke; at laſt with an unaſſur'd Voice he began. I know not what Opinion you will have of me,

H 2 when

when you have heard what I have to ſay, but I am puſh'd on by my Deſtiny, for ought I know, to reveal the Secrets of my Soul to you. There is no Philoſophy, continu'd *Sermodas*, can guard our Hearts from Love, and the Aſſaults of an amiable Face can batter down all our Reſolutions. I have long ſigh'd for a Woman in your Company, and find my Paſſion ſo violent, nothing can eaſe me but Returns of Love.

I WAS amaz'd at this Declaration, being it was what I never expected; for none of our Females could compare with the *Sevarambian* Women for Beauty. But there is nothing to be ſaid for that tender Paſſion. Moſt Women, be they ever ſo homely, one time or another have found Charms for their Admirers. I ask'd him which of our Women could boaſt of ſuch a Conqueſt. He told me 'twas the Miſtreſs of *Maurice*, and that, added he, has given me the Confidence to declare my Paſſion.

Paſſion. For as he is fallen in Love with another Woman, 'tis not to be ſuppos'd but he could part with her without any Pang. I ask'd him if he had ever declar'd his Paſſion to her. Far be it from me, ſaid he, to invade another's Property, I would ſooner have pined away in hopeleſs Grief, than to have declar'd it now, but for *Maurice*'s Affairs. My Intentions are honourable, and for what has paſt between 'em, I ſhall bury in Oblivion.

I BEGAN to call *Maurice*'s Miſtreſs to my Remembrance, and it occurr'd to me, ſhe was a very beautiful *Dutch* Woman, much the handſomeſt among our Women, which he having the firſt Choice (my ſelf relinquiſhing my Right) they had liv'd together ever ſince.

I WAS much concern'd for *Sermodas*, in imagining the Lady perhaps would not return his Paſſion, or be willing to remain in *Sporunda*, or, notwith-

H 3 ſtanding

ſtanding *Maurice* was ſo very much in Love with this *Scvarambian* Lady, he would not eaſily conſent to part with his *European* Miſtreſs. For Love in weak Minds, is too often the Frailty of Nature; and ſome Men are as willing to change their Miſtreſſes, as their Linnen. Thoſe we may properly call humane Brutes, and are indeed the greater Beaſts; which agrees with what a late Poet ſays, making a Compariſon between Man and Beaſt,

See where the Deer trot after one another,
Male, Female, Father, Daughter, Mother, Son,
Brother and Siſter, mingled all together.
No Diſcontent they know, but in delightful
Wildneſs, and Freedom, pleaſant Springs, freſh Herbage,
Calm Harbours, luſty Health and Innocence,

Enjoy

Enjoy their Portiou. If they ſee a Man,
How will they turn together all, and gaze
Upon the Monſter———
Once in a Seaſon too, they taſte of Love:
Only the Beaſt of Reaſon is its Slave,
And in that Folly drudges all the Year.

But my Friend *Sermodas* was warm'd with no baſe Deſires, his was a pure and lambent Fire, worthy himſelf. I muſt own I thought him wrong, as to the Object of his Wiſhes, but we muſt not always expect Reaſon in Love.

I PROMIS'D *Sermodas* to ſound *Maurice* the firſt Opportunity. He thank'd me for my Intention, and told me, whatever befell him, he ſhould never forget my Kindneſs. I beg'd this might be no Bar to gain the King's Conſent to our firſt Propoſal concerning

ing *Maurice*; and he gave me his Word and Honour, he would forward it all that lay in his Power, but would not hinder it any thing, tho' his utmoſt Happineſs depended on't.

AFTER taking a little Walk, we return'd to the Palace, debating as we paſs'd along the Affair in hand. I took my leave of *Sermodas*, and went to ſeek *Maurice*. I found him alone in his Chamber, in a very melancholly Poſture.

WHAT, ſaid I, my Friend, alone, and muſing; this ſuits but ill with your former Temper. All my Fortune paſt (return'd *Maurice*) had never Power to alter my Diſpoſition, but the Thought of what's to come almoſt drives me to deſpair; if the King ſhou'd not comply with my Deſires, I ſhall find no Remedy but in the Grave. Alas, (ſaid I) I have known many a Man, as far gone as you in Love, ſurvive his Paſſion

7 many

many Years. But do not think of Death, before you are ſure there's no other Remedy. I'll warrant you, if your *Dutch* Lady had not comply'd with your Amour, we ſhou'd have had you thinking on your Grave before now.

No, ſaid *Maurice*, to let you ſee how you are miſtaken, I have never had any criminal Converſation with that Woman, ſince I have had her. Why, you amaze me (ſaid I) and if I was not well aſſur'd of your Integrity, I ſhou'd hardly find Faith enough to believe you. I cannot think it is for want of Inclination, for to the beſt of my Memory, ſhe's both Young and Handſome. 'Tis true (return'd *Maurice*) ſhe's Young enough, and I always thought her Handſome, or I had not choſe her for my Mate; but there's no other Paſſion but Friendſhip between us, and ſhe has Virtue enough to vie with the Ladies of this Country. I muſt own, the Propenſity

penſity to Society of this kind, which attend the Young and Vigorous, made me fix upon her, when we made the Diſtribution of our Females; but the melancholly Story of her Misfortunes, and her own earneſt Deſire, hinder'd me from propagating any other Paſſion but Amity.

If it's true what you ſay, I think you have more Virtue than can be expected from a mortal Man, conſidering the Circumſtances we have lain under; and what you have told me ſo much amazes me, that I ſhall beg it as the greateſt Proof of your Friendſhip, to be let into the Story of her Misfortune, for there is no doubt but you know it. Yes, ſaid *Maurice*, and you ſhall learn it from her own Mouth. I only beg leave to wait upon her in the next Room, and prepare her a little for this Interview, my Stay ſhall not be long, we'll come to you immediately; on ſaying this he left me alone.

During

DURING his Stay, my Thoughts were taken up upon this Adventure. The Face is not always the Index of the Mind; for in *Maurice*'s Countenance could not be read he would abſtain from any thing his Deſires prompted him to, when it could be come at without Difficulty.

AFTER ſome ſmall Stay he enter'd, leading the Lady in his Hand. When the uſual Compliments among Strangers was over, ſhe ſeated her ſelf in the Window: When ſhe had paus'd a little, and wip'd the falling Tears from her Cheeks, ſhe began.

GENERAL, ſaid ſhe, Mr. *Maurice* is my Friend, and one I have ſo many Obligations to, that I can deny him nothing within the Bounds of Honour. He has deſir'd me to relate to you my unhappy Adventures; there's nothing in 'em Curious, but however, if you'll take

take 'em as they are, I am very willing to comply with your Requeſt.

I WAS born in *Amſterdam*, the Capital of *Holland*, of wealthy Parents, and of a good Family, if you will allow any of the *Dutch* to brag of their Deſcent. My Father was made Governor of *Batavia*, (his Predeceſſor being recall'd upon ſome Male-Adminiſtration) a Poſt perhaps the beſt in the *State's* Gift, where they live like great Princes, and not like thoſe who deal in Merchandize. My Father, when he went to his Government, took me along with him, my Mother dying juſt after ſhe brought me into the World. When we came to *Batavia*, he gave me all the Learning the Place would afford, that was proper to my Sex; and I would not have you think me vain, if I tell you I profited more than was expected.

WHEN I was about eleven Years old, my Father marry'd the late Governor of of *Amboyna*'s Widow, a Woman fam'd more for her Riches, than any other good Quality. And ſince her Huſband's Death, had come to reſide at *Batavia*, it being a Place of more Conveniency than *Amboyna*. This Lady had one Son, the Darling of his Mother, a Perſon poſſeſs'd of every thing that was the oppoſite of Good. He was born in *Amboyna*, but ſent to the Univerſity of *Leyden* in *Holland* for his Education. He came to *Batavia* with all the Accompliſhments of an affected Traveller, who brings nothing home but the Vices of the Places he has gone thro'. Before his coming, my Mother-in-Law had loſt that Name with me, and never having the Happineſs of knowing my own Mother, I had all the Affection for her, I thought due to a real Parent.

When this young Gentleman arriv'd, he caſt his Eyes on me, with Inclinations far wide of the Conſanguinity that

that ought to have been between us. He was too full of himſelf to imagine he ſhould meet with any Repulſe from me, and when he firſt declar'd his Paſſion, he did it in ſuch a manner, as if he thought I was under the utmoſt Obligation for the Favour he did me. The Repulſe he met with in his firſt Declaration, ſomething ſtartled him, but he had too good an Opinion of his own Merit, to imagine my Coldneſs proceeded from any thing but Cuſtom; yet his repeated Addreſſes began to open his Eyes, and he found by his Treatment, young as I was, I knew how to deſpiſe a Coxcomb.

I WAS freed from his impertinent Sollicitation for ſome time, inſomuch that I imagin'd he had forgot his Paſſion. But one Day he came into my Apartment with his Mother, (my Father being juſt gone to the Council-Room). I perceiv'd by her Countenance ſhe had ſomething of Importance to ſay to me, and

and my Heart ſoon ſuggeſted the Buſineſs. After ſhe had talk'd ſome time upon indifferent Matters, ſhe told me her coming to me now was chiefly upon her Son's Account, whoſe Paſſion was become ſo violent for me, his Life was become a Burden to him, begging me at the ſame time to receive his Addreſſes more favourably. I told her I was ſomewhat ſurpriz'd at her Sollicitation, imagining our near Relation was a ſufficient Bar to any nearer Alliance. She inform'd me that cou'd be no Impediment, for it was a thing very uſual in all Parts of the World. She was a Woman of ſuch a violent Spirit, not to brook any Contradiction; therefore I told her, my Obedience was ready to follow my Father's Commands. (Tho' I knew my Inclination could never admit of him for a Lover, having at the firſt Sight conceiv'd an invincible Averſion againſt him.) It's a good Child, ſaid my Mother-in-Law, I'll make it my Buſineſs to gain your Father's Conſent,

ſent, tho' we have not mention'd any thing of the Affair to him yet. After talking concerning this Alliance, and telling me how happy I ſhou'd be in ſo accompliſh'd a Perſon as her Son; ſhe went out, and left me with him. He began to diſplay his Thoughts in ſuch an affected manner, that I really imagin'd he cou'd have no other Paſſion than for his own dear Perſon. I beg'd he wou'd ceaſe for the preſent his Sollicitations, 'till I receiv'd Commands from my Father in his Behalf, which he promis'd me, and left me to my own Thoughts.

YOUNG as I was, I dreaded this Conjunction worſe than Death. However I was reſolv'd to yield my ſelf a Sacrifice to the Obedience of my Father, if he commanded me to receive him for my Husband, tho' I had Hopes he wou'd not agree to it, for to me it look'd like an unnatural Marriage.

I

I liv'd in the Plague of Doubt ſeveral Days, and all the Comfort I had was, that I had no Converſe with the Diſturber of my Peace. One Day wandring by the River Side, muſing on my Circumſtances, an *Alligator* ſprung out of the Water, and purſu'd me; my Maids that were at ſome diſtance from me ſcream'd out, which made me obſerve the Creature; I flew to avoid it as well as I cou'd, but my Fright took away my Strength, and I fell ſenſeleſs to the Earth; when I came to my ſelf, I found I was laid upon a Bed in a Fiſherman's Cottage, with my Maids, and a young Gentleman, a Stranger to me, ſtanding by me. I ask'd 'em how I had eſcap'd the Jaws of that voracious Creature! one of my Maids told me that the young Gentleman that ſtood by me had under Providence ſav'd my Life, for ſeeing me fall, he ruſh'd from a Thicket, where he had been following his Game, took me up in his Arms, and by running

ning in Angles, had eſcap'd the Monſter. I need not tell you this Creature has no Joint in its Back, and therefore takes near a Minute in turning himſelf, therefore any Perſon that is purſu'd by 'em, if they have Senſe in their Fright to turn to the Right, or the Left, may eaſily avoid 'em. I paid the Gentleman all the Acknowledgment for this ſignal Favour, I was capable of, in Words; but alas! I had not gaz'd upon him long ere I gave him my Heart in Recompence. He inform'd me, he was Son to the *Fiſcal* of *Batavia*, that he long had lov'd me, tho' he had never had the Confidence to diſcloſe his Paſſion to any one 'till this Accident. He gave me ſo many Proofs of the Sincerity of his Heart, and had ſo much Eloquence in his Declaration, that before we parted, I gave him a Promiſe of mine in Return, which indeed, was his before. I fixt a Meeting with him the next Day at an Acquaintance, both of his and mine; where

where we might have a farther Opportunity of converſing together.

WHEN I came home, my Brother-in-law came to congratulate me upon my Eſcape, and curſing his Stars it was not his Fortune to reſcue me from my paſt Danger, uttering at the ſame time ſuch a quantity of Rodomantado Speeches, one would have taken him for a Hero, if his Words wou'd have agreed with his Actions. I deſpis'd him before, but my ſmall Acquaintance with my amiable Deliverer encreas'd my Averſion.

WE met frequently at our Place of Rendezvouz undiſcover'd, and gave to each other the Promiſe of an unalterable Affection. All this happy time I was free from the impertinent Sollicitations of my hated Lover, which gave me Hopes they cou'd not ſucceed with my Father. Theſe Hopes flatter'd me if my favour'd Lover ſhou'd apply to

I 2 him

him in a proper manner, he might gain his Conſent, for his Fortune was equal to mine, his Father being one of the richeſt Men upon the Place.

THE next time we met, my Lover appear'd with the utmoſt Melancholy in his Countenance, which quite confounded me. It was ſome time ere I cou'd prevail with him to tell me the Cauſe of his Diſcontent. At laſt he told me with broken Sighs and Tears in his Eyes, that his Father had declar'd, he had agreed with one of the *Burgo-maſters* of *Amſterdam*, that he ſhou'd wed his Daughter, and had but that very Morning told him, he muſt prepare in a Month's Time to imbark for *Holland*, in order to wed the Lady; but he added he wou'd ſooner die than break his Faith with me. This News came upon me like a Thunder-clap, and in ſpight of all my Reaſon, I could not avoid ſhewing my Concern. This Diſturbance, ſaid my Lover, ſhews your Affection

Affection to me more than the most eloquent Language, therefore if you please, let us put it out of the Power of Fate to sever us. Let the Priest join our Hands, and leave the Conduct; of our future Fortune to Chance: Nothing can be equal to the Pain of parting for ever, and I have Sufficient, independent of my Father, to keep us from Poverty, tho' not enough to live in Splendor. I told him the Loss of Fortune to true Lovers was the least Ill that cou'd befall 'em, but the Curse of Parents sounded very dreadful to me. Who knows, said he, when we have put it out of their Power by marrying, but we may still be happy with their Approbation; knowing no Remedy, we may be forgiven. My Heart took his part so much that I consented, and the next Day we were wedded unknown to any one, but the Priest, one Friend of his, and one of my Maids, that I had confided in; but we were oblig'd, like the ancient *Lacedæmonians*, to meet in private. We continu'd our Commerce undiſcover'd three Weeks, and I thought my ſelf the happieſt Creature in the Univerſe, and to compleat it, my Lover told me News was brought from *Europe*, that the young Lady deſign'd for his Wife by his Father was dead.

THE Fruits of our Love began to appear, which brought new Terrors upon me, and I begg'd my Husband to conceal our Marriage no longer, for it wou'd ſoon diſplay it ſelf. He promis'd me to do it in a few Days. In the mean time, new Plagues began at Home, for my Father declar'd he intended to give me to his Son-in-law; he told me the Reaſon he had not ſpoke to me of it before, was, that he had endeavour'd to make him ſhake off his Paſſion for me, but to no purpoſe, therefore he commanded me to prepare for the Nuptials, the enſuing *Eaſter*. You may eaſily judge at the Shock this gave me. I beg'd my Father not to inſiſt upon

upon my Compliance, for I aſſur'd him I cou'd not think of Happineſs with him; but my Father was too obſtinate to be contradicted. He flung out of the Room, telling me he expected Obedience. When I met my Husband the next Day, we condol'd together our Misfortunes, and to add to 'em, he inform'd me, that he had mention'd a Marriage with me to ſee how his Father wou'd take it, but he fell into a Paſſion, a thing unuſual with him, and declar'd he wou'd never conſent to ſuch a Match, having ever had an Enmity to our Family. We ſpent the Time we ſtaid together in bewailing our Misfortunes, but came to no Reſolution. I paſs'd the enſuing Night in all the Torments of Deſpair, a ſure Omen of what befel me afterwards.

WHEN I ſtole out the next Day to our Rendezvous, I found a Letter there, inſtead of my Husband. I open'd it trembling with Apprehenſion, and read

to this Effect: "That mentioning to
"his Father our Marriage, he had forc'd
"him on board a Ship bound for *Hol-
"land*, not giving him Time or Op-
"portunity to ſpeak to any one; that
"he had prevail'd upon one of the
"Officers to leave that Letter for me,
"and if I had Love enough to run his
"Fortune, the ſame Perſon wou'd
"conduct me to the Ship where he
"was, and to help my Eſcape, he had
"ſent a Suit of Men's Cloaths, deſi-
"ring me to be ready the Dusk of the
"Evening the next Day, deſiring me
"to come alone.

My Grief at this unhappy News can better be imagin'd than expreſs'd by Words; but I had too much Affection not to prepare for my Flight, and no Reflection came over me, but that of being prevented. I went home, and with a heavy Heart prepar'd to follow all I held dear. I had a good Quantity of Jewels in my Poſſeſſion, that were my own Mother's; thoſe

thoſe I pack'd up, with what Apparel I cou'd conveniently ſend out by my truſty Maid. When I came to the uſual Place, I diſcover'd my Intentions to her, but ſhe vow'd unleſs I wou'd ſuffer her to accompany me, ſhe wou'd prevent my Eſcape, by acquainting my Father with my Deſign. I was eaſily prevail'd to accept of her Propoſal, being ſhe was a Perſon I dearly lov'd from my Infancy, but having no Diſguiſe for her made me very uneaſie. When the Perſon came, he ſeem'd unwilling to let her accompany me: But ſhe intreated him ſo movingly, that he ſaid he wou'd exceed his Commiſſion, and admit her along with us. When I was dreſs'd, we went with our Eyes overrunning with Tears to the Water ſide, and rowing almoſt all Night were put on board the Ship. The Perſon that conducted me, led me into the Cabin; I ſat ſome time, and was ſomething ſurpriz'd my Husband did not come to me. But my Conductor came in, and gave

gave me another Letter, whose Contents have liv'd ever since in Memory, by my often Reading.

"MADAM, I think it now high "time to undeceive you. The Person "that marry'd us was a Friend of mine, "and so far from being in Holy Or-"ders, that I believe he was never "three times at Church in his Life. I "must own this Action looks full upon "the Stroke of Barbarity, being I be-"lieve you are going to a Place from "whence you will never return; but "tho' you have left a good Estate be-"hind you, yet you have Charms e-"nough to make your own Fortune, "for fine Women are very scarce "where you are going. My Friend "will take great Care of you; and if "you should want a Midwife, and a "Nurse, before you come to the end "of your Voyage, there's Women e-"nough along with you. If it is a Boy, "pray Heav'n make him a better Man

"than

" than his Father; if a Girl, a wiser
" Woman than the Mother. When I
" told you ſome time ago, that my Fa-
" ther gave me Orders to Imbarque for
" *Holland*, in order to Marry, I told
" you Truth, and this very Day I ſet
" Sail. I don't expect the Lady I am
" going to ſee will have half your Beau-
" ty, therefore I fear I ſhall not con-
" verſe with her half ſo long; however,
" there's Variety enough there, which
" we want in *Batavia*. You know,
" in ſaving your Life, I had a Right
" and Title to your Body; and I think
" you are oblig'd to me for giving up
" that Title ſo ſoon. I don't doubt but
" this Epiſtle muſt give you ſome Di-
" ſturbance, but I have known two or
" three in your Circumſtance, have
" bury'd more than one Husband a-
" piece. Grief is as violent a Paſſion
" as Love, and the ſtronger it is, the
" leſs laſting. Haſty Fires are ſooneſt
" out, and the Horſe that runs ſwifteſt
" ſooneſt Jades. But I'll trouble you
" no

"no more, but to advise you to forget "me, as I shall you, while I am

Frederick Van Noort.

BEFORE I had read half the Letter, I sunk speechless on the Floor; and, as my faithful Attendant told me afterwards, it was some Hours ere they could bring me to any signs of Life. When I came to my Senses, I may properly say, I was ready to run distracted. The Thoughts of such an inhumane Act, beyond the Barbarity of the most savage *Indian*, made me wish for Death, as the only Remedy to my Misfortune. I beg'd the Person that convey'd me there, to bury me, and my Misery together, in the Bowels of the Deep; but he beg'd me to be patient, telling me Time would mitigate my Sorrows, and that such an ungrateful Wretch was not worth grieving for. To be short, this Gentleman gave me many Tokens of his Pity, which by Degrees ascended to Love. But alas! I had conceived

7 such

ſuch an Averſion for all the Male-Sex, that I reſolv'd for the future to avoid 'em, as I wou'd a poiſonous Serpent. How often did I curſe my fond Credulity, that led me to believe his ſoothing Words, wiſhing the Accident that brought me firſt to his Acquaintance had been the laſt Moment of my Life. My various Thoughts brought pointed Stings of double Death.

THE Ship ſet Sail the next Day for *new Holland*, where ſhe was bound to make a Settlement, having ſeveral Women on Board that went to raiſe their Fortunes; but I need not deſcribe 'em to you, ſince they are the ſame you ſav'd, and have now among you. We were drove into a Port on the Iſland of *Java*, where we were detain'd by contrary Winds upwards of ſeven Months. But the Time rather encreas'd my Woes, than leſſen'd 'em. The Burden I carry'd drew near the time of Delivery: And when the Pangs of Labour came

came upon me, I beg'd of Heaven to release me of my Woes, by putting an End to my Life. But notwithstanding my Grief, I was deliver'd of a dead Infant, with no other Help than my faithful Servant. We committed it to the Waves, first washing it with our Tears; and maugre my Grief, I recover'd my Strength, but my Misfortunes did not at all lessen. My Concern for my faithful Attendant was almost equal to my own, that she should be involv'd in my Unhappiness out of her Love to me. Tho' she bore it with an heroick Resolution, sometimes even rejoycing at her Fate, that had permitted her to accompany me in my Misfortunes. The Person that brought me on Board, began to be more eager in his Sollicitations, when he saw I began to recover my Strength, and what he call'd Beauty. But my Hatred and Sorrow was too violent to admit of any Addresses that Way, however I us'd him with good Manners. He was Supercargo of the Ship,

Ship, and one from the Make of his Person that might command Regard; but alas! none of the Sex had any Charms for me.

I HAD wore my Boy's Cloaths 'till I was deliver'd of my unhappy Burden, but I thought it then convenient to assume my own Person again.

THE Wind coming Fair, we prepar'd to Sail; the Supercargo going ashore for some Necessaries, quarrel'd with some of the *Javans*, and was mortally wounded. He was brought on Board, but expir'd the next Day. I must own his Death did not much grieve me, because I was rid of a Man, who for ought I knew might have in time proceeded to Force. We were several Days tost on the Ocean 'till we sprung a Leak, when we must all have perish'd, if your Vessel had not happily came in to save us; tho' I must declare, when I was told there was little Hopes of of escaping, my Concern was not for my self, but for my faithful Companion, who is since rewarded, in being Wife to *De Hayes*, one of your Officers, having lawfully wedded her at our first Arrival at *Sporunda*. As for the rest of my Fortune, you know as well as my self; I have only this to say, that when *Maurice* chose me for his Companion, I prevail'd upon him to cultivate a Friendship between us, and nothing else; and his Compliance with me has sufficiently convinc'd me, he is worthy to be a Friend. In the Confidence of that, I have beg'd him to use his Interest, that I may be permitted to be left behind, when you go from this charming Country, for all other Places will be hateful to me. Here the Lady ended, and I could not avoid shedding some Tears at the Relation of her Misfortunes. However, I fancy'd this seem'd to be a favourable Opportunity for my Friend *Sermodas*, and therefore declar'd the Passion he had for her. She seem'd ſeem'd ſurpriz'd at my Relation, yet I thought ſhe heard me more favourably than I expected, from her Averſion to the Male Sex. We had a long Diſcourſe upon it, and I inform'd her it would be the only means of having her Deſire, in being left behind. She cou'd have no Objection to the Perſon of *Sermodas*, for he was a very handſome Man, near forty Years of Age. I did not care to let the Affair cool, therefore I ſent to him immediately; and before we parted, there ſeem'd to be a good Underſtanding between 'em. When we parted with the Lady, I told *Sermodas* the Story of her paſt Life. He commiſerated her Misfortunes, but felt a ſecret Satisfaction at her Conduct. He gave me abundance of Thanks for managing this Affair.

The next Day the King call'd a Council, where *Maurice*'s Buſineſs was debated; and the Reſult was, If the Lady was willing to go with him, his Majeſty would give his Conſent. This was pleaſing News to 'em both; and the King, the more to honour 'em, would have the Marriage ſolemniz'd in the Temple of the City, and grace it with his Preſence.

The Day was fix'd, and the Preparations were as Magnificent, as if a Monarch's Nuptials were to be ſolemniz'd. *Sermodas* in a Robe of Cloth of Gold, and Garlands of Flowers upon his Head, as well as that of his Bride's, were the firſt Couple; and *Maurice* had on a Habit given him by the *Sevarambian* King, ſo rich in Gold and Jewels, our Eyes could hardly bear the Luſtre. The Brides were dreſt in White, the Cuſtom of the Country allowing no other Dreſs; but the Charms of their Beauty and Innocence was above all outward Imbelliſhments. Our unfortunate *Dutch* Woman's Perſon was equal to that of the *Sevarambian* Ladies, and ſhe had the Praiſes of every one as ſhe paſs'd on to the Temple. When the Ceremony was over, (which was much

the

the ſame we ſaw at *Sporunda*) we return'd to the Palace, where a noble Entertainment was prepar'd for the whole Court, at the King's Expence. After Dinner, the King did me the Honour to enter into Converſation with me; I then inform'd him of the Adventures of our *Dutch* Lady; and the Queen, being an Auditor, could not refrain Tears at the Relation. The new-marry'd Pairs had Apartments provided for 'em in the Palace, fit for the Reception of the greateſt Monarchs. Twenty Days were ſpent in Feaſting and Mirth, a Term only allow'd at the Marriage of their Kings. The Theatre of the Palace was open, (a thing I thought they were ignorant of) where were repreſented Comedies, Tragedies and Operas, with ſuch magnificent Decorations, as far exceeded thoſe of *Italy*. One of their Operas was the Loves of *Mars* and *Venus*, (for they are well acquainted with our Poetical Stories) where the Voices were ſo Charming they excell'd every thing of that Kind;

and the Words ſeem'd as well adapted to the Muſick, as is that of the *Italian* Language. To give the Reader a Sample of it, I have ſet down one of the Airs ſung by *Mars*, when he was courting *Venus* in a Cypreſs Grove:

Trema ſpleſſo pil Carmina
Nil Formaſo pelte Trano
Spum fel trotſo cronitano
Meluc cauſo tnuc te felſo.

The Elegance of the Language would be loſt in an *Engliſh* Tranſlation, however I'll give you the plain Meaning of the Words.

He tells her *her Eyes are Burning-Glaſſes that fire his Heart, which nothing can quench without Enjoyment.*

AFTER the time of Rejoycing for theſe Nuptials was over, the King gave Orders for a Ship to be provided to carry us to the Iſland of *Monatamia*, where we were to ſettle a Trade; but we were allow'd to come from *Europe* but with one Ship, every two Year, of ſix hundred Ton.

CHAP.

CHAP. VI.

The Author and Company Imbark for Monatamia. *Their Arrival, and Departure from thence to* Batavia. *They ſet ſail for* England. *A Conſpiracy on Board the Ship. The Author with others forc'd into the Long-Boat. Two Sailors murder* Maurice, *to enjoy his Wife. The Lady and one of the Sailors drown'd. The Author taken into a* French *Ship; his ſafe Arrival in* France, *and afterwards in* England.

IN a Month's time, every thing was ready for us to depart; for my own part, I wiſh'd that Father *Time* would have clip'd his Wings, and not have fled ſo faſt, for I ſhould with abundance of Satisfaction have ended my Days in *Sevarambia*, if it had been practicable. But then the Good of my Native Country pleaded for my going; for I was aſſur'd the Trade with theſe Excellent People wou'd be of very great Advantage to *England*. When the Day fix'd for our Departure was come, there were many Tears ſhed on both Sides; for my Men had behav'd themſelves ſo well during their Abode in *Sevarambia*, that they had gain'd the Eſteem of all that knew 'em. *Sermodas* with his new Bride (who had now forgot her former Griefs) wou'd accompany us to *Monatamia*, which the King being inform'd of gave him the Charge of the Ship, and Orders relating to our ſettled Trade in that Iſland. When I went to take my Leave of his Majeſty, and to give him Thanks for the many Favours he had conferr'd on us, he gave me ſo many rich Preſents as would enable me to live above Want, in any part of the World; and my other Officers, as well as the Men, receiv'd Preſents in Proportion, equal to their Station. We imbark'd *Auguſt* the 2d, and ſail'd down the River *Rocara* with the Wind and Tide, and at Night anchor'd before the City *Trumbello*, a Place famous for Trade with

with the Iſland of *Monatamia.* Here we took in ſeveral Merchants, and a skilful Pilot, to conduct us out of the Mouth of the River of *Rocara,* being the Paſſage was exceeding dangerous from the many Rocks within a Fathom of the Surface of the Water: but we got through without any Danger.

We ſteer'd S. S. E. all the next Day, but before Night it prov'd ſtark Calm. About Midnight a Breeze ſprung up, and the Ship had very good Way. The next Morning, the Iſland of *Monatamia* appear'd to us right a-head, and the Wind ſlackning, we lay by the next Night; for the Entrance of the Port, we was inform'd, was as dangerous as that of *Trumbello.* We ply'd off and on all Night, and in the Morning fir'd a Gun, to give 'em Notice to ſend us a Pilot. When he came on Board, he was ſomething ſurpriz'd to find ſo many *Europeans,* and 'till *Sermodas* appear'd, he ſeem'd backward in guiding us in, for it is almoſt a Wonder to ſee any

Foreign Veſſel there. *Sermodas* ſoon remov'd his Doubts, and he went immediately to the Helm. The Port is one of the fineſt in the World, form'd ſomething like the Harbour of *Portſmouth* in *England*, only much larger, and the Land higher about it, ſo that when you are in, you are Land-lock'd, and free from Storms. The Town bears the ſame Name as the Iſland, and is ſubject to the *Sevarambian* King, who ſends a Governor every three Year. It has many ſmaller Iſlands in its Juriſdiction, ſome two, three, or ſomething more Leagues in Circumference, and one very near as large as the Iſle of *Wight*. The Governor of theſe petty Places are called Kings, but I know not the Reaſon for it, unleſs it be in Ridicule.

SERMODAS, *Maurice* and I had ſeveral Conferences with the Governor, and had leave, if we thought fit, to make a Settlement there. We agreed to return from *Europe* as ſoon as poſſible

ſible with People for that Purpoſe, and ſome of our Men and their Wives deſir'd to remain there 'till we came back, which the Governour came into. Of ſeventy odd that were marry'd, but three remain'd with us to go for *Europe*. After ſtaying at *Monatamia* fourteen Days, we ſet ſail for *Batavia*, for we had ſeveral Sailors that liv'd there, who were not willing to go any farther, but however we were in no Fear we ſhou'd want Hands, for there we were ſure of meeting with enough.

I GAVE *Maurice* my Cabin, it being more convenient for him and his Lady.

WE arriv'd at *Batavia*, without meeting any Accident in our Voyage. Our Sailors ſoon forgot thoſe Virtues they had ſeen among the *Sevarambians*, and being moſt of 'em rich, they plung'd into the Vices, common to thoſe ſort of Men. To prevent which, I was reſolv'd to go from thence with the utmoſt Expedition. The Governour us'd us'd us with a great deal of Candour and Humanity, and beg'd me to give him a Journal of my Voyage, which I cou'd not deny him, first scratching out the Latitudes of Places; for the *Dutch* think it no Infringement on the Rights of other Traders, if they can trade themselves; and they are so powerful in the *East-Indies*, 'tis often in their Will to drive all others from their Settlements. I fixt the Day for sailing, but when it came, half of my Men refus'd to imbark, therefore I was oblig'd to apply to the Governour, who order'd me a Power to seize 'em, but they absconded, therefore I was oblig'd to stay longer, to supply that Want. When I had got my full Number of Men, we set sail from *Batavia*, bound for the *Cape of Good Hope*, in our Voyage to *England*. While I staid at *Batavia*, I had forgot to mention my Enquiry into the Story of the *Dutch* Lady. I was inform'd the *Fiscal*'s Son was gone from thence to *Holland*, as she related to us, and that the Governour's nour's Daughter, which was her ſelf, had abſconded from her Father, and had not been heard of for near two Years. The Governour had been almoſt inconſolable for her Loſs, as imagining ſhe had fled to avoid the Match he deſign'd her. The *Fiſcal* was dead about a Month before we arriv'd; however I inform'd the Governour by Letter, concealing my Name, of her firſt Misfortune, and her Happineſs and Tranquility ſince; letting him know at the ſame Time, it was not impoſſible but he might ſee her again (for ſhe and *Sermodas* had hinted to me, that if they could get leave of the King, they might within a Year or two make a Voyage to *Batavia*, to pay their Father a Viſit.) I ſaw the young Gentleman her Brother-in-law in the Palace, and he ſeem'd to me to be improved in his coxcomical Airs.

WE met with the Trade Winds in the uſual Latitude, and ſail'd very proſperouſly for ſeveral Days.

ONE

ONE Day after Dinner, as *Maurice* and his Lady were playing with me at *Ombre*, he told me, he did not very well like the Behaviour of ſome of the Under-Officers, who were frequently caballing with ſome of the new Sailors we had taken in at *Batavia*, and told me plainly he fear'd ſome Conſpiracy among 'em to our Prejudice. I was very much alarm'd at what he ſaid, and was reſolv'd to be on my Guard. He gave me ſome Reaſons to think that *De Nuit* was concern'd with 'em. I deſir'd him, if it was poſſible, to dive into the Affair, that we might take proper Meaſures to prevent 'em; but while we were conſulting the Means, *De Nuit* and about twenty of the Sailors ruſh'd into the Cabbin, and clapping a Piſtol to each of our Breaſts, ſwore we were all dead, if we made the leaſt Reſiſtance. I ask'd him with as much Preſence of Mind, as I was capable of, the Reaſon of this Proceed-

ing.

ing. He told me very insolently, that he thought it as much his Right as mine to command the Ship, assuring me at the same time, that from that Moment I shou'd lose the Title of General, which I had impudently assum'd, as well as that of Captain. I told him I was very willing to resign, when we arriv'd at the *Cape.* It may be so, said he, but I have no Intention to carry the Ship there, therefore if your Inclinations are so very strong for that Voyage, there's a Boat ready prepar'd to carry you and as many as are willing to follow your Fortune. I wou'd have expostulated with him, but it was to no purpose, for he wou'd not hear me. We were hurry'd away, and put into the Long-boat, that was ready out for that purpose. When *Maurice* and his Wife (all drown'd in Tears) and my self were in, the Wretch call'd from the Quarter-deck to the Men upon the Main-deck. If any, said he, have an Inclination to wait on the General, they

they are welcome. Two of my Men, whoſe Names were *Sturmy* and *Withers*, cry'd out they wou'd follow my Fortunes; telling him it was more honourable to ſtarve with me, than to live in Plenty with ſuch a Wretch as he was. Upon ſaying this, they went for their things, and came into the Boat to us. Some with Tears in their Eyes took leave of us, while others laugh'd at our Misfortune. *De Nuit* obſerving that, order'd the Rope to be cut that held the Boat, and we ſoon were left a-ſtern. They had given us Proviſions for two Months, with our Arms, and ſome Bedding, but alas! we had no Hopes of Eſcaping the mercileſs Waves, for by the beſt Accounts we were a hundred Leagues from any Land. They had given me one of my Trunks of Cloaths, as they had done the ſame by *Maurice* and his Wife, but as to our Gold that was too precious to be parted with. However I had moſt of my choiceſt Jewels, which I had ſew'd in the Lining of of my Gown, tho' I had few Thoughts concerning Riches at that Time. We appear'd to one another like ſo many Sacrifices to *Neptune*, tho' through all our Clouds of Sorrow, ſome glimmering of a Hope wou'd appear. We paſt the Remainder of the Day in a melancholy Silence. And the Terrors of the Night increas'd our Grief. *Maurice*'s Wife ſeem'd to bear her Lot with more Reſignation than any of us. We paſt the Night in the utmoſt Terror, and when the Day dawn'd, it brought us very little Comfort. We had a Sea Compaſs, but no Inſtruments to take an Obſervation, therefore we knew not well what Courſe to ſteer. One thing happen'd well for us, the Weather continu'd fair, and the Waves were moderate. *Withers* told me, he believ'd we were not many Leagues from *Madagaſcar*, and prevail'd upon us to ſteer North-weſt, and he did not doubt, thro' God's Providence, but we might reach it in three Days. The Thought

Thought of this made our Condition more ſupportable, tho' if we arriv'd ſafely, we knew not what Treatment we ſhou'd meet with; however 'twas better to truſt our ſelves with a barbarous People, than to the Mercy of the Waves. *Withers* inform'd us they were leſs barbarous than they were repreſented, and that he had met with ſeveral of 'em that were friendly to the *Engliſh*. The Weather continu'd fair, but we had ſteer'd North-weſt three whole Days, and no Sign of Land, which damp'd our Hopes again; but *Withers* ſtill continu'd in his Opinion, that we ſhou'd ſee Land in one Day more. But our Deſpair was heighten'd when we ſail'd on our Courſe four Days more, and ſaw no Land; 'tis true we had Proviſion enough to laſt us ſeven Weeks, but if a Storm ſhou'd ariſe, we had no Hopes of eſcaping in an open Boat. We did our Endeavour to comfort each other, but 'twas eaſily to be perceiv'd by our Countenance, the Hope

Hope we had. When Night approach'd, the Clouds began to thicken, and we perceiv'd evident Tokens of a Storm, which overtook us about Midnight. We then resign'd our selves to Heaven, and lay expecting our last Moments. We were toss'd about several Hours, and by degrees the Violence of the Tempest abated, but the Sea ran high, filling the Boat every Moment. However we were resolv'd to be wanting in nothing to save our selves, therefore threw the Water out again as well as we cou'd. Before Day the Weather prov'd calm, and the Sea less turbulent, and accordingly our Hopes began to strengthen. Just as the Day was breaking, we perceiv'd Land, right-a-head, and a strong Current setting in for the Shore; which, before the Sun rose, threw us upon it. We all leapt out, and gave Heaven Thanks for our happy Deliverance. The Place where we landed was between two Rocks, which had several Clefts or Holes in 'em. In some

ſome of theſe Holes we hid our Trunks, not knowing yet what Inhabitants we ſhou'd meet with. I perſuaded *Maurice* to dreſs his Wife in Men's Cloaths, otherwiſe her Beauty might bring us into many Dangers among a People, perhaps, that wou'd ſtick at nothing to ſatisfie a brutal Appetite; he lik'd my Advice ſo well, that he went aſide with his Wife, and put it in practice: after this was done, we climbed up the Rocks, but, to our melancholy Surprize, found we were upon a barren Iſland, without any Inhabitants, and not above two Leagues in Circumference; however, our Condition was ſomething better than the Night before. We rang'd about the Iſland, and found a Spring of excellent Water, which was of great Comfort to us, for that was what we moſt wanted.

Going to the farther Part of the Iſland, we obſerv'd ſeveral Pieces of a Veſſel, the Remains of ſome Shipwrack.

This gave us but a melancholy Proſpect of our own Condition.

About the middle of the Iſland, there was a Hill of a pretty Height, that overlook'd all the reſt of the Iſland. We went up to the Top, hoping from that Eminence we might diſcover ſome other Land. When I had gain'd the Top, the firſt thing I ſaw, was the Skeleton of a Man, whoſe Fleſh we ſuppos'd had been devour'd by the Fowls of the Air. Near him was a Bottle cork'd. Coming to ſee what was in it, I perceiv'd a Paper, which we took out. It was wrote with a Pencil in *French*, as follows. "If any Perſon is ſo unfor-"tunate as to come to this Place, and "read the Paper, he will know the Body "that fetch'd its laſt Breath here, is "that of *Frederick Van Noort*, who "in his Voyage to *Holland* was caſt "away in the Prince of *Orange*, on "this Iſland. From the Remains of "the Wrack a ſmall Veſſel was built,

L 2 "which

" which all the Company besides my " self went away from this Island with, " my self being left a-sleep on this " Hill, and as I suppose forgot: When " I awak'd, I saw the Boat at a distance, " but they were too far to be call'd " back. This Punishment was inflict- " ed on me from the Hand of *Heaven* " for my Sins, which to the last Mo- " ment of my Life I have heartily re- " pented of; especially for wronging " the Governour's Daughter of *Bata-* " *via*. If it should be the Chance of " any *European* to read this, let the " *Fiscal* of *Batavia* know he is child- " less, and has paid the Debt due to " Nature, by perishing for Want.

WE forgot our own Misfortunes, in reflecting on this melancholy Accident: yet, tho' we shed some Tears, I cou'd not help thinking he deserv'd a severe Punishment for those Injuries thrown upon the Wife of *Sermodas*.

WE

We had but little Time to reflect on any thing but our selves. We went from this Piece of Sadness to look after our Boat, which we pull'd on Shore, to see if there was any thing hurt about her, but by good Fortune we found her sound. We then call'd our little Body together, to consult what we shou'd do, whether we shou'd wait upon the Place to expect Relief, or venture once more to Sea, and we all agreed it wou'd be our safest Course to leave the Place while we had Provision, for there was none to be expected there. Accordingly we launch'd from this unlucky Island, and steer'd North-west, hoping we shou'd reach the *African* Coast, if we had overshot *Madagascar*. None of us cou'd imagine what this Place we had left shou'd be, for I had a very good Map of the World in my Trunk, and cou'd find nothing of it mention'd there, Therefore we call'd it the *Unlucky Island*; but we all conjectur'd it cou'd

L 3 not

not be a great way out of the common Courſe of ſailing. However we agreed to ſhorten our Allowance of *Proviſion*, for fear of the worſt, tho' we had undergone a great deal of Hardſhip already, for we had no Conveniency of dreſſing any Meat, therefore we were oblig'd to eat our Beef raw.

THE next Day, to our great Joy, we diſcover'd Land, which extended South a great way. We now began to think our Danger over, at leaſt that of the Sea. We came within two Leagues of the Shore before Night, and a ſtrong Breeze ſetting from the Land, we determin'd to lie by 'till the Morning. But finding the Water not very deep, we came to an Anchor. Having taken but little Reſt ſince we were drove from the Ship, we went to Sleep, leaving the two Sailors to watch by turns. About Midnight, I was awak'd by the Cries of *Maurice*'s Wife, and endeavouring to riſe, found I was ty'd Hand

Hand and Foot, and faſtned to the Maſt of the Boat. I was very much ſurpriz'd; but all the Efforts I made to untie my ſelf were to no purpoſe. I heard *Maurice* groan ſeveral times, and his Wife lamenting in the *Sevarambian* Language. She call'd to me, and begg'd my Aſſiſtance, but I gave her to underſtand in what Condition I was. I call'd to *Maurice*, but cou'd receive no Anſwer; yet I ſoon found by the two Sailors, that they had murder'd him, and intended to raviſh his Wife; and by her repeated Cries, I underſtood they were putting their damnable Deſign in Execution; but they were both ſo eager that a Quarrel aroſe who ſhou'd enjoy her firſt, and from Words, they fell to Blows. While they were diſputing, I heard her jump into the Sea, where ſhe was ſoon drown'd. The two Sailors were ſo buſie in their Aſſaults, they did not regard the Lady; their Strugglings were ſo violent, they both tumbled over board, and *Sturmy* not underſtanding ſwimming, met his Fate in the Waves; the other, with much ſtruggling, got into the Boat again, where he ſat ſometime without ſpeaking: Not hearing him ſtir nor breathe, I thought he was dead; but to be aſſur'd, I call'd out to him. He anſwer'd me with a faint Voice. I ask'd what was the matter? Alas, ſaid he, the Fiends of Hell have poſſeſs'd me, and hurried me upon the Brink of Deſtruction. Dear Captain, I had forgot you, but I might well do that, when I had forgot my Reaſon. Pray then, ſaid I, come and releaſe me; which he did, tho' he was long about it, for it was ſo dark we cou'd perceive no Object. I ask'd him the Meaning of what I heard. He told me, Love to the Wife of *Maurice* was his Motive of accompanying us, as well as that of his Companion's, tho' they knew not each other's Mind 'till they convers'd together at the *Unlucky Iſland*, tho' their Danger had taken off the Edge of their Appetites. But when the Fear of of Death and Starving was vaniſh'd, their Luſt return'd. So they made an Agreement to murder *Maurice*, and debated my Death, but he told me he had prevail'd to ſpare me, tho' with ſome Difficulty, therefore bound me in that manner while I ſlept, that I might not interrupt 'em in their horrid Deſign. I talkt to him concerning the horrid Deed; but he beg'd me to ſay no more, for the tormenting Thoughts of his own Conſcience, was ten thouſand Daggers in his wicked Boſom. I wou'd give the World, ſaid he, if I could call back four Hours of the paſt time; but if a ſincere Repentance can waſh away my Crime, it ſhall be the whole Buſineſs of all my future Days.

THE Thoughts of ſuch an horrid Action had overwhelm'd me with Melancholy. When the Day appear'd, I ſaw the Body of poor *Maurice* lying in the Stern of the Boat, ſtabb'd in ſeveral

ral Places; the Sight renew'd both our Griefs. We ſtript him of his Cloaths, and waſh'd him with our Tears while we were doing it, then threw him into the Sea.

WHEN the Sea Breeze aroſe, we made in for the Shore with heavy Hearts; for my own Part, I often wiſh'd I had ſhar'd the Fate of *Maurice*, for a Life like mine, that had run thro' ſo many various Fortunes, was hardly worth preſerving. When I conſidered what a Creature Man was, I thought it ſafer to herd with Brutes, who never prey, but for meer Neceſſity. How much I regretted leaving *Sevarambia*, where I am aſſur'd I cou'd have had the King's Conſent to have ended my Days there! Theſe melancholy Reflections brought us near the Shore, but we found it ſo full of Rocks, we durſt not venture in, therefore coaſted along; we cou'd not ſee any Inhabitants all the Way we ſail'd, In the Afternoon we ſaw out at Sea a Ship under

under Sail about two Leagues a-ſtern of us. The Sight gave us much Comfort, and we both agreed to ſtretch out that we might be in her way. *Withers* beg'd I wou'd not betray him, which I promis'd I wou'd not, if he continu'd in his Repentance. I have given you my voluntary Word already, ſaid he, and when I forget to think of the vile Deed with the utmoſt Horror, let me be given into the Hands of Juſtice. As the Ship approach'd us, we perceiv'd ſhe was *French* built. We made a Signal of Diſtreſs, and ſhe back'd her Sails 'till we came on board.

THE Captain us'd us with a great deal of Humanity, asking us how we came in that Condition. We told him the Truth as to *De Nuit*, but only mention'd *Withers* and my ſelf being put into the Boat. The Ship was call'd the *Maligna*, bound for St. *Maloes*, the Captain's Name St. *Andre*, laſt from *Siam*. When I deſcrib'd the Ship that turn'd turn'd us a-drift, he aſſur'd me ſhe was turn'd Pirate; for three Days before he had an Engagement with her, but by good Fortune, ſhooting her Fore-top-maſt by the Board, they got from her. In the Rencounter, the *Frenchman*'s Lieutenant was kill'd, and when I had related the Adventures of my paſt Life, he offer'd me his Poſt. I gave him Thanks, but beg'd he wou'd not take it ill, if I refus'd it, with no other Motive than that I fear'd I ſhou'd diſpleaſe ſome other Officer, who thought it might be his Due. He ſeem'd very well pleas'd with my Prudence, but wou'd force me to accept of his Cabbin. I met with ſuch civil Uſage from this Gentleman, that I ſhall always acknowledge it with a grateful Remembrance.

In our Voyage to the *Cape*, *Withers* fell ſick, and his Sickneſs ſo increas'd, that there was no Hope of his Life. I thought it my Duty to go to ſee him

as

as often as I could; he told me he was aſſur'd he cou'd not live, neither did he deſire Life; he hop'd he had made his Peace with God, and ſhou'd leave this troubleſome World with Joy. He left me his Heir, having no Family, and in three Days afterwards he dy'd. When I came to examine his Trunk (for he and *Sturmy* had brought all they had out of the Ship with 'em) I found upwards of two thouſand Pound in Gold Ingots.

WE arriv'd at the *Cape of Good Hope* without meeting any thing extraordinary in our way, where we ſtaid two Months to refreſh our ſelves, and clean our Ship. I need not deſcribe a Place that has been done ſo often. We left the *Cape* with a Fleet of Twenty Sail, of different Nations; and tho' there were ſome *Engliſh*, I had no Inclination to make any Acquaintance with 'em. When we came to St. *Maloes*, I offer'd to pay

pay the Captain for my Paſſage, but he wou'd not take any thing, nay offer'd to pay me for the Boat we brought on board him. 'Twas with ſome Difficulty I made him accept of a Diamond Ring, I found among *Withers*'s things; but he made me ſufficient Amends during my Stay at St. *Maloes*, forcing me to live in his Houſe, where I was magnificently entertain'd. From St. *Maloes*, we went to *Paris* together, where I ſold my Jewels and other things I had to diſpoſe of, which amounted together to thirteen thouſand Pound. This Money I employ'd in their *Miſſiſſippi*, and once reckon'd my ſelf worth ſixty thouſand Pound; but in the long run I made ſhift to get out of my thirteen thouſand Pound, two thouſand five hundred; ſo I came off a Loſer no more than ten thouſand five hundred, which I embark'd with for *England*. When I came home, my Daughters wou'd hardly be perſuaded I was their Father, for my Wife had been dead ſome

ſome time, but I ſoon convinc'd them, it was worth their while to remember me, becauſe it was in my Power to add to their Fortunes. Ever ſince I have remain'd at home, ſeriouſly reflecting on the paſt Actions of my Life, intending to ſink to my Grave in Peace and Tranquility. Expecting the Time without Fear, or Uneaſineſs; for as Death is a Tax laid upon us, I think the ſooner it is paid, the better; for what is there in this World worth living for? there's nothing new but Misfortunes, and even the happieſt Man is not exempt from 'em.

F I N I S.

some time, but Heaven convinc'd them, it was worth their while to remember me, because it was in my Power to add to their Fortunes. Ever since I have remain'd at home, seriously reflecting on the past Actions of my Life, intending to finish my Days in this Peace and Tranquility, expecting the Time when our Turn [illegible] Decease; for as Death is a Tax laid upon us, I think the sooner it is paid, the better; for what is there in this World worth living for? there's nothing new but Misfortunes, and even the happiest Man is not exempt from 'em.

F I N I S.

MEMOIRS

OF THE

Court of *Lilliput.*

Written by Captain *GULLIVER.*

Containing an ACCOUNT of the Intrigues, and ſome other particular Tranſactions of that Nation, omitted in the two Volumes of his Travels.

Publiſhed by LUCAS BENNET, *with a* Preface, *ſhewing how theſe Papers fell into his hands.*

LONDON:

Printed for J. ROBERTS, near the *Oxford-Arms* in *Warwick-Lane.* M.DCC.XXVII.

THE PUBLISHER TO THE READER.

THere are daily ſo many Impoſitions from the Preſs, that I am more than half afraid, the Reader will be apt to ſuſpect this is ſuch at his firſt taking it up: for which Reaſon I think it needful to inform him who I am, and by what means the following Pages came into my hands.

The Houſe I was born in, ſtood not above a Bow-ſhot from that wherein the Father of Mr. Lemuel Gulliver *liv'd; being much of the ſame Age with him, and going to the ſame*

School with him, we became extremely intimate: we sat on the same Form, had all our Exercises, and little Diversions together; the Trinkets which either of us were Masters of, were common to both, nor did we make any greater reserve of the Money we had at any time given us by our Parents, or any other Person. But our ill Fortune, at length, thought fit to interrupt a Friendship, which, had it continued in the same purity and sincerity it began, might have seem'd as great a Rarity, as any thing he afterward discover'd in his Travels.

But to return to my purpose: Mr. Lemuel *was sent to* Cambridge *at the age of fourteen, and I, who was some Months younger to* London, *and put Apprentice to a Stone-Cutter in* Westminster. *I will not trouble the Reader with any account of the hardships I endur'd in a seven years Servitude, which were so great, that I not only forgot the innocent Pleasures I had enjoy'd in the Society of that dear Companion, but also every thing else of the former Transactions of my Life; bending my whole Care and Study to please my Master*

Maſter and Miſtreſs, hoping thereby to alleviate ſome part of what I endured through their Ill-Nature, Pride and Covetouſneſs. I at laſt, by God's Grace, weather'd the point, and the ſevere Probation being paſt, ſet up for my ſelf in the next Street to my Maſter.

I then began to think of Mr. Lemuel, *but on making Enquiry for him, heard he was gone to the* Levant. *Soon after I alter'd my Condition, and in the Pleaſures of Matrimony, and the Care of my Affairs, again loſt all thoughts but ſuch as were conducive to thoſe two Ends: however, being told by ſome body, who had heard me ſpeak of my former Friendſhip for Mr.* Gulliver, *that he was return'd from his Travels and had taken a Houſe in the* Old Jewry, *I there renew'd my acquaintance with him; but his Circumſtances and Inclinations calling him a ſecond time abroad, and ſome vexatious Turns happening in my own Affairs, which oblig'd me to quit my Houſe, and go to my Wife's Relations in* Wales; *I heard nothing of my good Friend, till, after a long Revolution of Years, returning to* London, *I met with one who told me he liv'd liv'd at* Redriff: *I went to visit him immediately, he receiv'd me with great kindness, and my Wife being dead, and my Children dispos'd of abroad, would needs make me stay with him, and become a part of his Family; I consented, and left not his House as long as he continued at* Redriff.

During my stay, I saw Mr. Sympson *frequently with him, and was present when he gave him the Journal of his Voyages; but one Evening when we were sitting together, he told me he had other Papers which he believ'd might be of advantage to the Publisher. I took the hint, imagining with reason, that he would not have spoke in this manner, knowing my Circumstances, if he had not design'd to make me a present of them, which accordingly he did. Whether it was an effect of his Friendship for me, that he kept these as a Reserve, or whether he thought it improper to mingle with an account of the Manners and Customs of the several People he had been among, any Histories of their Amours, is uncertain: but this I know, that I have very well profited by the distinction he has*

has made, and hope the Bookfellers will do fo too : Neither do I think there is any great caufe to doubt it, fince the one is written with the fame Spirit and Veracity as the other, and may immediately convince the Reader that it is genuine. But if, after this, any fhould prefume to fay it is the contrary, I am ready to fhew the original Papers under Mr. Lemuel Gulliver'*s own Hand ; tho' if I pleas'd I might fpare myfelf that trouble, by fending thefe fufpicious Perfons to thofe worthy Gentlemen to whom I communicated them before they were fent to the Prefs : but I believe this will not be the cafe, unlefs with fome very ignorant People, whom it would not be worth the pains it would take up to undeceive. The fagacious part of Mankind will undoubtedly be pleas'd ; and as for the other, tho' I know my Friend would rather give a general Satisfaction than not, yet neither He nor I fhall be greatly difcontented if we fail in that part of our defire.*

But I have already apologiz'd beyond what I had Inftructions to do, and fhall therefore conclude with wifhing none

none may be ſo much Enemies to themſelves, as to be ſo to this improving and entertaining Hiſtory; of which I publiſh at preſent but that part which relates to Lilliput, *and ſhall proceed gradually with the Memoirs of the ſeveral Kingdoms he reſided at in their due order.*

LUCAS BENNET.

MEMOIRS OF THE Court of *Lilliput*.

CHAP. I.

The Author describes the Beauty of the Lilliputians *in general, and more especially of the Female Sex. Their great Propensity to Intrigue, and the Methods taken by their Lovers to seduce them from Virtue. An Account by what means he became acquainted with a Maid of Honour; the Service he did her, and the grateful Recompence she made him.*

I Believe the whole World affords not a Race of People more amiable in their Persons than the *Lilliputians*; few of the Men but have Complections more white and delicate than the fairest of our *European* Ladies; and Eyes so bright and sparkling, that if such were to be found in *England*, it would save our Poets, in their amorous Epistles, the pains of travelling to the Regions of the Sun, or digging the Bowels of the Earth for Diamond Quarries, to describe the Glances of their Mistresses: these having, in very deed, all that Radiance, which, because it is not to be seen in this part of the World, can be at the best but languidly express'd. Their Features are exact, their Limbs well turn'd; and one may perceive, in spite of the disadvantage of their low Stature, they may be said to have a noble Air and Mien in Miniature. The Females are very perfect in their Shape, tho' they go without Stays, and endure nothing from those cramping, torturing Machines of Bone, in which I have seen the *British* Mothers confine their female Brood. The Men also do every thing with a becoming

ming Eaſe; and although they have Dancing-maſters among them, who inſtruct them in the firſt Rudiments of Behaviour, when they addreſs to any one, know how to do it without ſticking too cloſe to the exact Rules of that courtly Exerciſe; they can approach you without a *Boree*, ſtep and retire without letting you know they have learn'd the *Rigadoon*; nor have they any occaſion for an Air out of an *Opera*, or a Speech ſelected from a Play, to make the favourite Fair ſenſible of the Paſſion they have for her. Nature, the beſt Inſtructreſs, is their Guide, and the Heart dictates to the Tongue. This is the Character which they in general deſerve; not but they have *Beaus* among them, who are the very reverſe of all I have ſaid, but they ſeem to be of a different Species from the reſt, are look'd on as ſuch, and herd only with one another.

NEITHER do the Women expect that multiplicity of Words which are the Pride of an *European* Lady; and as the most part of the other Sex are free from all Deceit in the manner of making known their Love, so these confess theirs without disguise, nay, sometimes condescend to make the first offer.

BUT there is no Rule without an Exception. Tho' the love of Truth, and an openness of Heart, seem the general Characteristick of the Nation, yet are there some who act on other Motives: There are Men who court but to betray, and Women who yield but through the Instigations of Interest. The Levity of the *French*, the smooth Deceit of the *Italian*, the sordid Avarice of the *Dutch*, the *Spanish* Pride, *Swedish* Ingratitude, and a mixture of all these Virtues, like the Disposition of my own dear Countrymen, may, in some particular Persons, be found in *Lilliput*, more especially

a-

Dutch

among thoſe of the new-created Nobility.

My extraordinary Size, and the Terror they conceived of me, preventing me from entring into their Aſſemblies, I could have been let into very few of their Secrets, if an Accident had not happen'd to introduce me into the acquaintance and intimacy of *Clefgarin*, one of the Empreſs's Maids of Honour. I was lying before the Door of my Houſe one of thoſe fine Nights of which there are a great number in this Country, indulging Meditation with a thouſand various Ideas, revolving paſt Tranſactions, and ruminating on the preſent, and what might be the future: In this Employment, I ſay, which is the Torment of the Gay and Proſperous, and the Wretch's only Comfort, were my thoughts wholly intent and buſied, when on a ſudden I heard a little Shriek, much like one of the ſmalleſt Notes of an *Engliſh Titmouſe*; and preſently after the ſame Voice

Voice ſeveral times repeated the word *Talgo*, which ſignifies ſomething more ſtrenuous than the moſt moving Expreſſion of Diſtreſs in any of the *European* Languages, at leaſt of thoſe I am acquainted with. I preſently knew it proceeded from a *Lilliputian* Woman, and was riſing haſtily to attempt her Relief; when ſpreading one Hand on the Ground, to the end that I might raiſe myſelf with more eaſe, I catch'd two of theſe diminutive Mortals between my Fingers; at which the Cries redoubled, and it being very dark, I was at a loſs how to behave, being fearful of adding to my Crime, by detaining them if innocent Perſons, and unwilling to loſe the reward of my good Service, if Criminals. I was in this perplexity for about half a minute, when one of them commanded me to let him looſe, on pain of having ten thouſand poiſon'd Arrows diſcharged againſt my Face next day. I was too well acquainted with the Accents of him that ſpoke, not to do as he order'd.

This

This was *Skyris Bolgolam*, a great Favourite with the Emperor, and whose Displeasure I fear'd more than any Nobleman's about Court. The Lady cry'd out to me to hold him fast, saying, he had attempted to ravish her as she was walking alone unsuspicious of any such Intent; protesting she would make the Empress acquainted with the Affront offer'd to her, and vowing the severest Revenge. I had the most tender Compassion for her, and could not resolve to abandon her to the Ruin she seem'd so much to dread; but on the other hand, dreading what might happen to myself through the Resentments of *Bolgolam*, I bethought me of a middle Course; it was, to give him his liberty, on condition he would give me his solemn Oath, never to fright that Lady again in the same manner; and to her I proposed a Vow alike binding, never to reveal to the Empress, or to any Person who should inform her, the attempt he had made on her Chastity; on which Condition

dition alone I told her I would continue my protection. Both ſeem'd very well pleas'd with this motion: *Bolgolam* performed firſt his Part of the Agreement, and was immediately ſeconded by the Lady. After which I made ſome excuſes for having detained him ſo long in that uneaſy poſition; repreſenting to him, that it was the buſineſs of every Man of Honour, to defend with the utmoſt of his power, a Sex who by their weakneſs are ſo much expoſed to Inſults; and that in my Country there was a Band of Knights choſen from among the nobleſt Families, on purpoſe for the protection of diſtreſſed Damſels. This I ſpoke prophetically; for tho' I knew that there was ſuch an Order inſtituted in the Reign of King *Arthur*, it had long ſince been loſt among us, and at that time not the leaſt hope or diſcourſe that it would ever be revived, as it has ſince been to the immortal honour of the Nation. *Bolgolam* ſeem'd to reliſh what I ſaid, and without any appearance of Re-

Refentment or Ill-humour, took his leave; though I have fince found, this Action of mine made him refolve to do me all the private ill Offices he cou'd.

THE Lady ftaid longer with me, attending for one who fhe freely confefs'd fhe had made an Appointment with in that Place: and tho' this was the firft time I had ever the honour of her Company, I eafily perceiv'd fhe was not among the number of thofe juftly called filent Women. She fat on one of the Buttons of my Coat-fleeve, and related to me her Name, her Quality, the Conquefts fhe had made over the Hearts of feveral young Noblemen of the Court; one of whom was him fhe expected to meet, but was now in fear that having heard the Rencounter between her and *Bolgolam*, he had retir'd, to avoid the difpleafure of that Favourite, by publickly avowing himfelf his Rival. And I could not forbear taking notice, that fhe appear'd more angry that he had at-

C tempted

tempted her at ſo unſeaſonable a time, than at the Attempt itſelf. Having given me a brief account of her own Life, which having nothing in it worth reciting, I ſhall omit, ſhe was beginning to enter into that of the Empreſs, who, it ſeems, had been formerly ſuſpected to have had an Amour with a young Knight, a Native of *Bleſuſcu*. She was juſt beginning to tell me the Severities that Princeſs had endured from the Jealouſy of the Emperor, and the cruel Death of her ſuppoſed Adorer, when her own arriv'd, and put an end to her Diſcourſe for that time. I was never of a humour to be pleas'd with Scandal, becauſe it ſeems to me to be the utmoſt depravity of Nature, to delight in rehearſing and hearing the Frailties of our Fellow-creatures; but this Lady expreſs'd herſelf with ſo agreeable a Volubility, and appear'd ſo little affected with the things ſhe ſpoke, that I could not look upon her as one who made her Reports thro' Malice, but merely for the pleaſure ſhe took in talking:

ing : and this Diſpoſition put me ſo much in mind of my beloved Country, that I could not help thinking, while ſhe was thus entertaining me, that I was at an *Engliſh* Viſit.

THE two little Dears tript away to finiſh their Love in ſome Myrtle-Grove, of which there are great plenty in this Kingdom, much about the bigneſs of thoſe Glaſſes with which we cover our Cucumbers and Melons in *England*, to ſhelter them from the inclemency of the *North* Air ; and I retir'd into my Houſe, to contemplate on this Adventure. I conſider'd, that wherever Luxury and Idleneſs preſides, there will be room for Pride, for Vanity, and Luſt ; and that led me to a reflection how much an elevated Station is an Enemy to Virtue ; and how greatly we deceive ourſelves in believing that Riches are the Source of Happineſs. To have it in our power to help the Afflicted, ſet the Priſoner free, oblige our ſuffering Friends,

C 2 and

and open the Eyes of Juſtice, to ſee the Merits of the needy Client's Cauſe, is indeed a Bleſſing we may laudably be ambitious to be poſſeſs'd of: but where are the exalted Minds who make this uſe of it? Do not thoſe ſeemingly happy Men, inſtead of ſtretching out their hands to the Diſtreſſed, lift them inceſſantly to their own Mouths in an eternal Round of Gluttony and Drunkenneſs? Do they not ſee the naked Wretch paſs unregarded by their door, while all the Splendor of the *Eaſt* is ranſack'd to adorn their own Perſons? Do not their neareſt Friends and Kindred lie periſhing in a Priſon, while gilt Coaches, and ſtately Pinnaces, are providing to procure themſelves variety of Air? Is not the Wit of Man ſtrain'd to the utmoſt pitch to find new Pleaſures for theſe expenſive Great-ones? And what does it all amount to in the end? Having poſſeſs'd and rioted in every vain Delight, Nature unſatisfied is craving ſtill; and finding nothing more, no new Amuſement, grows

grows ſick of what it has enjoy'd, and ſinks into a ſullen Diſcontent, and pining Languor; whence it is never to be rais'd, unleſs by the ſevere Remora's of a guilty Conſcience, either for acted Vices, or omitted Virtues.

WITH ſuch like Meditations, mix'd with ſome intervals of Sleep, I paſs'd my Hours till Morning; at which time one of thoſe Attendants, who, by the Emperor's Order, ſupply'd me with Neceſſaries, gave me notice, that three Ladies in a Coach were come to viſit me. I had had but an indifferent Night, and being a little indiſpos'd, took the freedom of entreating they wou'd command their Charioteer to drive into the Houſe, which they might eaſily do, if the Machine that brought them had been four times as high as it was; they very obligingly acceded to my deſire, and as ſoon as they enter'd, I ſaw the Wife and Daughter of the Principal Secretary of State, accompanied by *Cleſgarin*, my new and open the Eyes of Juſtice, to ſee the Merits of the needy Client's Cauſe, is indeed a Bleſſing we may laudably be ambitious to be poſſeſs'd of: but where are the exalted Minds who make this uſe of it? Do not thoſe ſeemingly happy Men, inſtead of ſtretching out their hands to the Diſtreſſed, lift them inceſſantly to their own Mouths in an eternal Round of Gluttony and Drunkenneſs? Do they not ſee the naked Wretch paſs unregarded by their door, while all the Splendor of the *Eaſt* is ranſack'd to adorn their own Perſons? Do not their neareſt Friends and Kindred lie periſhing in a Priſon, while gilt Coaches, and ſtately Pinnaces, are providing to procure themſelves variety of Air? Is not the Wit of Man ſtrain'd to the utmoſt pitch to find new Pleaſures for theſe expenſive Great-ones? And what does it all amount to in the end? Having poſſeſs'd and rioted in every vain Delight, Nature unſatisfied is craving ſtill; and finding nothing more, no new Amuſement, grows

grows ſick of what it has enjoy'd, and ſinks into a ſullen Diſcontent, and pining Languor; whence it is never to be rais'd, unleſs by the ſevere Remora's of a guilty Conſcience, either for acted Vices, or omitted Virtues.

WITH ſuch like Meditations, mix'd with ſome intervals of Sleep, I paſs'd my Hours till Morning; at which time one of thoſe Attendants, who, by the Emperor's Order, ſupply'd me with Neceſſaries, gave me notice, that three Ladies in a Coach were come to viſit me. I had had but an indifferent Night, and being a little indiſpos'd, took the freedom of entreating they wou'd command their Charioteer to drive into the Houſe, which they might eaſily do, if the Machine that brought them had been four times as high as it was, they very obligingly acceded to my deſire, and as ſoon as they enter'd, I ſaw the Wife and Daughter of the Principal Secretary of State, accompanied by *Clefgarin*, my new

new Acquaintance. As this Visit was wholly for the sake of Form, I had no Conversation with the two former worth repeating. Nor cou'd my talkative Virgin of Honour have an Opportunity in their presence of renewing the Discourse she had began the Night before; but pulling out of her Pocket a little Piece of Gold about the same bigness as one of those sort of Patches which the Ladies of our Country call a Speck, told me in a sort of a Whisper, while the other two were engaged in admiring the prodigious largeness of a Pin-cushion I had happen'd to let fall in the further side of the Room, That she thought she cou'd do no less than make me that Present for the Protection I had given her. I laid it on the Palm of my Hand, being obliged to keep it with the utmost Circumspection before my Eye, lest I should not find it again, while with my other Hand I search'd for a piece of Paper to wrap it in. I perceiv'd that there was something on one side of it

which

which differ'd it from the other that was plain Gold, but could form no Idea of what it was, till ſhe inform'd me that it was her Picture at full length, drawn by the greateſt Artiſt in the Country in Miniature-Painting. With great Care and Diligence I preſerv'd this Curioſity, and at my return to *England*, made a Preſent of it to the Univerſity of *Oxford*, to be placed in their Repoſitory of Rarities, by that wonderful Cherry-ſtone on which is engraved three hundred Faces. I parted not with it, however, till I had view'd it in a Magnifying-Glaſs, and ſeen indeed that it contain'd the moſt beautiful Figure I ever beheld in my whole Life; the Shape, Features, nay, the very Embroidery on the Garment, as exact and diſtinct as thoſe in the largeſt Pictures we have drawn. If any one ſhou'd make a doubt of the veracity of this, it is eaſy for him to convince himſelf, either by going in Perſon where it is kept, or by writing to any of thoſe learned Students, whoſe Piety and

Wiſ-

Wiſdom will not ſuffer them to deceive others, nor be themſelves deceiv'd.

After this, I had the company of *Clefgarin* almoſt every day, who ſtill entertain'd me with one diverting Story or other, as often as ſhe found me alone; but I hope the Reader, after what I have declared concerning my love of Virtue, will ſuffer no cenſorious thoughts to enter into his head to the prejudice either of mine, or this Lady's Reputation, who if ſhe had not been too greatly influenced by her Paſſion for that young Lover already mentioned, might have been a very eminent Example of Chaſtity, for any thing that I know to the contrary. And beſides, the inequality of our Stature rightly conſider'd, ought to be for us as full a Security from Slander, as that between Mr. *P——pe*, and thoſe *great* Ladies who do nothing without him; admit him to their Cloſets, their Bed-ſides, conſult him in the choice of their Servants, their Garments, and

make

make no ſcruple of putting them on or off before him: Every body knows they are Women of ſtrict Virtue, and he a harmleſs Creature, who has neither the Will, nor Power of doing any farther Miſchief than with his Pen, and that he ſeldom draws, but in defence of their Beauty; or to ſecond their Revenge againſt ſome preſuming Prude, who boaſts a Superiority of Charms: or in privately tranſcribing and paſſing for his own, the elaborate Studies of ſome more learned Genius.

THIS, to maintain the Impartiality of an Hiſtorian, I am obliged to ſay of the *Lilliputians*, that they are extreme in all their Paſſions; and nothing, methinks, can be more wonderful, than that in ſo ſmall a Body there ſhould dwell ſo large a ſhare of Soul: They ſeem indeed all Spirit, and ſeldom will undertake any thing without a Reſolution which enables them to hazard the greateſt Difficulties for the attainment of their Deſires. Hence it

D fol-

follows, that the Women, forgetful of their Sex, and affecting wholly to despise what we call *Decorum*, no sooner feel the Fires of Love kindle in their Hearts, than they seek ease by revealing it to the inspiring Youth: and the Men, when prompted by Desire, wait not a slow Consent by tedious Courtship, but boldly endeavour to force the Joy they wish. But this Disposition will more plainly appear, by relating some Adventures of which I was informed by *Clefgarin*, in the course of her Visits to me.

CHAP.

CHAP. II.

Clefgarin *makes the Author acquainted with a very odd Amour between two Perfons of Condition. Some Remarks he makes on it. The whole Court comes to vifit him. He endeavours to divert them, by fhowing the ufe of a little Machine he had in his Pocket, but it happens otherwife, to the great fhame of the* Lilliputian *Ladies. Various Conftructions made on this Accident. He fears to lofe the Favour of the Court, and be expofed to the Malice of his Enemies.*

ALTHO' I underftood the *Lilliputian* Language well enough to difcourfe with the Natives, yet I cannot pretend to tranflate it fo as to make it agreeable to an *Englifh*

D 2 Ear.

Ear. Neither do I approve that Cuſtom among Authors, of making long Speeches for the Perſons of their Hiſtory, and then endeavouring to paſs them on the Reader for genuine. I ſhall not therefore attempt to ſay, that *Clefgarin* gave me the Intelligences I am about to communicate poſitively in ſuch or ſuch words, which it is impoſſible I ſhou'd remember after ſo long a ſpace of Time; and I ſhould juſtly forfeit my Character of Veracity to pretend to it: it is enough I relate the ſum of what ſhe told me, and leave to the wiſe Men of the Age, the Art of Cavilling about the *Manner*, till the *Matter* is forgot.

In one of the Viſits that this Lady made me, ſhe told me that a certain Gentleman of a great Eſtate in *Lilliput*, I think ſhe ſaid his Name was *Shefinbaſto*, was married to a Lady of equal Fortune called *Deffarheſal*. She was one of the moſt beautiful Women in *Mildendo*, the Metropolis of this Empire:

pire: They liv'd together for ſome time in the greateſt appearance of mutual Affection that could be; and might ſtill have done ſo, had the Virtue of *Deſſarbeſal* been at all of a piece with the Perfections of her Perſon.

Koppockitaſh, a young Native of *Blefuſcu*, being come to reſide at *Lilliput*, as a Place of greater Diverſion, and conſequently more agreeable to the Gaiety of his Genius, happen'd to ſee the charming *Deſſarbeſal* at the Temple of *Wannacuk*, a Deity in great eſtimation among the People of theſe Kingdoms. He became as much in love with her as a Man of his Temper could be, for he was among the number of thoſe I have deſcribed in the foregoing Chapter, a fluttering, noiſy, empty, vain, inſenſible Animal; from which 'tis eaſy to infer, that the reputation of having acquir'd the Favour of ſo fine a Woman as *Deſſarbeſal*, was of infinite more conſequence to him, than being in reality

happy

happy in her good Graces. To compaſs this, he induſtriouſly found out what Places ſhe moſt frequented, and never fail'd of being there; contriv'd to ſit near her at all publick Aſſemblies; play'd with her Fan, which was made of the third part of a Butterfly's Wing; talk'd to her in a low Voice, as if he fear'd to be over-heard by the Company, though what he ſaid was not of the leaſt ſignification, and tended neither to good or ill. This Behaviour would have certainly gain'd his Deſigns, had they been on a Lady leſs celebrated for her Virtue; but ſhe was look'd on by all the *Lilliputians* as ſo great a Pattern of Modeſty and conjugal Affection, that all he did was of no other effect than to render him more ridiculous than ever.

ENRAG'D at his ill ſucceſs, he reſolv'd to puſh his Fortune at once, and having order'd her to be watch'd to a Place where ſhe went one day, he waited for her till ſhe came out, at the end of of the Street, in his Coach; and as ſoon as ſhe appear'd in hers, made himſelf be drove ſo cloſe to it, that the Wheels touch'd each other: her Coachman, apprehenſive of ſome ill Accident by the Juſtle, ſtood ſtill, believing the other wou'd draw off in reſpect to his Lady. This was what *Koppockitaſh* wanted, and immediately ſtarting up, threw himſelf with an admirable agility out of his own Coach into hers, in the ſight of both their Servants, and ſeveral other People who were paſſing by. The Surprize that *Deſſarheſal* was in, made her ſhriek out as loud as ſhe cou'd, on which, having immediate ſuccour, he was compell'd to quit her, without any other benefit by this Adventure, than having it in his power to boaſt he had had Courage to attack in ſo bold a manner, a Woman of *Deſſarheſal's* Condition and reputed Virtue.

EVERY body muſt think an Attempt of this kind muſt make a great noiſe in the

the World; nothing, it ſeems, was more the publick Chat; and thoſe who pretended to be the niceſt Judges in the Punctilio's of Honour, were in great expectations of hearing that *Sheſinbaſto* had endeavour'd to revenge the Affront put upon his Lady, by calling to a bloody account the preſuming *Koppockitaſh*: but many Days paſſing over, and no ſuch thing occurring, they begun at length to ſay no more of what had happen'd.

But *Deſſarheſal* forgot it not, ſhe had related to her Husband all that had befallen her; nor fail'd to heighten the Boldneſs of *Koppockitaſh* by all the Aggravations ſhe was able; but finding him unmov'd, and that inſtead of awaking him to Indignation, he only endeavour'd to calm that which he obſerv'd in her, telling her he was ſatisfied of her Love and Virtue, and that it was not in the power of *Koppockitaſh*, or any Man in the World to make him jealous; ſhe took it ſo ill, that from that moment the Af-

female writer?

fection ſhe had for him was perverted into Contempt and Loathing; ſhe thought it an Indignity to her Beauty that he appeared ſo tame, and began in her heart to doubt his want of Courage. The daring Spirit of *Koppockitaſh* now ſeem'd lovely in her eyes; the little Follies of his former Behaviour paſs'd with her for ſo many Indications of the Gallantry of his Humour, and the Imprudence of his late Attempt, for the Violence of his Paſſion: that is, ſhe was inclined to like him, and therefore could eaſily find Excuſes for every thing he had done.

HE, on the other hand, perceiving there was nothing to be fear'd from her Husband, was eaſily perſuaded by his Vanity, that he ſhould ſome time or other triumph over the Wife, to which end he wrote to her, 'tis to be ſuppoſed, in the ſofteſt and moſt elegant manner; but be that as it may, her Heart already prepared for his purpoſe, yielded itſelf an eaſy Prey, but having ſtill ſome Remains

E of

of regard to her former Reputation, ſhe would not conſent to meet him, but in ſuch a way as ſhould make the diſcovery of it next to an impoſſibility.

SEVERAL private Aſſignations were made and kept between them, and *Deſſarheſal* grew ſo infinitely fond of him, that it was with pain ſhe ever ſuffer'd herſelf to be ſeparated from him: they notwithſtanding had their meetings very private; and tho' *Koppockitaſh* did not fail to give intelligible hints of his Happineſs, wherever he came in company, yet was very little credit given to what he ſaid, ſo high an eſteem had the former Behaviour of *Deſſarheſal* ingrafted in the Minds of all who knew her.

AT length, her Paſſion riſing to the moſt extravagant height, and his deſire of publiſhing her Frailty, not inferior; both, to gratify a different View, join'd in the moſt abhorr'd Deſign that ever was heard of in the World. Good Hea-

ven

ven preserve our *British* Dames from such irregular Tendernesses, our Beaus from such dangerous Vanities, and our Island, so famed for Modesty, Piety, and Gentleness of Nature, from producing any Examples of the contrary, like this of the *Lilliputians!*

IT was agreed between them, that *Shesinbasto* should fall the sacrifice of their mutual Contentment; and in this manner did they contrive this execrable Design: It was the part of *Koppockitash* to procure Assassins, who shou'd enter with him at midnight the House of that unhappy Husband, and murder him while sleeping in his Bed; and of *Desfarhesal* to prepare every thing in order to escape with him, after the Deed was done, to *Blefuscu*; where it was their intention, (hers at least) to pass the remainder of their Lives.

NEITHER were negligent in their several Employments; *Koppockitash* easily

E 2 found

found the means to provide himſelf with Aſſiſtants for this horrid Enterprize, and *Deſſarbeſal* was buſy in packing up her Jewels, Plate, and Money. There was a neceſſity for her Woman being in the Secret, becauſe ſhe could not make theſe Preparations without her knowledge; and one Male-ſervant, whoſe buſineſs it was to lock up the Gate when all the others were in Bed, the Key of which he always kept to prevent any nocturnal Rambles, to the ſcandal of this well-order'd Family. Theſe two did ſhe by great Bribes and Promiſes oblige to be of her Party, and the latter of them was to open the Gate to *Koppockitaſh* and his Followers, on his making a certain Sign agreed on between themſelves.

THUS far every thing favour'd the Wiſhes of this guilty Pair, and the Day arriv'd which was deſign'd ſhould be the laſt the injured *Shefinbaſto* ſhould ever ſee, without the leaſt appearance of any

croſs

croſs Accident to impede, or diſappoint their Undertaking. But *Yargomaſh* (for ſo was that Servant called) reflecting ſeriouſly on the Affair he was ingaged in, found it ſo full of Horror, that ſtruck with a ſudden remorſe, he reſolv'd not only to have no hand in it himſelf, but alſo to prevent the execution of it by any other; and without any heſitation ran to his Maſter, who happen'd to be at that time alone in his Cloſet, fell on his Knees before him, and lifting up his Hands and Eyes, cry'd out for Pardon. Theſe words, and the poſture he was in, made *Shefinbaſto* at firſt think he was run mad; but finding he perſiſted in it, and perceiving no other marks of Frenzy in him, demanded what he meant: to which the other reply'd, that he durſt not ſatisfy him till he had promis'd him forgiveneſs. This his Maſter was unwilling to do, as not knowing the nature of his Crime; but the Fellow ſwearing by all the Gods the *Lilliputians* worſhip, that if he did not, the Secret
ſhould

ſhould die with him, he was at laſt prevail'd on to grant what he ſo earneſtly required ; on which *Targomaſh* reveal'd at full the black Deſign, and how far he had been tempted to be a Partner in it.

Clefgarin told me, that *Shefinbaſto* was the moſt cool and temperate Man alive, and that he heard ſo ſurprizing an Account with a calmneſs very much to be wonder'd at, conſidering the nature of the thing. He paus'd awhile on what had been told him ; then bade the Fellow, as he would wiſh to merit the Pardon he had gain'd, by no ſuſpicious Word or Action, to let *Deſſarheſal* imagine ſhe had been betray'd. Which the other having ſworn to do, he went out, and hir'd ſix or ſeven of the moſt reſolute Men he could pick out, to be ready at a moment's warning, well arm'd. Theſe having order'd to wait at a convenient diſtance from the Gate, he ordered *Targomaſh*, at his return, to let into the Houſe privately, and place them in ſome

Room

Room where they ſhould not be ſeen by any of the Family. The repenting Servant executed his Commiſſion with ſo much dexterity, that they all enter'd, and were placed in ambuſh, without being ſeen by any one but himſelf. This was no ſooner done, than *Shefinbaſto* went to the Chamber of his falſe Wife, and finding her with her Woman, ('tis probable diſcourſing of their intended Deſign) he upbraided her in Terms as ſevere as he could find words to form, tho' by far more gentle than her Crime deſerv'd. The moſt daring Guilt, when once detected, grows humble, fawning, and ſubmiſſive; ſhe threw herſelf at his Feet, wept, begg'd, ſwoon'd, uſed all the Arts of Female Flattery, and feigned Contrition, but all in vain, he was not to be moved; but having ſearch'd her Cabinet, and taken thence all the Papers he could find, lock'd her in the Room with the vile Aſſiſtant of her Deſigns.

I

I believe the Reader will eaſily conjecture, the Cogitations with which he entertain'd himſelf till Midnight, were not very pleaſing; but what they were, as well as many other things in which my Information is deficient, I ſhall leave to Imagination to ſupply; it being entirely oppoſite to my Principle, to ſet down any thing which has not been well atteſted for Truth. But not to run into impertinent Digreſſions, the Hour being come, and the appointed Signal given, *Yargomaſh* open'd the Gate, at which *Koppockitaſh*, with two or three of his Companions, ruſh'd in. The reſt had follow'd, had not *Yargomaſh* given the Alarm too ſoon, and *Shefinbaſto*'s Men appear'd, and fallen on thoſe who were already enter'd.

Koppockitaſh drew his Hanger, and would have made ſome Flouriſhes, but Affectation now gave way to Fear, and he made a ſhift to eſcape, leaving thoſe he he had engaged in his Caufe to get off as they could; who being eafily feiz'd, were carried before *Shefinbafto:* and after having been examined, were fent under a Guard of three or four of the Men, to one of the ftrongeft Rooms in his Houfe, where they were confined beyond all poffibility of efcaping.

I had no opportunity of hearing the Conclufion of this Story: As *Clefgariu* was in this part of it, we faw the Emperor, Emprefs, and a great number of Courtiers coming to vifit me. She ftept behind a Tree to avoid being found alone with me, till they were feated, then mingled with the Train, and was not obferv'd which way fhe came. Although I was very fenfible of the Honour I receiv'd in being permitted to entertain this auguft Affembly; yet I felt at their appearance a kind of Palpitation of my Heart, which I could not then account for, unlefs it proceeded from the Vexation I conceived at

F the

the Interruption their Presence gave me; but I had soon after cause to believe it was an Omen of the Misfortune which was then near approaching me.

BEFORE I left *England*, I was acquainted with a very ingenious young Man, who was a sort of a Projector. By his great Study, and Application, he had contriv'd a little Machine, call'd a Powder-Puff; the Body of it was Leather, plaited in small Folds, so as to gather Wind; the Top and Bottom fine Wood, with circular Holes at each end, fill'd up with Lawn strain'd hard, that by the least movement of the Hand the Powder would fly lightly out, without discommoding the Ladies Hair, or Gentlemens Perriwigs, as common Puffs are apt to do. But I need not enlarge on the Description, since I find the Invention succeeded so well, that at my return I saw them lying on the Windows of every Toy-Shop in *London*. But with what Ingratitude are frequently the

the Labours of the Wiſe rewarded! Inſtead of ſeeing my worthy Friend in a Coach and Six, as I expected to do, (for I could not have imagin'd ſo important and uſeful a Piece of Ingenuity could have eſcaped having annexed to it ſome very great Penſion) I met him in a tatter'd Coat, his Cheeks fallen, and all the Marks of Anguiſh on his Face. I deſir'd him to go and eat a bit of Meat with me, it being about Dinner Time; at which I perceiv'd he was very much revived, and waited not for a ſecond Invitation. On my asking him the reaſon why he was ſo much neglected, when his Project had prov'd ſo beneficial to the Publick; he anſwer'd, that there was but little Encouragement now-a-days for the moſt noble Undertakings, and that he muſt be content with the Fame of having been of ſome ſervice to his Country, without hoping any other Recompence, and that this was the Caſe of many other publick-ſpirited Men, as well as himſelf. This led me into a ſerious Reflection on the Unhappineſs of thoſe, who having but a Competency of their own, run it out in Projects and Experiments for the Good of a Kingdom: He who obliges three or four particular Perſons, may perhaps make one Friend among them; but he who obliges a Nation, finds his Reward only in himſelf.

I beg my Reader's Pardon for this Digreſſion, into which the remembrance of that worthy Patriot, the Puff-Maker, has unwarily led me. He had juſt compleated this admirable Invention before I went to travel, and would needs make me a Preſent of one, that I might make known by that Teſtimony to how great an Excellence in Machinery our Countrymen are arriv'd. I had preſerv'd this Rarity in a Pocket made on purpoſe for it, and with great difficulty concealed it from the *Lilliputians* when they ſearched me. But being now in the

the Emperor's Confidance, I thought I could not oblige him more, than by ſhowing him this incomparable Piece of Workmanſhip. I pluck'd it out, and related to him the Virtues of it, at which he was extremely ſurpriz'd. The Empreſs and all the Ladies were charmed, and readily confeſs'd, that to waſt Powder through the Hair, was infinitely more curious than any thing they could have imagin'd. Some of them deſired I would ſhow them in what manner it was done. And fifty *Lilliputian* Slaves being diſpatch'd for that purpoſe, return'd with as many Loads of perfum'd Powder, each bringing a ſilver Box full, about the bigneſs of a Grain of Oats. I empty'd all into the Machine; but five or ſix Ladies, among whom was *Queintavalite*, Siſter to *Flimnap* the Treaſurer of *Lilliput*, happening to ſtand a little too near, as I inconſiderably began to play it, were blown down by the too powerful Wind of it. The young Lords ran

in

in immediately, partly out of respect to offer their Assistance, and partly thro' Curiosity, their Fall discovering some Beauties they would gladly have conceal'd; though less distinctly than it would have done, if their Garments had been kept out, and hollow from their Limbs by those Ribs of Whale, which our *English* Ladies think add so great a Grace to their Air and Motion.

But whatever pleasure this Accident might afford the young Nobility, I perceived the graver part of them were much offended. The Empress thought herself affronted in the Persons of her Women, through either my Negligence, or Presumption, and complain'd of it to the Emperor, in terms which very much affected him. For my part, I stood like one confounded, and had not a Word to offer in my defence; which gave an opportunity to those who envy'd me, to represent the Action

Action as done with Design; but some others endeavour'd to excuse it as an Inadvertency. The Emperor said little either to the one or the other; but taking the Empress by the hand, led her to her Coach. The whole Court follow'd; some of them who I knew had no Good-will for me, as they departed casting a scornful Look on me; which gave me to understand, I had lost all the Interest I had with those who had hitherto protected me from their Malice, and threw me into the most terrible Disquiet I ever remember to have known in my whole Life before; with reason dreading a Power which I knew was absolute, and believing myself destitute of any Friend to plead my Cause. I accus'd myself for not endeavouring to vindicate my Innocence in the Affair, while the Royal Presence gave me an opportunity; but it was now too late to remedy that Inconvenience, and I was oblig'd to have

have recourſe to all the little Philoſo-phy I was maſter of, to enable me to ſuſtain ſo unexpected and ſo great a Misfortune.

CHAP.

CHAP. III.

The Author laments the loſs of Cleſgarin, *who is diſcovered in her Intrigue, and baniſhed the Court. He makes ſome Reflections on the nature of Love, and the Ingratitude of both Sexes to each other, when once that Paſſion is worn off. The Secretary of State's Wiſe makes him a Viſit, relates to him an Amour lately diſcovered between a Man of Quality, and the Siſter of an eminent Tradeſman; and gives him ſome hope of recovering the Good Will of the Emperor.*

IN theſe Diſquiets did I remain ſome days, in which time I had leiſure to make ſome Reflections on the Condition of a diſcarded

Favourite, eſpecially when he falls not into Diſgrace for the ſake of a particular Party: in ſuch a caſe, indeed the Faction, whoſe ſide he has taken, will, in ſome meaſure, contribute to mitigate his Misfortunes: and even the Sovereign himſelf, looking on him as a Perſon conſiderable enough to be feared, will not proceed to any Extremities againſt him, unleſs he puts an end to all Apprehenſions from him by lopping off his Head; and that too is commonly done, without giving him any warning to do any thing in his own Perſon, or his Friends, to embroil the State, and hinder the Execution. But from me there was not the leaſt Shadow of a Danger. My Houſe was ſurrounded with a great number of Guards arm'd with poiſon'd Arrows; who, if I had made any attempt to ſtir beyond my Precincts, would have immediately ſhot at me. I was therefore treated with a Contempt, which, after ſuch great Proofs of Reſpect as I had lately been

ac-

accuſtomed to, was extremely grating. I had now no Viſits from any body; and when I ſaw any of thoſe who I had thought moſt my Friends paſs by in their Coaches, or on Horſeback, they turn'd away their Heads, and look'd another way. Even thoſe appointed to attend me, and bring me in my daily Allowance of Proviſion, uſed me more in the manner of a Priſoner, than a Gueſt. Never Man was more forlorn, more miſerable than I at that time; the Impertinencies of *Clefgarin* wou'd have now been Muſick to my Ears, but ſhe, as well as the reſt, had abandon'd me; and I accus'd her in my mind of Inconſtancy, and Forgetfulneſs of the many Promiſes ſhe had formerly made me of Friendſhip. I thought the Intereſt ſhe had with the Empreſs, might have been of great ſervice, if ſhe had exerted it: and tho' I was never very poetical, I ſhould certainly have been tempted to make Verſes on the Inſtability of all human Dependance, if my

G 2 Pocket.

Pocket-Book had not been full of more material Notes and Obſervations, which I had from time to time made on the Manners and Cuſtoms of this Country, and which are at large ſet down in my Book of Travels, publiſhed by Mr. *Sympſon*. But I was ſoon after convinced I had done this Lady wrong; for happening to ſee the Empreſs paſs by to take the Air, with a great Retinue, I ſaw not *Clefgarin* among them; on which I asked one of my Guards if ſhe were indiſpos'd, that ſhe was left behind: and he inform'd me, that ſhe had been baniſhed the Court, having been found in the Palace-Garden with *Bleſtritch*, a young Nobleman, in a Poſture very unbecoming the Modeſty of her Character and Title; and that *Bleſtritch* having afterwards been queſtioned concerning his ſeducing a Maid under the immediate Care of the Empreſs, he alledg'd in his defence, that he had been far from any ſuch Intent, if ſhe had not made the firſt Advances,

and

and produced ſeveral Letters under her own hand to prove the Truth of what he ſaid.

THIS clear'd her from all blame as to her forſaking me, ſuch a Misfortune being ſufficient to engroſs all her Thoughts; but I conceived the higheſt Indignation againſt *Bleſtritch*, for his ungenerous Treatment of her. I found, as *Dorax* ſays in the Play, that

> *Ingratitude's the Growth of every*
> *Clime.*

And ſure when one conſiders of it, nothing can ſeem more ſtrange than that one finds between the Sexes; it looks, methinks, as if that Paſſion which excites them to the Enjoyment of each other, might more properly be called Hate, than Love, ſince the ſame Conſequences flow from it. Does one ever ſee a Man part from his Miſtreſs, or a Woman from her Gallant, without loading them with Reproaches, magnifying

fying every little Fault, and depriving them of all thofe Charms which at firft attack'd them? Are they not lefs obliging, if after fuch a feparation they chance to meet, than they would be to any other Perfon in the World? To forfake one Object for another, may be called only Inconftancy; but to expofe, and refufe thofe Proofs of Friendfhip one would give to an indifferent Perfon, muft certainly be the Effects of Averfion. On the whole, therefore, it muft be inferr'd, that Love being an extreme Paffion, cannot be fucceeded by one fo cool, when compar'd with that, as Friendfhip is; and Hate being altogether as violent, fupplies its place. All this is common to both Sexes; but as to the Men, who in the Affairs of Love run no hazard, it cannot be wonder'd at, that they fhould fo eagerly purfue the Pleafures of it: but the Women, who have fo much to fear, fo much to lofe, methinks fhould not fo eafily be brought into the Snare. I had at that time

time many Reflections of this kind; but I know they would be little agreeable to my own Sex, or instructing to the other, and shall therefore forbear communicating them; nothing being more impertinent, than to give Advice unask'd, especially to Persons to whom Nature affords but a scanty Portion of Consideration.

I had been eight days without seeing any body from the Palace; but at the end of that came *Debalklick*, the the Wife of *Keldresal*, Principal Secretary of State. She told me, that it was not forgetfulness of me which had occasioned her absence, and excused herself and Husband, on the account of some private Affairs of her own, that I doubted not her Veracity in it. She also assured me, that *Keldresal* had used his utmost Interest with the Emperor to restore me to favour, and that she hoped the matter was as good as done. We fell afterward into a a gay Converſation. Amongſt other things, ſhe told me, that *Fuergoliſthaſſo*, a young Lord, whom I had often ſeen in the Emperor's Train, had like to have been kill'd by *Barbebigell*, an eminent Citizen of *Mildendo*. The Adventure happened in this manner.

Barbebigell had a very beautiful Siſter called *Sewawnawick*; her Father at his Death had left her Miſtreſs of a very plentiful Fortune, ſhe vying in Jewels and rich Clothes with moſt of the Court-Ladies, and took a pride in ſhowing herſelf among them, and receiving the Compliments which were made her by the young Courtiers. She made many Conqueſts, but ſhe was inflexible to all Sollicitations but thoſe made her by *Fuergoliſthaſſo*. He eaſily ſaw the Deference ſhe paid him, and grew more preſſing for the Confirmation of that Paſſion, which ſhe had made no ſcruple of letting him ſee. He pleaded with ſucceſs, ſhe yielded the

the laſt Proof in the power of Woman to beſtow. Love was indulg'd to the utmoſt height, but the Conſequence was no way pleaſing to either of them. She was with Child, and grew diſcontented at the Pain and Danger which are inſeparable from that State, and the Infamy which it ſeldom fails to bring on a Woman who ſubmits to it, without having been introduced by the Ceremony of Marriage. Nor was he more at eaſe; he was by nature extremely covetous, and doubted not but ſhe wou'd think herſelf not obliged to contribute wholly to the ſupport of this Increaſe of her Family; he was troubled to find himſelf obliged to give ſome ſmall Preſents; and ſhe, that he allow'd no more.

nd theſe Diſquiets on both ſides, created a mutual Diſguſt. To add to that of *Sewawnawick*, ſome malicious Perſon having perceived the alteration of her Shape, communicated it to *Barbabigell*, from whom ſhe very carefully conceal'd it: on which he examined her, but ſhe

H de-

denying it with many Imprecations, he made uſe of the Authority of a Brother, and broke open her Cabinet; where he found Letters, which not only confirmed the Truth of what he had been told, but alſo inform'd him to whom it was ſhe ow'd her diſgrace. He was infinitely griev'd to find it was a Perſon, whoſe Quality took away all hope of redreſſing his Siſter's Misfortune, by compelling him to marry her, or of revenging her Ruin by his Death with any poſſibility of ſafety to himſelf: for the Laws of *Lilliput* are never to be diſpens'd with for the loſs of a Peer. this way, (even tho' he be in effect the moſt wretched or vicious Creature in the world;) but extremely mild, when the Delinquent is call'd to account for the Murder of a common Man. And for this reaſon, he forbore ſending a Challenge to *Fuergoliſthaſſo*; but not able to ſuffer the ſight of a Misfortune, for which there was no probability of a Remedy, he oblig'd *Scwawnawick*

wick to quit his Houſe, which he forbad her ever to enter, or call him by the Name of Brother.

THIS poor Creature in vain lamented his Unkindneſs, he was not to be mov'd, and ſhe was forced to depart. The firſt thing ſhe did after her Baniſhment, was to ſend for *Fuergoliſthaſſo*, to whom ſhe imparted what had befallen her; at which he fell into the utmoſt Rage againſt *Barbahigell*: For you muſt know, the Nobility think it rather an Honour, than a Diſgrace, when they deſcend to the Embraces of a Citizen. And reſolving to be reveng'd on him for ſeeming to contemn what he accounted an honour done to his Family, and Siſter, he went the next day to the Houſe of this inſenſible Man, and deſired to ſee him; but being deny'd admittance, bid the Servant who anſwered him to tell his Maſter, that he wanted to ſpeak with him for his good; that he had no concern in what manner he behav'd with a Sister, but would advise him how he treated a Woman, whom a Man of his Quality was inclined to favour. This Message being reported to *Barbabigell*, he grew beyond all Patience; and reply'd by the mouth of the same Servant, that he was Master of his own House, and would see no other Persons in it, than such as he thought fit; but he would write to his Lordship, and appoint a place where he would hear what he had to communicate. On this, my Lord withdrew; and the next Morning receiv'd a Letter from him, which *Debalclick* repeating to me, I set down in Characters in a part of a Leaf in my Pocket-Book, which happen'd to be vacant, and have with great pains and labour translated into *English*.

MY LORD,

" WHEN my Sister had so little
" regard for her Honour, as to
" resign it on your Temptations, I
" ceased to think her worthy my Concern;

" cern; but ſhall ſo far remember what " is owing to myſelf, as not to ſuffer " tamely an Inſult ſuch as I have re- " ceived from you. I believe the great " Park, where the Emperor is accuſ- " tomed to hunt, will be a proper " Place to decide which of us leaſt de- " ſerves to be affronted, and will ex- " pect you there, arm'd with a Bow " and Arrow to-morrow ſoon after " Sun-riſe."

Barbabigell.

THE Lord, who imagin'd not that a little *Cit* would dare to think of revenging himſelf on a Man of his Quality, was at firſt a little alarm'd; and being not very fond of expoſing his Perſon, where there was a probability of Danger, would have avoided the Combat, by ſaying, it was a leſſening his Rank to fight with one ſo much beneath him; but then conſidering that ſuch an Evaſion might, among ſome People, be look'd upon as Cowardice, he reſolv'd to to accept the Challenge, bethinking himſelf at the ſame time of an Expedient to prevent Miſchief; which was, to apprize the Keepers of the Park, that a Duel was intended to be fought there, to the end that they might be ready, as ſoon as the Antagoniſts appear'd, to ruſh in, and keep them from coming to an Engagement.

THE time appointed being arriv'd, they met; *Barbabigell* had his Bow immediately prepar'd, but *Fuergoliſthaſſo* ſeemed ſomewhat ſlow in his Motions, and began to talk much after the manner of the *French* Dueliſts, who kill one another with abundance of Ceremony and Good-manners. The other, however, being more fiery, was for finiſhing the Buſineſs; and plainly aſſured his Lordſhip, that as he came not thither to be entertain'd with Diſcourſes, he would waſte no farther time in them, and that if he did not retire to a convenient diſtance, he muſt expect that

that he would make uſe of the advantage: As he ſpoke theſe Words, he went back as far as was neceſſary to take his Aim; which the Lord perceiving, followed his Example, tho' with an aking Heart, curſing in his Mind the delay of the Park-Keepers. Both now with Arms extended ſtrain'd their Bows, and ſwiftly flew the whizzing Arrows; that ſent from the Hand of *Fuergoliſtbaſſo* fell on the Graſs unhurtful, but *Barbabigell's* graz'd on the Embroidery on the Shoulder of the Peer, and on its fatal Point bore off at leaſt two Silver Roſebuds, and a Sprig of Jeſſamin: But this Misfortune, tho' at another time would have been look'd on as a great one, was now but ſlightly regarded, a more terrible one being in view; the furious *Barbabigell* drew a Sword, whoſe fatal Shine made the Beau tremble; but his Fears were ſoon over, the wiſh'd-for Park-Keepers appear'd, and put an end to the Fray. *Fuergoliſtbaſſo* ſeem'd enrag'd at the diſappointment,

and

and told his Enemy, that he ſhould find another time to puniſh his Inſolence, but more prudently went out of Town the ſame day, for fear of being compell'd to make good his Words, and return'd not till he heard that *Barbabigell* had receiv'd Orders from the Court to proceed no farther in this Buſineſs.

THE Brother's Inſolence ſerv'd as an Excuſe for him to break off with the Siſter; ſhe no longer had a Reputation to loſe, nor a Virginity to forfeit; and the ſecond part of the Pleaſure of an Intrigue, to a Man of his Lordſhip's Character, is expoſing and ridiculing the Creature ſo undone. He plentifully indulg'd his Humour and his Vanity in this point, and *Sewawnawick* had not only the Expence, but all the Melancholy of her Condition alſo to go through, without the leaſt aſſiſtance or ſympathy from him, or ſcarce that miſerable Relief, the Pity of the World; moſt People condemning her more for the

the Choice ſhe made in ſuch a Partner in her Crime, than for the Crime it ſelf.

WHEN *Dabalclick* had concluded this Hiſtory, I took the freedom to ask her concerning the Affair of *Koppockitaſh* and *Dafferheſal*, having a great Curioſity to know in what manner *Shefinbaſto* behaved himſelf. But ſhe told me that the matter was ſtill in debate, that ſhe was kept a cloſe Priſoner in her Chamber under a ſufficient Guard, and *Koppockitaſh* continued in private, having never been ſeen ſince; but that ſince his Amour with the Wife of *Shefinbaſto*, thoſe who pretended to be moſt acquainted with his Circumſtances, reported that he had ſquander'd away his Eſtate, and ſeem'd to inſinuate that his late Attempt had been inſtigated more by a motive of Intereſt than Love. As for what would be the Conſequence, there were various Conjectures; but

I none

none could be certain they had hit upon the right, or could be able to gather any thing from the reserved Temper of *Shesinhasto*.

CHAP.

CHAP. IV.

Debalclick *continues her Converſation with the Author, acquaints him with the Marriage of a certain General, in two days after the deceaſe of his former Lady; his own Death, and how his Widow became the Bride of an Apothecary; and afterwards relates the Hiſtory of a Lady who ſets up for a Wit, and the Succeſs of her Works. The Author is reſtored to favour, the Emperor ſends for the Powder-Puff, the various Advices the* Lilliputian *Council give concerning the Uſe of it, and which of them was taken.*

THis Lady perceiving I was very much pleaſed with the Entertainment ſhe gave me, continued with me a conſiderable Time, and

I 2 hav-

having ask'd me if I had not at my first landing seen General *Tolbuclin*, gave me an Account of him which very much surpriz'd me. I very well remember'd that it was he who commanded the Party that had taken me Prisoner in the manner described in my Travels: He appear'd to be pretty well advanced in Years, and had all that Gravity which is becoming in Age. But she told me, that at that time, his Lady, who was a Woman of great Quality and Merit, lay dangerously sick, and soon after died; and that instead of having his House hung with Black, the Sun excluded, and mourning Tapers supplying the place of Day, as was expected from a Man of his Station in such a Calamity; those who went to visit him some days after the Funeral, found every thing in the same manner it was accustom'd to be, when the Lady, whose Death they came to condole, was living. So odd an appearance could not but surprize all who saw it, tho' Complaisance oblig'd oblig'd them to conceal it. They were beginning however to praiſe the Virtues of the Deceaſed, and lament the loſs of ſo excellent a Perſon; but the General ſoon put an end to theſe Condolements, by telling them that Congratulations were more ſuitable to his preſent Condition; and as he ſpoke, roſe from his Chair with as much Agility as the Gout, with which he was very much troubled, would give him leave, and hobbled into another Room, whence he immediately return'd, leading in a Woman of a comely Appearance, who he preſented to them as his Wife, declaring that he had made her ſo before the Funeral of his former. So odd a Proceeding in a Man of his Reputation, made every body curious to enquire into the Motives which had occaſion'd it; and ſome who pretended to have dived into the particulars of his Behaviour, for the laſt eight Years, would have it, that he was married to her long before his firſt Lady died, it being allowed among the

the Great to have a Wife for each Hand; and that fearing the Violence of that Diftemper, with which he had a long time been afflicted, would fome time or other take him from the World, fhe made ufe of the Afcendant fhe had over him, to oblige him to acknowledge her as his Wife, immediately on the Death of the other: Not that it was love of his Perfon that induc'd her to defire he fhould be thus fpeedy in his Declaration: His Age and Infirmities made fuch an Imagination ridiculous; befides, fhe had a more vigorous Lover, who fhe hoped might one day be the better for the Widow of a General. *Debalclick* told me, fhe one day overheard a young Fellow, who was of no higher rank than an Apothecary, and this fine Lady in Conference, as they were retired, thinking themfelves in full fecurity, in one of the Grotto's in the Palace-Garden: She repeated to me the Expreffions fhe heard between them, fome part of which I have tranf-

lated,

lated, and will, I am certain, be agree-able to ſome of my acquaintance, who I know make love in much the ſame manner.

Lady. Have I caught thee in my Arms, my own Soul! my deareſt Jew-el, Sugar and Roſes is in thy Lips.

Apo. Aye, ſo there is in thine, my Life.

Lady. Come to my Arms, and let me hug thee cloſe, thou Precious.

Apo. Aye, ſo art thee.

Lady. Thou Treaſure of my Life.

Apo. Aye, ſo art thee.

Lady. Thou ſweeteſt, deareſt, lovely-eſt of thy Sex.

Apo. Aye, ſo art thee.

Lady. I love thee more than Life.

Apo. And ſo do I thee.

There was abundance more of the ſame kind, which for fear I ſhould not do juſtice to the original, I have not ventur'd to tranſlate; beſides, for many of the tender Words that enſu'd, I could find

find nothing in the *English* Phrases; *Pudsey*, *Nickey*, *Honeybud*, *Dove's-Eyes*, or all the little loving Names that I have ever been acquainted with, will not come up to the superlative Follies of this Conversation: which I cannot say that I can gather any more from, than that the Lady had by far the greatest command of Language, the Lover being no more than her Eccho; and for want of Words of his own, return'd those she spoke, which it seems serv'd his purpose as well: for the General dying in a few Months after he had own'd her as his Wife, she was left at liberty to make a present of herself, and the great Substance he left her in possession of, to this Darling of her Soul; which she accordingly did, following the Example of her former Husband, not to give her Friends too much Trouble in offering her Consolation.

THE Reader must understand, that there is no Trade or Calling whatsoever

ever in *England*, that there is not the ſame alſo in *Lilliput*; but I know of none in which they ſo much abound as Bookſellers and Poets: Women there ſet up for Writers, before they have well learned their Alphabet, and Bookſellers build fine Houſes out of needy Authors Brains, juſt as they do here: The Preſs is the laſt Reſourſe of the one, and the firſt Enriching of the other. But having mentioned this, I cannot find in my heart to omit a Story *Debalclick* told me among many others, of a Lady who took a method to make her Works ſell, which was as extraordinary in its kind, as any thing I ever remember to have heard.

An honeſt plain Man, I think formerly a Grocer, who, as he ſaid, by loſſes in Trade, but according to the Report of the World, through the Extravagancies of his Wife, who laviſh'd the beſt part of his Gains on a young *Blefuſcan*, of whom ſhe was infinitely fond,

K hav-

Women authors

having been oblig'd to ſhut up Shop, was forced to live for ſome time in a Condition no way agreeable to the gay Humour of her that had brought him to it: To remedy this, ſhe bethought her ſelf of an Expedient, which if it did not anſwer her Husband's End, to bring him out of his Misfortunes, would her own, in procuring for herſelf variety of Company, Treats, and ſome Preſents. The *Lilliputians* have that extreme fondneſs for antient Writings, that it is a Saying among them, That no Man ever eſtabliſhed a living Reputation for his Works till after himſelf was dead; ſhe therefore prudently conſidered, that to attempt any new thing, of which there were ſo great variety every day, would be ſo little to be wonder'd at, that tho' a great number ſhould read it, few would have Curioſity to ſee the Author: ſhe therefore takes to pieces one of the moſt celebrated Pieces of the laſt Age, and gives publick Notice in the News-Papers, that ſhe was about

to

to new print it in a Language more adapted to the preſent Mode of Converſation, and that whoever was willing to ſubſcribe toward the great Expence of ſuch an Undertaking, might come and view part of the Work at her own Houſe.

THIS was an Enterprize of ſo bold a nature, that it aſtoniſh'd the whole Town; every body concluded that ſhe was either mad, or conſcious ſhe had a Genius, and Depth of Thought beyond what is uſually found in a Perſon of her Sex. Crouds of People were daily at her Houſe, and ſome, tho' but few, (conſidering the Numbers which Curioſity brought there) ſet down their Names among the Liſt of her Subſcribers; but this laſted but for a ſhort time: *Debalclick* told me, ſhe never heard of any Perſon who made her a ſecond Viſit; diſguſted either with the Freedoms which they ſaw the *Blefuſcan* take with her, or at her monſtrous Vanity, in attempting a thing ſhe had ſo little the Capacity to perform. She took notice of the Contempt the wiſer part of mankind regarded her with, and the Indifference ſhe perceived in the moſt gay and amorous, and felt all the Vexation imaginable for ſuch a Diſappointment. To repair this Misfortune, or, as the common ſaying is, to force a Trade, ſhe ſent her Husband, who has ever been a moſt obedient Animal, among the Coffee-Houſes, to invite the Gentlemen to his Houſe, and cry up the Wit and Beauty of his Wife: This acquired her ſome few more Cuſtomers, and having, by the aſſiſtance of her *Bleſuſcan* Gallant, at laſt finiſhed the Undertaking, ſhe committed it to the Preſs; whence it came out large enough indeed in bulk, in proportion to the Original, but as far unlike that in Spirit, as ſhe had endeavoured to make it in Language. The Succeſs however ſo far anſwered her Deſires, that a certain Lord, who, tho' fearing the Jealouſy of his

his Wife, he excufed himfelf from honouring her Works with his Name, in private gave a Subfcription very confiderable, and has not only done her the Favour of many Vifits himfelf, but has alfo introduc'd fome others, whofe acquaintance has been of very great Service to her Affairs.

THIS was not the only Stratagem of her prolifick Brain, it rather ferv'd but as an Introduction to another more gainful one: The name of Author gave her a pretence of being known in the great World; fhe talk'd of nothing but Lords and firft Minifters, and as there are always a number of unhappy Perfons, who are folliciting for Penfions, Bounty-money, or Places at Court, or in Offices, fhe undertook to plead, and make Intereft for them, for a good Confideration. She wanted not Artifice to keep their Expectations ftill warm, while they continued in a Condition to make her any Prefents, and when fhe found

found their power of doing ſo began to fail, had always an Excuſe ready which ſcreen'd her from their Proſecutions, tho' not from their juſt Complaints. *Debalclick* aſſur'd me, that by this means ſhe ſupported herſelf, her Husband, and *Bleſuſcan* Lover in ſo handſome a manner, that thoſe of her acquaintance, who were ignorant of her Proceedings, imagin'd ſhe had an Eſtate fallen to her.

BUT I hope, notwithſtanding the number of People, who in *Great Britain* are at a loſs how to get their Bread, none of them will take this Hiſtory for a Precedent; ſince I ſcarce believe a Stratagem of this nature would ſucceed in *London*, as it did in *Lilliput*, where no kind of Impoſitions are ſearched into with that exactneſs, nor puniſhed with that Severity: People may there defraud, cheat, ruin and betray who they pleaſe, the Emperor and his Miniſtry exempted; but the leaſt Suſpi-

Suſpicion of a Miſdemeanour againſt any of thoſe, is death inevitable. How happy therefore are we, who live under ſo glorious a Conſtitution, who in the meaneſt State of Life, receive an equal benefit of the Laws with thoſe that enjoy the moſt exalted one; and where no partial Favour or private Intereſt can be a Privilege for Injuſtice.

THESE Reflections reminding me to what Misfortunes my wandering Diſpoſition had reduc'd me, join'd to the Solitude of my preſent; for in many days I had not ſeen the Face of any but *Debalclick*, and thoſe appointed to attend and guard me, made me exceeding melancholy: how often, and how fervently did I pray to be once more reſtor'd to my dear Country; and how many Reſolutions did I make, that whenever I became ſo bleſt, I would give over all thoughts of rambling! As an addition to my preſent Calamities, I had

had alſo the fears of being treated in a worſe manner than I had yet been; and as I ceas'd to hope any future Favours from the Emperor, I thought I had ſufficient Reaſon to dread a great deal from his Diſpleaſure. *Debalclick* omitted nothing to chaſe ſuch an Imagination from my Mind; but it was rooted there, and I continued inconſolable.

BUT I ſoon found the Effect of thoſe Interceſſions, which that excellent Lady and her Husband were daily making for me: A few days after ſhe had been with me, *Libriber* and *Mamugar*, two great Officers, came to my Houſe; I no ſooner ſaw them, than I read in their Countenances the worſt part of my Misfortune was over; they told me, that the Emperor commanded me to ſend that miſchievous Machine, which had been the cauſe of ſo much Confuſion, that it might be examined by his Engineers, in order to have ſome others made by it, it, of a ſize more ſuitable to the Stature of the *Lilliputians*; and added, that being now convinced, I had no real Intention to affront thoſe Ladies, who had the ill Fortune to be expos'd by its too potent Wind, he was willing to pardon the Effects of my Inadvertency. I proſtrated my ſelf on the Ground, in token of my Gratitude and Humility, and a Carriage made of thirty five Deals, artfully fix'd together with Pegs, in breadth about a Foot, and in length a Foot and a half, and drawn by 20 Horſes, being arrived, I laid my Puff upon it, and tyed it faſt with a Packthread Cable, that it might not fall off. I entreated *Libriber* and *Mamugar* to preſent my moſt humble Duty to his Majeſty, with my Thanks for his gracious Pardon: they aſſured me they would deliver what I ſaid, and took their Leave.

I had now again as many Viſitors as ever, which confirm'd me that I was

L in

in good earneſt reſtored to the Emperor's Favour, and it was not long before he came in Perſon, attended by all his Court, into the Plain before my Houſe, and ſtretch'd his Hand for me to kiſs: I fell flat on my Belly, to receive the Grace, and renew'd my acknowledgments for his unbounded Mercy: He ſeem'd pleas'd with my Submiſſions, and aſſur'd me of the continuance of his Eſteem: All the Lords paid me their Compliments in their turns, and I learn'd perfectly by this change of my Affairs, how unſtable the Condition of a Stateſman is. The Emperor, among other Things, condeſcended to inform me, that his Engineers had given in their Judgment very much in favour of my Puff; ſome were of opinion it would be of great ſervice to blowing up the Fires, others had found out a much better Uſe for it than even the Projector of that excellent Invention ever thought of; it was to employ it in their Kitchens, to ſcatter fine ground

ground Meal on the Meat as it was roaſting, and for that purpoſe there were great numbers of them order'd to be made for the Service of the Cooks Royal. I think myſelf oblig'd to give this particular Account of the Value ſet on it in *Lilliput*, becauſe I have been inform'd ſince my Return, that my Countrymen have been ſo ſtupid as to reject the Contrivance as a thing of little merit.

CHAP. V.

The Author is magnificently treated by a Nardach *or great Lord: The happy Agreement between him and his Wife. The Author enters into a Diſcourſe of Marriage: no Medium in that State. A Story of a Lady of the Court, and the Methods ſhe took to prevent her Huſband from giving her any ill Treatment. The Author diſcovers an Intrigue between the Wife of* Flimnap, *High Treaſurer of* Lilliput, *and a young Lord.*

BEing reſtored to the Favour of the Emperor, I was alſo of conſequence again entitled to the outward Reſpects of all thoſe who had any dependance on him: But there was a a great Lord call'd *Bohinlin*, who had always expreſs'd a great deal of Civility to me, and I dare ſwear was heartily glad of my Re-eſtabliſhment; he no ſooner heard of it, than he ſent to deſire I would come to viſit him, which I accordingly did: but by reaſon of my not being able to enter his Houſe, the Entertainment was ſpread on a Table, without the Walls of his Court-Yard, where he and his Wife being plac'd in Chairs ſuitable to their ſize, I lay down on a thouſand Carpets, which were ſpread on the Graſs, and leaning my Head on one Hand, with the other I received the Tuns of Wine, and Diſhes of Meat, which were brought to me by the Servants. After Dinner, we enter'd into a very pleaſant Converſation: *Bohinlin* had a good Underſtanding, and talk'd very elegantly on whatever Subject he made choice of. By his Diſcourſes I was inform'd of many things, concerning their Laws, Religion and Manners, of which before I

was

was ignorant; but tho' he was a grave and reserv'd Man in other things, he could not forbear, when speaking on the most serious matters, turning every now and then to his Wife, and embracing her with a Tenderness, which one might easily see was not affected. But as often as he did this, he would beg my Pardon: Excuse me, my good Friend, said he, that my Love for this dear Creature, breaks in upon the Thread of my Discourse, and occasions Interruptions which may seem impertinent; but, said he, it is her Virtues that have endear'd her to me, and render'd her personal Charms infinitely more valuable: her Modesty, Meekness, Tenderness and Love!——I have all that I can wish in her, because I am very sensible by her diligence to please, that she has all she wishes for in me! We have in effect but one Soul, one Will, and if ever our Opinions disagree, it is but like various Thoughts rising in one Mind, and which-ever, on deli-

deliberation appears moſt reaſonable, is aſſented to by the other, without any tenacious aſſuming on the one ſide, or reluctance on the other: Thus is our Life one continued Concord, without one jarring Sound; and you cannot blame me, noble *Fleſtrin*, ſaid he to me, (for that was the Name they had given me) for having a Senſe of this great happineſs ſo much at heart, that I cannot ſometimes help ſpeaking of it. I aſſured him, I was ſo far from taking it ill, that nothing afforded me a greater ſatisfaction, than to behold that perfect Amity in a married State: I ſet the Tenderneſs between this agreeable Couple againſt the fooliſh Fondneſs *Debalclick* had deſcribed between the Lady and the Apothecary; and tho' the ſame Paſſion was the Source of both, yet that Paſſion being influenced by different Motives, produc'd different Effects: the one had in it all that was amiable, the other nothing but what was ridiculous and nauſeous. I then began

began to reflect on the Behaviour of ſome married People I had known in *England*; and tho' it had often ſeem'd ſtrange to me, that I ſhould be very well pleas'd at the Love I obſerv'd in one Couple, and as much diſguſted at that which I ſaw in another, I now learn'd the Cauſe whence it proceeded, and found it was not the matter, but the manner, which render'd their Endearments either agreeable or the contrary to a Stander-by. When two Perſons of good Underſtanding, and that love one another, are join'd in Marriage, the tender Expreſſions they make uſe of are pleaſing to others as well as to themſelves; but when the rude and unpolite make any Attempts to demonſtrate their Affection, it gives us an Idea ſo much to the diſadvantage of that Paſſion, that we even deteſt the Marriage-State, becauſe it gives them an opportunity to trouble us with thoſe Fooleries, which would elſe be conceal'd behind the Curtain.

We

WE fell after this into a Discourse of Marriage in general, in which *Bohinlin* very eloquently prov'd, that there is no Medium in that State; that a Parity of Dispositions, Years and Fortune, and a mutual Passion, render'd it the greatest Blessing that Mankind could know; and that wherever any of these were wanting, it made the Persons so join'd, not only a Curse to one another, but very vexatious also to all the World beside.

YET are there some Wives, said the Wife of *Bobinlin* smiling, who take Measures to prevent any ill Treatment from the unaffectionate Husband: *Frelobar* had so little Affection for *Brambinsfin*, even when he was first married to her, that he rose the next Morning after the Ceremony before Day-break to go to a Hunting Match, which she took in such ill part, that all the Tenderness she before had for him was converted

M into

into Contempt: She doubted not but ſo early a Neglect would in time grow into Rudeneſs and ill Treatment; reſolving therefore to be beforehand with him, ſhe no ſooner open'd her Eyes, than ſhe did alſo her Mouth in Scoldings and Revilings, which when he endeavour'd to return in the ſame manner, ſhe repeated more loudly; and by often practiſing, grew at laſt ſo perfect a Termagant, that finding himſelf unable to cope with her, he was glad to let her rail herſelf out of breath, without making any Reply to what ſhe ſaid; was fearful of doing any thing which might ſtir ſo terrible an Alarm, and thought it a Bleſſing if he could purchaſe her Silence at any rate. Thus does ſhe rule by Fear, tho' not by Love, and the greatneſs of her Station having render'd her an Example to thoſe who think it agreeable to ape their Superiors, even in their moſt notorious Vices, have made this Behaviour ſo much a Faſhion, that now-a-days a Woman no longer finds her

her Husband never ſo little deficient in the Ardours ſhe expects from him, than ſhe preſently takes the ſame Method to make him fearful to offend her.

I know not what I ſhould do in ſuch a caſe, replied *Bobinlin* ; no Miſery, in my opinion, being equal to that of being condemn'd to liſten to theſe inceſſant Clamours : but I am apt to believe, that if my Poſts and Buſineſs in the World would not permit me to quit ſuch a Woman, I ſhould invent ſome Stratagem or other, either to make her dumb, or my ſelf deaf.

THIS naturally turn'd the Diſcourſe on the difference of Women's Tempers, on which the beautiful Wife of *Bobinlin*, whenever it came to her turn to ſpeak, diſclos'd ſo much fine Wit, and juſt Senſe of that Obedience, which is the Duty of a Wife, and ſo gracefully deſcrib'd the Amiableneſs of Softneſs in a Woman, that I found it was not with-

M 2 out

out great reaſon her Husband had given her ſo many Praiſes.

I was ſo highly delighted with my Entertainment, in the Company of theſe two excellent Perſons, that it was not without the extremeſt regret I ſaw the Sun decline, and the pale Moon appearing at a diſtance, to remind me it was time for me to take my Leave; which having done, I could not reſolve to return to my Houſe, till I had firſt indulg'd my Meditation in the adjacent Fields, which being extremely lonely, I was in no danger of meeting any of the Natives; thoſe of the vulgar ſort of them, notwithſtanding the marks of Favour, with which I had been grac'd by their Emperor, having not yet been able to overcome their Fear, whenever they ſaw me walking or ſtanding on my Legs.

THE happineſs in which *Bobinlin* liv'd with his Wife, made me long to be once

once more with mine, with whom I had pass'd some days pleasantly enough to make me desirous of enjoying more of them; but the little likelihood I could perceive of ever being likely to return, either to her or my dear Country, made me extremely melancholy: it also added to my Trouble, that I had no means of imparting the discovery I had made of this Empire to the Government of *England*, the Glory of whose Thanks for such a Service, would have been a sufficient Compensation for all the Hardships and Dangers I had gone through in it.

As I was contemplating on this and other various Affairs, I continued walking, till I had pass'd through more than a hundred of their enclos'd Fields; the Hedges which made the Boundaries of them, being not above an Inch and a half from the Ground, I step'd over without regarding there was any thing in my way, as I did also over many Ditches

Ditches of about the ſame breadth ; and I know not how much farther I might might have ſtray'd, had I not perceiv'd at a ſmall diſtance from me, ſeveral little Lights, which every now and then mov'd up and down, like our *Engliſh* Glow Worms in a froſty Night, or like thoſe wandring Fires, which are frequently ſeen in marſhy Grounds, and lead the unthinking Traveller out of his way. I had no apprehenſions of danger from ſuch an *Ignis fatuus*, and went nearer to the place where they were: I then perceiv'd my wandrings had brought me to a Caſtle, which by the magnificence and largeneſs I doubted not but was the Habitation of ſome great Man: I had no buſineſs to knock at a Door I could not enter, nor was it a ſeaſonable Hour to make Viſits ; the *Lilliputians* being extremely regular, confining their Diverſions, as well as Buſineſs, to the Day, and devoting the Night wholly to Sleep ; it being an Article of their Religion, to do nothing that may

may ſeem to invert, or in the leaſt break in upon the Order of the Creation. As I approach'd, I found, by ſtooping down, and looking through the Windows, that thoſe Lights which I had ſeen, were carried up and down by the Servants in ſeveral Rooms, who were preparing for Bed : I had a proſpect diſtinct enough to diſcern the Faces of them, and remembred to have ſeen ſome of them among the Train of *Flimnap*, High Treaſurer of *Lilliput*, by which I conjectur'd this to be ſome Country-Seat of his; but I was more confirm'd, when looking into a fine Chamber, richly adorn'd, I perceiv'd his Wife in a looſe Undreſs, ſitting on a Couch, with a young Lord by her, whoſe Face I very well knew, as alſo his buſineſs there, having had ſome hints of this intimacy from *Clefgarin*, during the time of her viſiting me. The Lady appear'd in a kind of a Diſorder, as if in ſome reſentment againſt her Lover, who by kneeling, looking tenderly on her Face, and ſeve-

ral

ral other Geſtures of Submiſſion, teſti-fy'd his unwillingneſs to offend. At length her Countenance grew more ſe-rene, ſhe ſuffer'd him to kiſs, embrace her, and ſoon after to pluck off her Clothes and carry her to Bed, where he ſoon follow'd. I had neither Curioſity nor Deſire to know what farther paſs'd between them, but withdrew with as much haſte as I could from the Window, without making any noiſe; but I was ſo unhappy as to ſtumble againſt an Oak, over which I fell, breaking the Tree at the ſame time, which made ſo great a noiſe, that the Servants of *Flimnap*, not being yet aſleep, were immediately rouz'd, and at their Windows to ſee what had occaſion'd it. They imme-diately diſcern'd me, and thinking I had ſome ill Intent, ſet up a loud Cry: the Lady herſelf was alarm'd, perhaps ima-gining it was occaſion'd by the unexpe-cted coming of her Husband; but her Fear was in a ſhort time converted to Rage, when ſhe beheld me; and tho' I omitted

omitted nothing which I thought might convince her of the Grief I was in, for having caus'd this Disturbance in her Family; she continu'd extremely incens'd, and after having vented her Displeasure, in some opprobrious Language, she shut the Window, and would listen to me no further.

I made the best of my way home, heartily vex'd at the Accident, as indeed I had good cause; for whether it were that this Lady could not forgive the Disturbance I had occasion'd her, or that she suspected I had seen something more than she was willing should be known, I cannot determine; but I was soon convinc'd by the ill Offices her Husband afterward did me, that she had incens'd him against me.

FROM this time forth I made a Resolution never to wander beyond my own Precincts, being by woeful Experience convinc'd how dangerous it is

N to

to know more of the Great than they desire ſhould be reveal'd; and that to have the power of doing theman injury, is certain to draw the ſevereſt from them; at leaſt it is ſo in *Lilliput*, where indeed right and wrong are ſo confounded, that Strength alone can give the deciſion. I was for ſome time debating within my ſelf what Courſe I ſhould take to mitigate her Reſentment; I was at firſt of opinion to acquaint her Lover with my knowledge of his Happineſs, and by giving him my ſolemn Oath never to reveal what I had ſeen, make him my Friend; but I rejected this Deſign as too full of Danger, and reſolved by no Word or Action to let either of them ſuſpect I had diſcover'd their intimacy. I never could be able to judge whether it was to the ſuggeſtions of my good or ill Genius, that I gave over that Deſign, but am apt to believe it was the latter, ſince I could not have had Enemies more inveterate

veterate than both were to me, if I had proceeded with as much inadvertency as I really did with circumſpection.

CHAP. VI.

The Author is invited to ſee ſome of the Diverſions of the Country, which were particularly Rope-dancing and Tumbling. He deſcribes the Manner of them, and of the Theatre where theſe Exerciſes were performed. Keldreſal *acquaints him that they had formerly other more elegant Entertainments, and gives him the reaſons why they were left off, and theſe introduc'd. A Lady falls into a Swoon at the Feet of the Emperor as he ſits on the Throne: He offers to raiſe her, but the Empreſs ſeems diſſatisfied, and the Reaſons why, related to the Author by his Friend* Keldreſal, *and alſo the*

the Marriage of a great Lord with one of the Empreſs's Maids of Honour.

MOST of the People of Quality who had come to viſit me, had frequently expreſs'd a great deſire that I ſhould be preſent at the publick Diverſions of the Country, extolling them in a very high degree, and telling me that it was impoſſible I could ever have ſeen any thing ſo fine in my own Country; becauſe, ſaid they, what appears ſo very beautiful among us, muſt needs be monſtrous, and appear rather terrifying than delightful to the Eye, when perform'd by Creatures of ſo vaſt a bulk as you are. I daily heard ſo much of theſe kind of Diſcourſes, that I was at length oblig'd in complaiſance to affect an Inclination of ſeeing what they ſo highly prais'd; and *Keldreſal* being more importunate than the reſt, I conſented to go, if by any means there could be a Window left open

open in the Theatre that I might look in. He ſent immediately to the Perſon who had the management of theſe Performances, and gave orders that ſome contrivance ſhould be made, that I ſhould ſee every thing as commodiouſly as poſſible; and indeed he acquitted himſelf ſo well of the Commiſſion given him by *Keldreſal*, that I found I could ſee over the whole Place, either ſtanding or ſitting on the Ground, and leaning my Body a little forward. He told me there was to be a great Performance that day, and that the Emperor, Empreſs, and the whole Court intended to grace it with their Preſence. I reſolv'd therefore not to neglect this Opportunity; and having notice at what time they were to begin, I went ſomewhat before the Company came, on purpoſe to take a view of the *Theatre*. It was in form not much unlike our Play-Houſes in *England*; but the Boxes were more richly adorn'd, and the Thrones whereon the Emperor and

and Empreſs were to ſit, rais'd a conſiderable height above the reſt, which Diſtinction I very much approv'd of-for methinks a Prince who is in reality ſo vaſtly exalted above his Subjects, ought not at any time, much leſs in a publick Aſſembly, to ſit on a level with them: And indeed I queſtion not but it is very much owing to the great State with which this Emperor always appears, that he is treated by the *Lilliputians* with that Reverence. The Boxes in which the Nobility ſit, are extended on the right and left ſides of the Thrones, the Men ſitting on the Emperor's right Hand, and the Ladies on the Empreſs's left. The Princes and Princeſſes of the Blood-Royal are placed in a little Gallery behind the Thrones, and the great Officers of the Houſhold, with the Maids of Honour, ſit on the Steps of the Thrones. The Gentry and Commonalty are mingled promiſcuouſly together, Men and Women, in a large ſpace like our Pit; but they never

ver sit in the presence of the Emperor or Empress. On the Stage were fix'd two Poles of Wood, about the bigness of two Knitting-Needles; to which was fixed a Rope, at least a foot and a half from the Ground, a Ladder, like the Lattice of a Bird-Cage, was set for the Performers to mount; several gold Hoops, which I should have taken for Wedding-Rings in *England*, were fastened to the Ground; and those, as I was inform'd, who could pass through them with the greatest Agility, and Swiftness, received Marks of Favour from the Emperor's own Hand, according to their Dexterity.

I had no sooner satisfied my Curiosity in viewing the House, than the Company began to come in; the Pit was immediately fill'd, nor were the Boxes long empty: But the Musicians did not touch their Instruments, till the Trumpets at a distance proclaim'd the Royal Family were on their way thither: then

then they began to tune them, and as ſoon as the Emperor and Empreſs appear'd, ſaluted them with a Concert, which indeed was exceeding pleaſing. As ſoon as they had taken their Places, *Keldreſal*, willing to hear what my Sentiments would be on the Entertainment, entreated their Majeſties Permiſſion that he might be near me; which being granted, he came out, and communicating his Intentions to me, I ſat down on the Ground, and placed him on my Hand, where he had the opportunity of obſerving every thing as well as myſelf.

EVERY body being placed according to their degrees, the Show began; but I was ſoon ſick of the monkey Tricks and Poſtures in which the Actors ſeem'd to endeavour to vie with each other, who ſhould moſt diſtort his Body, or appear to have leaſt of the human Form; I therefore turn'd my Eyes from the Stage on the Aſſembly, which

O I

I confefs I thought very beautiful; the various-colour'd Habits, and the different Airs, and Manner in which they were difpos'd, the Magnificence of the Houfe, rich Canopies and Carpets, made the Profpect feem to me, like a fine Fan in an *European* Lady's Hand.

Keldrefal foon perceiv'd that I was more taken with the Company, than with the Skill of the Actors, and took notice of it to me. I had not yet learn'd enough of the Arts of Courts to be able to difguife my Thoughts fo far, but that he knew they turned with the utmoft Contempt on fuch Fooleries: and being very much my Friend, told me, he would not have me difclofe my Mind too freely on this head before the Emperor, or any Perfon who might be fufpected fhould inform him of it, thefe being the only Diverfions he approv'd of, or would encourage in *Lilliput*. I thank'd him for his Advice, and affur'd him I would not fail to obferve ſerve it; but could not forbear teſtify-ing ſome ſurprize, that a Prince in all other things ſo polite, ſhould have ſo little Elegance in his Taſte of Diverſion. But *Keldreſal* ſoon inform'd me, that it was owing to his Policy, not want of Genius. We had, *ſaid he*, in former Reigns, ſome very famous Poets, who compos'd ſuch exact Repreſentations of human Life, that it was impoſſible for any Perſon of what Humour ſoever to come often to the *Theatre*, without ſome time or other ſeeing his own Character ſo lively diſplay'd, that he immediately knew it, in ſpite of the Prejudices and Blindneſſes which Self-Love throws before the Eyes. In theſe Satires of the Foibles of human Nature, the Great were equally involved with the Vulgar, nor did any Man's Gold or Titles buy off the juſt Remonſtrance of the poetick Cenſure; which at length giving diſguſt to ſome Men in power, and beſides it being look'd upon as a thing of dangerons conſequence, that the Vices of the Great ſhould be ridicul'd by the meaner ſort; theſe kind of Entertainments were diſcouraged by degrees, and at laſt wholly forbid; and this new way of Entertainment introduced as more proper to create Mirth, and altogether unhurtful, either to the Peace of Mind, or Reputation of the Spectator. This, *continued he*, is the true reaſon of perverting the Stage to Uſes for which it was not originally deſign'd; but as this is not allow'd to be ſaid publickly, you muſt keep it as a Secret: The common Opinion being, that the Art of Poetry is ſo far loſt, and degenerated from what it was, that there are no living Authors capable of writing any thing fit to be repreſented before an Aſſembly ſo auguſt as this.— Tho', *added he*, I am very ſenſible that no Nation ever did, or ever can produce Genius's more ſublime and noble, than may be found at this day in *Lilliput*. I could not forbear teſtifying ſying my Concern for thoſe unhappy Gentlemen, and the Suppreſſion of an Art which in all Ages has been eſteem'd ſo valuable, and is of ſo great ſervice both to repelling the Vices of a People, and encouraging the Virtues. But he again bid me beware how I ſpoke on that Affair, and ſeemed ſo cautious of being overheard to have talk'd to me concerning it, that I perceiv'd he anſwer'd my Interrogatories with pain, and for that reaſon held my tongue, turning again towards the Stage, and Actors, as much as I was able to endure. But I was ſoon eas'd of the Conſtraint I put on myſelf, by an Accident which drew the Eyes of the whole Aſſembly another way.

A Lady, who ſeemed of Condition, by having been placed among the Nobility, quitting her Seat to ſpeak to ſome Perſon who ſtood near the Throne, juſt as ſhe approach'd that whereon the Emperor ſat, fell at his feet in a Swoon. He

He no ſooner ſaw her, than he ſtooped to raiſe her, imagining no more at firſt, than that her Foot had ſlipt by ſome Accident; but the Officers of the Houſhold ſaving his Majeſty that trouble, perceiv'd the Condition ſhe was in, made a ſign to the Ladies, who crowded about her in a moment, and applyed proper means for the recovery of her Senſes; which being done, ſhe continued ſo ill, that ſhe was oblig'd to leave the Houſe. The Empreſs, whoſe Face was covered with Frowns from the firſt moment the Emperor had taken notice of her, having ſpoke ſome Words to him in a Voice too low for any Perſon but himſelf to hear, quitted the Place with all imaginable ſigns of Diſcontent. The occaſion of it was too obvious not to be perceiv'd by every body, and I had nothing to fear in letting *Keldreſal* know how much I was ſurprized, that ſo great an Empreſs ſhould behave in ſuch a manner, it being an Argument of the meaneſt and

and most degenerate Soul to grow jealous on every trifling occasion, and endeavour to engross even the Complaisance of her Husband. He shook his Head in token of being asham'd that she had been guilty of so great a Weakness in Publick, but went so far as to inform me, that tho' their State made those great Princes appear for the most part to live in a perfect agreement, yet were their private Hours rack'd with perpetual feuds and discontents: A mutual Jealousy reigns in the Breasts of both, and the one cannot testify the least Complaisance for a deserving Subject, but the other is presently uneasy. The Emperor indeed has discover'd some Symptoms of an amorous Disposition; he has at this day one of the finest young Ladies about the Court great with Child by him, and has been more than suspected to have an Intimacy with the Wife of a certain Lord: the Empress, on the other hand, is said not to have been ungrateful for the Effect of her Charms;

Charms ; and it is not therefore to be wonder'd at, that both Parties ſhould live in a continual diſtruſt of each other. Nor is this to be imputed to an exceſs of tenderneſs of either ſide ; Jealouſy is not occaſion'd by Love, the Husband's Honour is concern'd in the Actions of his Wife, and the Intereſt of the Wife in thoſe of her Husband : This you know is the Caſe among common People, why ſhould it not alſo be ſo among Princes ? He ſaid no more, nor did I think it fit to preſs him, perceiving it was a Theme on which it did not pleaſe him much to ſpeak ; and thinking myſelf infinitely favour'd in the Confidence he ſeem'd to have of my Diſcretion in revealing to me ſo much as he had of the Secrets of his Prince. He afterwards inform'd me of ſeveral Amours between Perſons of the firſt Quality, which becauſe they had nothing more remarkable in them, than what one may every day hear of in *Lon-*

London, I have not thought it worth while to relate.

I could not avoid, as I was viewing the Aſſembly, taking notice of an old Lord, who I had often ſeen with the Emperor, and who now ſat near him; he had till now always appear'd a Perſon of great Sagacity and Wiſdom; and having been taught always to reverence hoary Hairs, I had the greateſt reſpect for him: but I now thought he behav'd in a manner, which might juſtly forfeit all that the World had conceiv'd for him; his Eyes were continually rivetted on the Face of a young Beauty who ſat oppoſite to him, and who by her Air, and the languiſhing Glances ſhe caſt on all the young Nobility, who were addreſſing her with their Eyes, I perceiv'd to be a very Coquette. Good God! cry'd I, is it poſſible that a Man who has already one Foot in the Grave, can look with Deſire on any thing? Can he covet what he is paſt the power of

P poſ-

poſſeſſing? *Keldreſal* laugh'd very heartily at this Exclamation of mine, and as ſoon as he had given over, The Lady knows by this time, ſaid he, whether your Obſervation be on juſt Grounds or not, for I aſſure you ſhe is his Wife: They were married ſome days ſince, to the aſtoniſhment of the whole Court, as the News of it is now to you; but becauſe I think there is ſomething in the Story more extraordinary than you will often meet with, I will acquaint you with the particulars. This lovely young Creature, continu'd he, was Maid of Honour to the Empreſs *Badgarlin*; the eldeſt Son of this old Lord, was infinitely in love with her, he made his Addreſſes to her, but not on honourable Terms; they were ſuch however as had made ſome Impreſſion on her Heart in his favour, and he had undoubtedly carry'd his Point, if his Father, being told that he frequently viſited her, and that 'twas thought it would be a Match, had not conceiv'd the higheſt

eſt indignity at it; he look'd on her Birth and Fortune ſo vaſtly inferior to his, that not all her Charms were ſufficient to make amends for the Diſproportion; he not only forbad his Son ever to ſee her more, but alſo would needs make a Viſit to the young Lady himſelf, to aſſure her that if ſhe married his Son, he would diſinherit him, and do every thing in his power to make them both unhappy in every other Circumſtance. With theſe Reſolutions it was he went; but he no ſooner had caſt his Eyes on her, than he became a Rival to his Son, and inſtead of treating her with Threats and Contempt as he had deſign'd, fell at her Feet, proteſted he could not live without her, and entreated her to have Compaſſion on him. The Girl had Ambition, and that juſt Pride which all Women ought to have in the preſervation of their Virtue; and reminding her that the young Lord ſollicited her but on diſhonoura-

P 2 ble

ble Terms, made her eaſily conſent to the Father. They were married, to the ſurprize of every body, who had heard the Contempt with which he treated her, when any mention was made of her becoming the Bride of his Son. Her Ambition is now gratified to the utmoſt Extent; but ſhe has other Paſſions which her old Husband is wholly incapable of ſatisfying: She has Beauty to create Deſire, and a Heart capable of being ſenſible of it herſelf; and you may gueſs in part by her Behaviour in this publick Place, that ſhe takes Liberties in private little to the advantage of her Husband's Honour.

THE Entertainment broke up juſt as *Keldreſal* had done ſpeaking, on which he took his Leave, and mingled with the Courtiers that attended the Emperor. I kept my place, till the whole Train had paſs'd by me, fearing to tread on any of them; every one ſalu-

ſaluted me with great courteſy, and I had no other reaſon than to be very well ſatisfied with what I had heard and ſeen.

CHAP.

CHAP. VII.

The Author in his return home meets with Clefgarin; *she accompanies him to his House, and gives him an Account of many singular Adventures; in particular, of a* Squahib, *or Priest of* Lillipur, *and the Daughter of a* Blefuscan *Lord. She takes her Leave, and he lies down to rest, but perceives an old Picture on the Walls of his House, which he had not observed before; he draws near, and discovers certain Figures which he is very much at a loss to know the meaning of. His Reflections thereon.*

I Have already taken notice, that the *Lilliputians* go to Bed very early, for which reason they have all their Diversions by day: the

the Sun was yet ſo high when I left the Theatre, that I thought it too warm to walk; for which reaſon, I retir'd to my Houſe, which was very airy by reaſon of the many Windows, which let in Wind, but were fenc'd from the Sun-beams, by certain Branches of Trees, which grew on each ſide, and ran up the Walls, after the manner of our Laureſtines or Honey-ſuckles. I was ſcarce enter'd, before my old Acquaintance *Clefgarin* came to make me a Viſit; I was rejoyc'd to ſee her, and tho' nothing in my own Country, where I had ſuch variety of agreeable Amuſements, was more diſagreeable to me than a talkative Woman, yet in a place ſuch as that where I then was, I was glad of any thing that might help to paſs over the ſolitary Hours, and make me for a little time forget the dear Delights I had left behind.

After ſhe had given me a full Relation of her own Misfortunes, which I

I was before inform'd of by others, innumerable were the little Hiſtories ſhe gave me of Ladies who had err'd in a more unpardonable manner than ſhe had done, yet ſtill retain'd the favour of the Court; but I ſhall paſs by the greateſt part of them in Silence, as having nothing in them ſurprizing or entertaining to an *Engliſh* Reader. But there were ſome things ſhe told me, which I believe, at leaſt I hope, were never parallell'd in a Country ſuch as that to which I have the honour to owe my Birth.

I have hitherto avoided making any mention of the Religion which is profeſs'd in *Lilliput*, becauſe all the Accounts I could be able to get of it were very dark and indiſtinct; but I perceiv'd they held ſome Tenets of the *American Indians*, ſome of the South Continent of *Arabia Petræa*, and others they borrow from thoſe People who inhabit the farther part of the Land of *Magellan*:

I

I saw that several of their Articles of Faith border on those of the Nations I have mention'd; but it cannot be supposed that they are owing to them, because, as I have already taken notice in my Book of Travels, they never heard, till I inform'd them, that there were any other Kingdoms in the World, than that of *Blefuscu* beside their own. This I learn'd, however, that they worship a Being who they say gives them all good things; but they pay infinite more Worship to one whom they fear; they seem to pray to Heaven for Blessings, and to Hell not to torment them; to the latter they offer Sacrifices every day, and but very rarely to the other; by which 'tis plain, they are influenc'd more by Fear than Gratitude: yet have they pretended Holy Men in great number, whose Office it is to preach Virtue, and decry Vice; these are call'd *Squabibs*, are held in great Veneration by the People, and pretend to a kind of Infallibility. It was of

Q one

one of the moſt conſiderable among them, that *Clefgarin* gave me the following Relation.

A young Beauty, the Daughter of a *Blefuſcan* Nobleman, diſcovering a more early Inclination to Marriage, than was conſiſtent either with the Modeſty of her Sex, or the Circumſtances of her Father, who at that time was not in a condition to give her a Portion equal to her Birth: her Parents, finding their Admonitions of little effect, and that ſhe ſtill diſcover'd an extraordinary Diſpoſition to the Society of the other Sex, at laſt ſent for a *Squahib* to diſcourſe with her, believing what he ſaid would make a greater impreſſion on her Mind. They were left alone together, and he began with many grave Remonſtrances, that it was not the Province of Womankind to diſcloſe the leaſt Tenderneſs for any Man till he had proved himſelf worthy of it by his Conſtancy and Love; and that a Child ſhould never think

think of difpofing of herfelf, till commanded to do fo by her Parents; with many other fuch like Arguments becoming his Office. The Girl liften'd to him with a good deal of patience for fome time, but in the end told him pertly, that fhe was above Diffimulation, which fhe look'd upon to be the worft of Vices, that fhe believ'd fhe had no Inclinations but fuch as were agreeable to Nature, and therefore neither would nor ought to be afham'd of them. This Anfwer, fo full of Spirit, gave her fuch Charms in the eyes of the *Squabib*, that he grew enamour'd of her, and inftead of preaching the Doctrine for which he was admitted by her pious Parents, now made it his Bufinefs to cherifh Sentiments fo much to the favour of his new Defires; and perceiving fhe liftned to thefe kind of Difcourfes with fome warmth, he took the boldnefs to kifs her, put his Hands in her Bofom, and take other Freedoms which *Clefgarin* left to my Imagination to guefs; but

Q 2 which

which I dare not preſume to wound the chaſte and modeſt Reader with revealing: it ſhall ſuffice to ſay, he obtain'd of her every thing he wiſh'd. After which, as was agreed between them, for the continuation of his Viſits, he told her Father, that his Precepts had, as yet, been capable of making no great Impreſſion on her; but that he hoped he ſhould in time be able to make her a new Creature; on which he was deſir'd to renew his Viſit Days: a million of Thanks, and a Preſent, as conſiderable as the Scantineſs of their Fortune would admit, were his recompence for the trouble he had taken.

THE good Mother, who had been greatly afflicted at the Diſpoſition ſhe obſerved in her Daughter, had a fancy to hear in what manner ſhe would reply to the Exhortations made her by the *Squabib*; and the next time he came, ſhe went into an upper Room, where ſhe

ſhe contriv'd to make a little Hole, through which ſhe might hear and ſee every thing that paſs'd. The amorous Couple paſs'd their time as before, and the poor Woman was ſo much aſtoniſh'd, ſhe ſcarce could believe her Eyes; but being at laſt too well convinc'd, ſhe ran immediately to her Huſband, and acquainted him with the ſurprizing Truth, who, alſo diffident at firſt, ran up Stairs to aſcertain himſelf more than he could be by the report of any Perſon. Never was Man more confounded, for they ſtill continued their wanton Play, till he cried out to them to give over, telling them he would be reveng'd on both, for the diſhonour they had brought upon his Family: He branded the *Squabib* with the Names of Hypocrite, Villain, Impoſtor, and the like, and the young Girl with all that can expreſs Infamy in her Sex. The Delinquents had nothing to ſay in their defence, and the old People had out their Railing with-

out

out any interruption ; but their Stock of Breath, as well as Expreſſions, being pretty near exhauſted, they grew more calm; and conſidering that what was done was paſt recall, began to caſt about in their Minds how to patch it up, or, as the ſaying is, make the beſt of a bad Market: they told the *Squabib*, that ſince he had ſpoil'd the Goods, he muſt endeavour to get them ſold as well as he could; and ſince he could not repair the Injury he had done their Daughter, by marrying her himſelf, (the Prieſts of *Lilliput* not being allow'd to take a Wife) he muſt provide a Husband for her with all ſpeed. This he promis'd to perform, and on that Condition they ſuffer'd him to depart.

HE knew too well the Puniſhments to which he ſhould be expos'd, in caſe this Adventure were divulg'd, not to be very induſtrious to have it conceal'd, which he could hope for by no other means, than thoſe the Parents of his pretty

pretty little Miſtreſs had propos'd. He therefore gave ſuch extraordinary Commendations of her, to a young Gentleman whom he had under his Care, and who was not very well acquainted with the World, that he fell greedily into the Snare, and thought himſelf the happieſt Man in the World to have ſo virtuous a Creature for his Wife.

THEY are lately married, ſaid *Clefgarin*, and the cunning *Squabib* has again re-eſtabliſh'd himſelf in the Favour of the old People, and enjoys the ſame Freedoms, without ſuſpicion, with the Bride, as ſhe had permitted him to take before ſhe was made ſo. Yet, continued ſhe, becauſe every body is not acquainted with this Affair, and ſhe has the Sanction of Marriage, ſhe has the aſſurance to talk of my Misfortune, as if it were a Prodigy, when Heaven knows I am in reality leſs guilty than herſelf.

I

I believe this Lady would never have been weary of reciting to me Adventures of this kind; for besides the natural Love that all Women are born with, to hearing themselves speak, she had that irresistible Motive, to expose the Faults of her Neighbours, hoping thereby to make her own seem less; but my Guards coming in with Supper, reminded her it was time to take leave, which as soon as she had done, I sat down on the Ground, and eat what was brought me, and soon after retir'd to my Mat, whereon I was accustom'd to sleep: But the Day being not yet quite shut, I lay contemplating on many melancholy Incidents of my past Life, and grew so exceeding splenetick by thinking too deeply, that I know not if I should not in a little time have arriv'd to that height of Vapours, as to have fancied myself a Bottle, or a Goose-Pye, if I had not met with an interruption, which was perfectly providential,

to

to rouze me from that unmanly Diſtemper. At the farther end of my Apartment I ſaw ſome little confus'd Spots and Lines drawn athwart each other in a Mathematical manner, which, tho' I had liv'd here for many Months, I had never obſerv'd before: I was prodigiouſly ſurpriz'd, becauſe I knew that ſince my arrival none had been at work in the place, and I could not conceive how it ſhould have been there even one day unperceiv'd by me, who at my firſt coming had made an exact ſcrutiny into every part of the Houſe, the deſcription of which I have related in my Book of Travels, and but by accident omitted this I am now ſpeaking of. I roſe and drew near to the Wall, which was compos'd of Stone, but plaiſter'd over with a kind of white Varniſh, ſome of which being rubb'd off by accident, as I imagine by myſelf, for I uſually hung up my Coat in that place when I went to Bed, on a little Spike, which I found in the Fields, and had been I ſup-

R poſe

poſe ſome part of a *Lilliputian Paliſado*, and 'tis probable by plucking it off too haſtily, had made this Fraction in the outſide Covering of the Wall, and by that means diſcover'd the Figures I ſaw, and which as I approach'd increas'd my Wonder. I never ſaw in *England*, a Globe more exactly drawn, I do not believe the niceſt Mathematician could have found fault with the ſmalleſt Line: How, ſaid I to myſelf, can theſe People have ſo juſt a notion of the Poſition of the World, yet imagine there are no parts of it habitable but that they poſſeſs, and the ſmall Iſland of *Blefuſcu?* But what amaz'd me moſt, was a vaſt number of black and deform'd Bodies which ſeem'd to hang in Air, each arm'd with a Bow and Arrow, as if in act to ſhoot the Globe: I could not for my Life conceive the meaning of this, and hoping an Explanation by looking farther, I pick'd the Varniſh off for a conſiderable ſpace, but could find nothing but thoſe horrid

rid Figures, multiplied one behind another.

I do not remember ever to have ſuffer'd more from Curioſity than I did at this juncture. I continu'd ſtill picking the Varniſh off, till darkneſs put an end to my Work, but was then compell'd to give over and return to Bed, where inſtead of taking that Reſt for which the Night was ordain'd, I paſt it in various conjectures on what I had ſeen; ſometimes imagining that in former times that Kingdom had been poſſeſt by other ſort of People than it now was, and ſhould have been tempted to have believed that Painting had been done by an *European* Hand, if the ſize of the Temple in which it was, had not convinc'd me it could only be of ſervice to a *Lilliputian* Race. The more I meditated, the more I was confounded in my Opinions; and finding it impoſſible to form any which I could promiſe myſelf was juſt, I made uſe of

R 2 my

my Philoſophy, to reſolve to be content till I could find ſome Perſon endued with a ſufficiency of Good Nature, and Knowledge of former Tranſactions, to inform me of what I ſhould never be able to find out myſelf.

CHAP.

CHAP. VIII.

Keldresal *visits the Author, and acquaints him with the meaning of the Figures on the Wall. The strange Allegory of the* Lilliputians. *The reason why all such kind of Descriptions, either in Writing or Painting, were now forbid among them.* Debalclick *and some other great Ladies come to see the Author; an odd Story related by one of them concerning two Lovers.*

WITH the same Cogitations in which I had past the Night did the Morning find me; at which time, before I had quite swal-

low'd

low'd the two hundred Manchets and three Tuns of Wine allow'd me for my Breakfaſt, *Keldreſal* came to viſit me: could not have wiſh'd for a more proper Perſon to explain what I ſo much deſir'd to know. I had had many Proofs of his Friendſhip for me, and knew he had a perfect Underſtanding in the Annals of his Country; I made no doubt therefore, but that it would be both in his Power and Inclination to oblige me in this Requeſt, and as ſoon as the firſt Civilities were over, made him look on the Wall, and diſcover'd to him my impatience of knowing the meaning of what it contain'd. He appear'd much ſurpriz'd at what I had done, and told me that had I been a *Lilliputian* born, or had liv'd among them long enough to be acquainted with their Laws, to have brought thoſe Figures to light, would have drawn on me ſome very ſevere Puniſhment; but as I was a Stranger, and had been guilty only through Ignorance, 'twas probable I might obtain Pardon from the Empe-

Emperor, if he ſhould happen to know it; however, he adviſ'd me to conceal what I had done, and eraſe the Figures, if by any means I could, ſo as they might not be ſeen by any that came to viſit me. It ſeem'd very ſtrange to me, that it ſhould be a Crime to look on Pictures, which one might eaſily ſee had been long ſince drawn, and which appear'd to have no reſemblance of Treaſon in them; and begg'd he would inform me of the Reaſons which made me guilty, if he could poſſibly do it without becoming ſo himſelf. He anſwer'd, that that would be an impoſſibility, becauſe that it was to prevent any Diſcourſe of them that ſuch kind of Imagery was forbid; but to convince me of the good Opinion he had of my Integrity and Diſcretion, he would venture to reveal what if he were known to do, would perhaps coſt him his Life. I was beginning to give him ſome Aſſurances of an eternal Secrecy; but he would not ſuffer me to proceed, telling me that my own Honour was a better

better Security than all the Vows I could make. I thank'd him for ſo obliging a Confidence, and prepar'd to liſten to the Explanation I ſaw he was about to make, which he immediately did in theſe or the like Words. This Place, ſaid he, which is now allotted for your Apartment was formerly a Temple, and the moſt magnificent one in the whole Kingdom: this Painting that you have ſo miraculouſly diſcover'd, was done by the greateſt Artiſt of his Time, from a Draught given him by the firſt and perhaps the greateſt Philoſopher, Mathematician, and Geographer that ever the World produc'd: He divided the Globe by ſtrait and oblique Lines, in the manner you ſee it here decypher'd, foretold the Change of Weather, counted the number of the Stars, and prefix'd certain Times for the riſing and ſetting of the Sun in ſuch and ſuch Seaſons of the Year. He was greatly applauded for the ſucceſs of his Labours, and our Hiſtory informs us, that

that never Man receiv'd more ſubſtantial Proofs of Eſteem and Admiration. This brought the Art or Study of Mathematicks ſo much in faſhion, that all our young Nobility and Gentry bent their Minds this way; and preſently after roſe up a number of imaginary Proficients; Vanity, and a deſire of broaching new Opinions, and rendering themſelves remarkable, made every one affect to have made new Diſcoveries in the Regions of the Air. Vaſt Treatiſes were in a ſhort time compoſed, and different Syſtems were every day ſet forth; ſome as diſtant from all Probability, as they all were from one another. Every one had a particular Set of Followers, who appear'd ſo well convinced of the Truth of what they profeſs'd, that they declared themſelves ready to endure Martyrdom for the Conviction of the reſt. This puzzled the Minds of the People ſo much, that they knew not to which to give Credit, and frequently occaſion'd Diſtinctions among them, to

S the

the ruin of many a noble Family; for which reaſon, and alſo that the immoderate Application to Philoſophy took our Youth from the more uſeful Studies of War, Politicks, and Mechaniſm, *Golbaſto Momarin Eulame Guclo*, the Father of our preſent Emperor, made an Edict, ſtrictly prohibiting the uſe of Mathematicks for the future, except in ſuch Branches of it as were neceſſary for Navigation, or for Weight and Meaſure, with a Penalty of two thouſand *Gredulgribs* (each of which in Gold is as big as a Silver Penny *Engliſh* Money) affixed to the Conviction of the Crime after the Publication of this Order; and if the Delinquent was found incapable of paying ſuch a Fine, his Life muſt anſwer for his Fault. All the Books of Argument relating to this Science were immediately burn'd, all the Paintings of it demoliſhed, or plaiſter'd over, as you ſee it was here, and the ſame Puniſhment allotted for any one who ſhould conceal the one, or by any means preſerve

ſerve the other, as for him who ſhould be guilty either by writing or painting a new one of the ſame kind. By this means, *added he*, Aſtronomy, Geography, and many other Branches of this noble Science, are intirely loſt, or lie dormant in the Breaſts of thoſe who dare not tranſmit them to their Poſterity.

ALTHO' no Man is a greater Admirer of theſe kind of Studies than my ſelf, yet I confeſs I could not avoid thinking it very prudent in the Government of *Lilliput* to ſuppreſs them, when they began to encroach on the practical and more uſeful Buſineſs of Mankind while they live in the world: For, on mature Conſideration, what is it to us, by what means it firſt received its Formation, or how it is ſince influenced and directed, if we are provided with all things needful in it? And how void of Reaſon muſt we appear to a diſintereſted Obſerver, to loſe that time in viſionary Speculations, which is too little

S 2 to

to be employ'd in the endeavour of acquiring what alone can defend us from Insults, and Contempt, and the want of those Necessaries, without which Life is so far from being desirable, that it becomes a Burthen? In the midst of these more serious Reflections, I could not forbear laughing at a sudden Thought which just then came into my Head, that if such a Law were put in force in *England*, what a loss our Ladies would be at, for the Amusements they meet with in having their Fortunes told. But I had no leisure now to indulge Meditation; and perceiving that *Keldresal* had made no mention of any thing but the Globe, I intreated he would continue his Favours to me, in letting me know the meaning of those Figures which were drawn about it, and for whom they were design'd. He presently told me, that by those horrid Shapes were meant the various Vices which poison Human Nature; which were allegorically described, by having all their Bows ready bent,

bent, as if inceſſantly at work, to plague and corrupt the Breaſt of Man: The number of them being infinite, they were always painted, he ſaid, in that manner; and the more you gazed on a Repreſentation of that kind, the more you ſtill perceiv'd, the whole Space being all fill'd up with them. At firſt I comprehended not the meaning of what he had ſpoke; but going cloſer, and applying my Perſpective, I ſaw diſtinctly that indeed there was no Void, but between the Wings of the one was couch'd another ſmaller Figure; nor was even the Hair, Pore, the minuteſt Part, without a thouſand little Demons of inferior Quality. Theſe, I judged, were the Weakneſſes which attend any great Vice, and are ready to ſteal in their Infection, where the more perſpicuous Darts are repell'd. Thoſe of the large ſize, which at firſt ſtruck my Eye, I ſuppos'd to be the Cardinal Sins, ſuch as Ambition, Luſt, Avarice, Cruelty, Pride, Contempt of the Gods, and wilful Perjury.

ry.

ry. I communicated what I thought to my obliging Friend, who told me I was perfectly right in my Conjectures; but again, strictly charg'd me to blot out the Picture, as soon as I had enough consider'd it to be able to retain as much of it in my Mind, as I thought would be of service either to the Amendment of my Morals, or Satisfaction of my Curiosity. I assur'd him, that I would obey him; after which he bid me farewel, being obliged to attend the Emperor at his Levee on some extraordinary Business.

As soon as I had waited on this kind Friend to the Door, I returned to my Picture, gazing on it with the greatest pleasure that ever I had known in my whole Life, to behold such an infinite number of little Figures, the largest of them not exceeding half the bigness of one of those Pins which the Ladies call Minikins, others like Atoms in the Sun-Beams, too small for sight without the help

help of a Magnifying-Glaſs, was ſomething ſo very curious, that I could have ſpent my whole Life in admiring ſo prodigious an Effect of Art. But as all Pleaſures have their ſhare of Pain, mine was ſufficiently embitter'd when I conſider'd that this wonderful Piece muſt be demoliſh'd: could I have taken it down, and brought it to *England* with me, I ſhould have thought it a greater Treaſure than all the Wealth of *America*; but that was impoſſible, not only on the account of the King's expreſs Command, that no ſuch thing ſhould be preſerv'd, but alſo becauſe it was painted on the Wall, which there was no removing, without pulling down the Fabrick, and by that means betraying the Theft. I could not reſolve, however, to ſcrape it out till I had had my fill of gazing on it: and for that reaſon, being told the Wife of *Keldreſal*, and ſome other Ladies were come to ſee me, went out to receive them, making an Excuſe that I did not invite them in, be-

because I said the Persons appointed to attend me, had not yet made my Apartment in that Decency which was necessary to receive Persons of their Rank.

It was a very fine Day, and they being in a Coach, I sate down on the Ground, and took it up, Horses and all, and set it on my Knees, that I might the better hear them, and be able to discourse with them. They seem'd to approve of my Proceeding, and we enter'd into a very gay Conversation.

Debalclick being, according to her custom, extremely facetious, gave a Life to the Company; and as she was never without one entertaining Story or other, among abundance of others, favour'd me with one, which I think fit to relate, because it may convey an Idea of some part of that Vivacity and sprightly Wit with which the *Lilliputian* Women very much abound, especially in any Ex-

Exigence which requires a readineſs of Thought and Invention.

A young Lady, who by her own Accompliſhments, and the handſome Fortune it was in her Father's power to give her, was entitled to great Expectations, among the number of thoſe that addreſs'd her for Marriage, ſet her Heart on one, who in point of Wealth was the moſt inferior of any of them. She made no ſcruple of revealing the Inclination ſhe had for him to her Father; but he ſaw not with her Eyes, and told her at once, that he had rather ſee her dead, than the Wife of a Perſon he look'd upon ſo much beneath her, and that if ſhe married in that manner, nothing but her Love ſhould be her Dower. Though the Paſſion with which theſe young People regarded each other was very great, yet they prudently conſidered, that Love of itſelf was unſubſtantial Diet, and that a Lady would make but a very indifferent Figure in

T the

the Circle, or her Husband in the Senate, whoſe Treaſure conſiſted in that alone. They reſolved therefore to wait with Patience, till the Death of this rigid Father ſhould give them liberty to compleat their Loves, each making a ſolemn Vow never to look with deſire on any other Object. The Father being of a great Age, gave them not the pain of a tedious Expectation. He dy'd in a few Months, and left his Daughter a very great Portion; but on this condition, that ſhe ſhould not marry with *Fridomar*, (ſo was her Lover call'd.) How terrible a Diſappointment this unexpected Clauſe gave them who were concerned in it, may eaſily be judg'd! She had a Brother, to whom the main part of the Eſtate deſcended, and who was alſo to be poſſeſs'd of her part of it, in caſe ſhe diſobey'd the Injunction: Both of them endeavour'd to bring him to Terms, offering the half of what ſhe was to be Miſtreſs of, if he would conſent to their Nuptials. But, like moſt Heirs, he he was reſolutely bent to perform the Will of his dead Father, where he found it his Intereſt to do ſo, and remained inflexible both to his Siſter's Tears, and the Entreaties of *Fridomar*.

But now comes the proof of what a Woman can do, when once ſhe is reſolved upon it; ſhe found that no other Man in the world but *Fridomar* was forbid: and had heard of a Perſon, who, by reaſon of his great Age, and Incapacity of getting his living, had for a long time been a Dependant on the Charity of thoſe that knew him in a better State. This Man ſhe eaſily perſuades to become her Husband, on certain Conditions drawn betwixt them, that he ſhould claim no other Privileges of that State, than to be well provided for, and taken care of during the little time he had to live; which, according to the Courſe of Nature, could not be long. In a word, ſhe was married with great Solemnity to this poor

Alms-Man, bedded with him in the ſight of ſufficient Witneſſes, and her Brother was compell'd to pay her Fortune the next day. The Caution of the Father extended not to a ſecond Marriage, and nothing now remains to compleat the Happineſs of *Fridomar*, but the Death of the old Bridegroom; who, poor Wretch! will in all probability expire ſomething ſooner, by the ſudden change from Want to Plenty, than if he had continued in a Condition, which, by being long enur'd to, was become a ſecond Nature.

ONE of the Ladies that came with *Debalclick*, and heard her tell this Story, was what we call in *England* a *Prude*, and very much condemned the Miſtreſs of *Fridomar*, for going to ſuch an extravagant length. It was immodeſt, ſhe ſaid, for a Woman to confeſs ſo great a Paſſion for a Perſon of the other Sex; and for her part, ſhe could not

not imagine what Charms there were in thoſe Creatures call'd Men, that ſhould inſpire ſuch Affections. But *Debalclick*, who was a Woman of a vaſt deal of Wit and Spirit, rallied her ſo handſomely on this Affectation, that ſhe was glad to drop it, and appear like the reſt of the Company.

THEY ſtay'd with me till Dinner-Time; which, after they were gone, I took without doors, to prevent the Perſons who ſerv'd me from taking notice of the Picture, which I could not find in my heart to demoliſh yet-a-while. I eat my Supper alſo in the ſame manner; and no more Company coming that Day, I went to bed, without having done any thing to blemiſh what I took ſo much pleaſure in beholding. But having a very ugly Dream that Night, though I was never ſuperſtitious, I reſolved to put a Conſtraint on my Inclinations, and do as as I was ordered by *Keldreſal*: and with my Knife ſo disfigured the Painting, that it was impoſſible for the ſmalleſt Line to be diſcovered.

CHAP.

CHAP. IX.

Various Occurrences happen, which lose the Author the Favour of the Court. He resolves to go to Blefuscu. *Obtains permission to do so: but before his Departure, is inform'd of the Proceedings of* Shefinbasto *and* Dafferhesal, *a different way from that he heard before. He departs from* Lilliput, *and arrives at* Blefuscu, *where he stays too short a time to be able to make any considerable Observations: And takes leave of the Reader for this Voyage.*

IT was well for me I obliterated the Painting on the Wall; for early the next Morning *Skyresh Bolgolam* (who I never thought much

much my Friend, especially since the Adventure of *Clesgarin*) came to my House. His Errand was from the Emperor, who had been by some Enemies of mine, and perhaps by himself, incensed against me for having entertained certain Ambassadors from *Blefuscu*. But I will not trouble my Reader with the Repetition of that Affair, it being already related in my Book of Travels, as also the Ill-Will this Minister had to me. His Business now was to order me not to stir from my House, without a particular Leave obtained from his Majesty; which Message having deliver'd, he went away: Nor was I at all griev'd to lose his Company, tho' I was very much so, to hear I had forfeited the Favour of the Emperor. I did not, however, despair of regaining it by the Interest of *Keldresal*, and several other other good Friends I had at that time. Nor was I much deceived, a few days restored me to my Liberty: But this gave me the Expe-

rience,

rience, that I had Foes which were very powerful and inveterate, and reminded me of the Unſecurity of my Condition, ſince Friendſhip, where there were no Expectations of a Return, might poſſibly in time grow weary of doing good Offices: But Malice was always induſtrious to compaſs her Intent, and for that reaſon wiſh'd myſelf freed from the Dependance of the one, or Fears from the other. Some few days after, I had permiſſion to walk abroad; the Royal Palace was on fire, whether by deſign, or accident, I will not pretend to ſay, but it happened of ill conſequence to me, as I have informed the Reader in my Travels: The Empreſs, inſtead of thanking me for the timely Aſſiſtance I brought to quench it, becoming my moſt implacable Enemy for the Means by which I did it. The Emperor, however, was more inclined to pardon me, and in ſpite of the Suggeſtions of my Enemies,

U per-

permitted me the Continuance of my Liberty; and on my earneſt requeſt, by *Keldreſal*, and ſome others who favour'd me, gave his Royal Aſſent for my leaving *Lilliput* whenever I could find an opportunity. I had for a long time entertained a Curioſity of ſeeing the Kingdom of *Bleſuſcu*: and having been very ſtrenuouſly preſs'd by the Ambaſſadors which came from thence, not to leave that part of the world, without calling there, I reſolved that ſhould be my firſt Voyage. But I communicated not the Time, in which I intended to make it, to any Perſon living; and it was well for me I did not, Articles of High-Treaſon being then drawing up againſt me, which would undoubtedly have been ſent to ſtop my Proceedings, had any notice of it reach'd my Enemies.

But while I was laying Schemes in what manner I ſhould beſt leave *Lilliput*,

liput, I was not without my uſual Sett of Company and Entertainments. Among other Things, I heard from a great Lady an account of the Affair of *Shefinbaſto*, *Koppockitaſh*, and *Deſſarbeſal*, vaſtly different from that which had been given me by *Clefgarin* and *Debalclick*, who it ſeems were both of them very great Friends of *Shefinbaſto*'s. I was now informed, that all that had been reported of the intended Murder, and Robbery of that Gentleman, was intirely fabulous, and that *Koppockitaſh* was the only injured Perſon: That it was true indeed, he had made an Attempt on *Deſſarbeſal*, when ſhe was in her Coach, but that it had only been the Effects of Wine, and that he thought no more of it, till ſhe, by her Husband's orders, who contriv'd with her to get a Sum of Money out of him, writ to him a Letter of Encouragement; that when he afterwards appointed a meeting with her,

Shefinbasto surprized them together, and obliged him to pay him down a thousand *Spruggs* to buy off the Prosecution he might else have commenced against him at Law, for making an Attempt to bastardize his Family: That in some time after, *Dessarbesal* writ to him again, complaining of her Husband's ill Treatment of her, and conjuring him to deliver her from the Confinement in which she pretended to be kept; that being enamour'd of the Woman, and pitying the Calamities he imagined she suffered wholly on his account, he assured her in his Answer of doing every thing she would have him, and fixed a Night on which he would come privately and take her from her Husband's House; that the Persons he brought with him were only Friends, which were to assist him in case of a Surprize, but intended no hurt either to the Life or Fortune of *Shefinbasto*. All this was now

now affirmed with the ſame Confidence by one Sett of People, as the before related Story was by another; and indeed by what was ſaid on both ſides, it was impoſſible for me to determine which was the Truth: but which-ever of them could produce ſuch Letters as both pretended to have in keeping, muſt undoubtedly carry the Cauſe. The Tryal was to be before ſix Judges appointed for that purpoſe; but my Affairs would not permit me to tarry the Deciſion; though it certainly muſt be a very remarkable Conteſt, and would have afforded good Entertainment to my Country-Men, who ſet a great Value on Books of Tryals ſuch as this. I might indeed, in ſo great a diſtance of Time and Place, have made the Hiſtory more compleat, by making a Cataſtrophe of my own, and abſolutely fixing the Guilt on that Party I was leaſt inclin'd to favour: but my Love of Truth would not ſuffer me to impoſe

poſe upon the Publick for any By-end of my own; and if any Reader finds in himſelf a Curioſity of knowing more than I am able to diſcover, either of this, or any other Fact I have mentioned, he muſt be content to ſuffer the Pain of it, or take the ſame Voyage I did to inform himſelf.

THOSE who pretended to aſſert the Truth of this Story, as laſt mention'd, told me that it had of late been very much the Faſhion for Men to debauch their own Wives to ſome great and wealthy Men, thereby to enrich their own Fortunes, and get rid of the Women they grew weary of poſſeſſing. Their Law in that point agreeing with ours, to grant a Divorce on the proof of Adultery; and, like ours alſo, allows this Privilege only to the Rich: the Poor being wholly unable to pay the Expence, are compell'd to drag the matrimonial Chain, till Death releaſes them

them from the Bondage, tho' with the most known Prostitute, and untameable Shrew that ever Man was plagued with.

It seems, methinks, in all Countries, as if the World were made only for the Great, and that it is not enough that they have the richest Habits, the most luxuriant Feasts, the only Respect; in fine, that they ingross all the Joys of Life: but Law must also be their Slave, and Power give them a Privilege over Right, and either deter, or silence all the Complainings of the Needy injured. Yet so it is, and ever will be, while, as I remember to have heard spoke on the Stage in some Play,

Gold is a greater God than Jupiter.

I beg my Reader's pardon for this Digression, especially on a Theme which every

every one is ſo well acquainted with, that it may juſtly be thought impertinent to add more than has been already ſaid, though to little purpoſe; for while he who has it, is poſſeſs'd of ſo many Advantages, none but thoſe who want it will declaim againſt it; and how much the Diſcourſes of ſuch unhappy People are regarded, may every day be obſerved.

WHILE my Thoughts were yet in the ballance how I ſhould leave *Lilliput*, I received private Intelligence, that I ſhould ſpeedily be impeached of High-Treaſon. I had ſeen enough of the Maxims of that Court, not to know that whenever they had a mind to find a Man guilty, they had ways enough to make him appear ſo, and that Innocence was no Protection againſt Decrees of State: For which reaſon, I delay'd no longer; but going to the Sea-ſide, took that Method for my Eſcape, which

which I have at full related in that Book publiſhed and ſet forth by my good Friend Mr. *Sympſon*.

PERHAPS it may be expected, that I ſhould give as full an Account of *Bleſuſcu*, as I have done of *Lilliput*; but the ſhort ſtay I made, together with the Fears that the Malice of my Enemies would purſue me there, kept me from making any great Obſervations of the things I ſaw; which indeed were not many, becauſe I ſeldom ſtirred from the place allotted for me near the Palace of the Emperor, unleſs it were to walk on the Sea-ſhore, and caſt a melancholy Look towards *Europe*; which, tho' I paſſionately longed once more to return to, I ſaw no hope of doing.

I muſt confeſs, that though I was treated with all imaginable Courteſy and Kindneſs by this good Monarch,

X and

and his Peers, I paſſed the time of my being there with an inceſſant Diſcontent, and ſecret Repining; inſtead of thoſe grateful Acknowledgments I ought to have made to the almighty Diſpoſer of all things, that I had ſo happily eſcaped the Snares laid for me by the *Lilliputians*; I murmur'd that I was no farther from their reach, as if the ſame Power which had till now ſo miraculouſly preſerv'd me, would not ſtill do ſo if I relied on him: but I know no part of Chriſtian Duty more difficult to be practiſed, than that of Faith.

THE Manners, Cuſtoms, and Habits, as well as the Bulk and Stature of the People of *Bleſuſcu*, are much the ſame with thoſe of *Lilliput*; nor are their Laws and Religions very different. There is, however, a ſecret Animoſity in the Nature of both to each other, though that of the *Bleſuſcans* is is very much heighten'd by the Complaints which the *Big-Endian* Exiles of *Lilliput* have made, concerning the Illegality of the Miniſtry, which drove them thence. The Reaſons of their Baniſhment, I have no need to repeat, having given a full account of them in my Travels.

DURING my abode in the *Blefuſcan* Territories, I had frequent Converſations with thoſe unhappy Gentlemen, who, though many of them had fine Senſe, diſcover'd a certain Raſhneſs and Impatience of Temper, which could not be agreeable to ſo deſpotick and arbitrary a Monarch, as that of *Lilliput*: But through all the Zeal that they expreſs'd for their Principles, I was inform'd by good hands, that the greateſt part of them were at that time privately ſolliciting for Pardon, and Permiſſion to return home; and that theſe too were not of the meaner ſort, but of thoſe whoſe Countenance and Perſuaſions had influenced the others, whom they now took no farther notice of, leaving them to extricate themſelves, as well as they could, from Difficulties, into which they had been brought meerly through their Inſtigations.

THIS made me frequently reflect on the Folly and Stupidity of all Followers of a Faction, who, if it ſucceeds, have no ſhare in the Glory or Profit; but if it fails, are ſure to be Partakers of the Obloquy, and, for the moſt part, are the only Perſons on whom thoſe Puniſhments fall, which their Superiors, either through Intereſt, or by being conſiderable enough to be feared, avoid.

I heard of a Perſon of great Note, who having engaged a good number of his Tenants and Servants in the *Big-Endian* Faction, at laſt finding means to

pro-

procure his own Pardon, left theſe poor Wretches with no other Dependance, than on the Charity of the *Bleſuſcans*, thoſe of their own Party not having wherewith to relieve them. I could not forbear uttering ſome Expreſſions, which teſtify'd my Deteſtation of ſuch an Act of Barbarity, but they told me nothing was more common; and I bleſs'd Heaven that I was born in a Country where ſuch inteſtine Broils but rarely happen, and where Chriſtianity and Honour obliges every one to relieve, to the utmoſt of his power, the Diſtreſſes he has occaſion'd.

I obſerved too another Misfortune among theſe Exiles; which was, that tho' they ſuffered for the ſame Cauſe, the ſame Calamities, they endeavour'd not to leſſen the Weight of their Diſtreſſes by a perfect Agreement among themſelves, they rather ſeemed to lay the blame of their Miſcarriages on one another,

other, and ſometimes would carry their Reproaches to ſo great a height, that it grew up to fatal Quarrels. They were little regarded by the People they were among, and indeed ſuffered to inhabit there more to keep a rival Power in awe, than for any Good-will to them or their Opinion.

THIS was the only part of their Politicks, which it fell in my way to diſcover, tho' I believe they want it not in other things; for they are reputed to be a very wiſe People, and I doubt not if I had tarry'd any time among them, but many things would have occur'd to my Obſervation worthy of the Attention of a Reader. But my good Fortune ſending me, when I leaſt expected it, the means of returning home; I had the Grace not to refuſe the Bleſſing, and took my leave of that part of the World, with a Pleaſure, which, it it is my belief, no Traveller that has ſpent much Time in foreign Countries but has been ſenſible of, when on his Return.

FINIS.